THESE MIRRORS PROVE IT

Also by Holly Prado

Nothing Breaks Off at the Edge (New Rivers Press)
Feasts (Momentum Press)
Losses (Laurel Press)
How the Creative Looks Today (The Jesse Press)
Gardens, a novel (Harcourt Brace)
Specific Mysteries (Cahuenga Press)
Esperanza: Poems for Orpheus (Cahuenga Press)

THESE MIRRORS PROVE IT

Selected Poems and Prose, 1970-2003

HOLLY PRADO

cahuenga
PRESS

ACKNOWLEDGMENTS

Grateful acknowledgement is made to the following publications:

1970s: New Rivers Press, Momentum Press, *Bachy 12, rara avis, Three Rivers Poetry Journal 11/12, Tinderbox, Contemporary Women Poets: An Anthology* (Merlin Press), *First Person Intense: An Anthology* (Mudborn Press), *The Lamp in the Spine, The Streets Inside: Ten Los Angeles Poets* (Momentum Press).

1980s: The Jesse Press, *Blue Window, Boxcar, "Poetry Loves Poetry": An Anthology* (Momentum Press), *Temblor, The Colorado Review, Village Idiot, Redstart, The Kenyon Review, APC Newsletter, Peninsula.*

1990s: *Bachy 16, Bachy 18, Invisible City, The L.A. Weekly, Sulfur, Rhododendron, Caprice, The Colorado Review, The Jacaranda Review, The Talking of Hands: An Anthology* (New Rivers Press), *Diamonds Are a Girl's Best Friend: Women Writers on Baseball: An Anthology* (Faber and Faber), *The Tule Review, Grand Passion: An Anthology* (Los Angeles Poetry Festival), Cahuenga Press, *Sic (Vice and Verse), Solo, The International Poetry Review, Beyond the Valley of the Contemporary Poets: Fourth Annual Anthology,* Skylight Books' Postcard Series: Skylight's 30 L.A. Poets for Poetry Month, 2000, Puddinghouse Press, "Sense of Site" Postcard Series 2002 (Writers at Work and The Los Angeles Cultural Affairs Dept. and the Durfee Foundation), *The Year's Best Horror and Fantasy, 1999* (St. Martin's Press), *Exquisite Corpse.*

2000s: *Lummox Journal, L.A. Woman: Literatur von Los Angeles Ladies: An Anthology, Spread: Democracy Issue, Dufus #4: The Baseball Issue, Spreading the Word 11: An Anthology of Winners of the Fin de Millenium L.A. Poetry Contest 2000, Cimarron Review, So Luminous the Wildflowers: An Anthology* (Tebot Bach), *Beyond Baroque Magazine, Psychological Perspectives: a Semiannual Journal of Jungian Thought.*

Front cover photo by Philip F. Johnson, October 10, 1948
Photo of the author (back cover) by Allison Schallert
Typesetting and book design by Greg Boyd, Asylum Arts
Printed by McNaughton & Gunn, Inc., Saline, MI

Cahuenga Press is owned, financed and operated by its poet-members James Cushing, Phoebe MacAdams Ozuna, Harry E. Northup, and Holly Prado Northup. Our common goal is to create fine books of poetry by poets whose work we admire and respect; to make poetry actual in the world in ways which honor both individual creative freedom and cooperative support.

Cahuenga Press, 1256 N. Mariposa, Los Angeles, CA 90029

CONTENTS

The 1970s

The 1980s

The 1990s

The 2000s

For Harry E. Northup
"So may it always be"

For our son, Dylan Northup

And for my parents

Gladys Helen Johnson (1900-1954)
Philip Farnsworth Johnson (1900-1975)

And for Eleanor Johnson

With thanks to the generous writers in my writing workshops whose creative energies sustain my own. In particular:

Rae Wilkin
Barbara Crane
Linda Berg
Toke Hoppenbrouwers
Jill Singer
Pamela Shandel
Kathleen Bevacqua
Marlene Saile
Rachel Kreisel
Joan Isaacson
Marie Pal
Edith Kornfeld
Margaret Walsh
Sara Bragin
Maggie Bryant
Sidney Higgins
Lisa Frankel
Mary Barnes
Arlene Andrew
Olivia Sanchez-Brown
Ginger Emerson
Erin Douglass
Valerie Savior
Joan Wood
Shaké Rose
Jason Greenwald
Gina Battaglia
Richard Heller
Vicki Mizel
Jane Wheatley-Crosbie
Gloria Lewyn
Kathy Berkowitz
Aletheia Morden
Kathleen Tyler
Judy Accardi
Cesca Brenner
Sharon Toriello
Wendy Markowitz
Bill Banks

Also, deepest gratitude to these friends of the creative soul, whose lives have been my inspiration and encouragement:

Alison Townsend
Elaine Brooks
Margaret Johnson
Judy Oberlander
Marla Lanagan

THESE MIRRORS PROVE IT

THE 1970s

INTRODUCTION
(1970)

what's part of her
what's not

THE ART MUSEUM: A CORRIDOR OF MIRRORS
(a sculpture by Lucas Samara)

reflective
tone

I step into myself
that nose a shock
and my grandmother's short legs
two hundred of them without shoes
my brain
so many folds
peonies in the cemetery   *Look up*
the opera carmen
boxes within boxes like a chinese puzzle

I sink into the lines
between sections of mirror
then come back again
someone pushes for his turn
a blind boy   *Mirror in*
his eyes roll behind dark glasses   *ourselves*
when he laughs there's a small mirror
in his throat
I see my voice
a line of sound that moves
like an electrocardiogram
a camera hangs around his neck
he doesn't bother to lift it
when he takes a picture

I read somewhere
that Africans were terrified
when they saw a movie of their tribe
taken the year before
on the screen was a man who had died
my mother wears my hair
here in the mirrors
her 1928 wedding dress is brown velvet
the long sleeves
are tight around my wrists

19

a few feet away
a kid of ten or so
removes the glass screws
that hold the mirrors
once he sees himself
the image is caught
catalogued by the museum
they manipulate the mirrors
give you someone else's chin
or eyebrows
no one can tell him
it's not the museum's fault

people at the end of the corridor
come in through the back
one child calls it the house
the house is open he says
I used to wave at actors in movies
they seem to see the audience
don't they
and when you play a record
the performer has to stop whatever he's
doing
to sing for you
these mirrors prove it

NOTHING BREAKS OFF
AT THE EDGE
(1976)

THE GARDEN

rilke has said that
each man will take with him
from the earth
one word that he loves most

I have been thinking all evening
just in case
and can't go beyond
lizard

RAINMAKING

someplace in new mexico I slept for twelve hours in my sleeping bag in the back seat of my car in my clothes. I woke up feeling clear and rested— the sky was pink and I ate a piece of cheese and a lot of crackers. when I got to the rest area with a john, a woman and her little girl were there. the little girl had brought her doll in to pee, too. the mother had a change of clothes on hangers and was washing up. she was taking care of what needed to be done. women know how a clean shirt gets dirty—how food gets eaten, plants and moons live and die.

I drove all day toward los angeles. all of my feelings were religious— mother mountains and ghosts of indians, geronimo, cochise hold-outs marked along the road. there was a dead animal, too large for a dog, at the edge of the desert. he was still bleeding. I couldn't help looking at him. for the whole trip I felt that I was giving myself up to a cycle of some kind. I didn't understand, but I liked living it out: the sense of larger ways outside of the city. even the ritual of driving seemed to fit—shifting gears, passing trucks, stopping for gas without getting out of the car—all a gathering of symbols that I didn't recognize but felt was dictated and important. (like that woman who says beethoven visits her and composes music through her.) I had seen my friend j.b. in alamogordo, new mexico, for three hours. then I got in my car and started home again. why 800 miles for that? an excuse to be on the road with my symbol/self/ woman?

I've never wanted to just give myself—hand myself out—and have always kept some stuff for me inside. women are protected by their menstrual cycle. when they menstruate they aren't required by the tribe to respond to sexual demands—they become virgins again for a few days, and become their own personal selves: what they are mysteriously inside. I've done that. not just once a month. saved myself for myself—not to have it all absorbed by a man or friends or the kids I teach or the people in line at the market. even when I want to push toward other lives. when my husband and I split up six months ago, I wanted to start giving again right away. a woman's thing. to find her life in a man. know him so well that she enters his moods and lives in them instead of in herself. it can be very nice. the woman who lives downstairs from me is pregnant. she is really full of the baby. sometimes I can feel her pregnancy through her ceiling/my floor. the roundness. she and her husband and the baby. magic three: magic heaven-earth-underworld. magic family. she's taking a pottery class, too. pregnant and making round pots to be filled with weeds, milk. I like having her there, under my place, holding it up with all that life. but I don't feel barren because she's fertile. I need to be in that other virgin self for awhile. my own secret. creature. like this trip.

always a question: how to balance the transmission of life and energy and love but keep rich levels of yourself inside. does one feed the other? I used to think so. now I feel more positive about the idea that all of us should live alone away from everyone for at least two years. not to be a reflection of a style or some other man's beauty. real initiations—you go out in the forest or up on the mountains and stay until you know something—are entrances.

so there I was, driving through new mexico feeling it all in my arms and back, not understanding the road or myself but glad to be there with the ghosts. winter is supposed to be the dead time, but it seems to be the clearest time for hearing voices.

some crows flew up in the road—shining in the air. they kept folding and unfolding—almost purple. they were quiet, but I know that sometimes a crow will go off by himself and sing. they have a song that's different from the cawing that they do. a crow will find a deserted spot—even away from other crows—and sing. what we see is just a fragment of the mystery. magic formulas always change. I'm not really all of the things that have happened to me or what I have made of them. but there are those voices, doors closing, stars that can't be seen in the afternoon, salt, buttermilk, two dogs running down the hill with their tails up, blood, bones, parables, the urine that leaves me, my sign of the zodiac which is the bull: the crescent moon/ horned beast/ feet to the ground. that twelve hours of sleep was perfect. it's taken me a month to think about it, but that was the place I turned into another start of something. I even dreamed during that night. the daughter of one of my friends was with me. she had a little-girl purse open on the seat of the car. there was a clean white handkerchief inside.

JANUARY 30TH:
LARGER THAN OTHER PLANTS

I bought some brown shoes in mexico that are woven like a life of hard times. somebody left without finishing them. at first, one would hardly go on my foot, and slowly I've realized that they aren't even a pair. some small holes on top are in different places on the right shoe/ left shoe. the back of the left shoe has a piece of leather missing that should be there. the shape of the tops: the left is pointed/ the right is rounded. I didn't see these things, but now that I have, I wonder why any shoes should have to match. I see that each foot is different. I should listen to my left foot with great kindness. there's a growth between the little toe and the toe next to it that deserves care. the foot never complains/ never whimpers or tries to make trouble. and my right foot has a sense of humor. it walks toward the mud/ puts itself on the slippery rock/ has a misshapen big toenail. my feet give energy: a dance: the steps repeated but never in quite the same place. shapes of weeds that come to live between the radishes, turnips, cauliflower of the new february garden. the order that swings through the sky and catches me so that I can't shake it off—on a sunday like this I can only give myself up to it. I've surprised myself ever since I've been awake— interrupting myself with ideas: herb tea/ making yogurt/ talking about catholicism/ drawing with a green pen/ making a second excuse not to visit friends/ reading a list of images I wrote last tuesday that don't seem what they did: sparrow, house, cactus, bed, wolfman. everywhere there's something to be looked at carefully. every brown eye in the skin of the pineapple with its four short hairs. I thought there were only two. the pears with brown skins—like vegetables. you don't need a piece of bread or even a dish to put them in. full of remembered-forgotten taste and never easy to eat. hard meat against your teeth. two wrinkles at the side of my mouth that are just like my father's and my aunt jeannette's: farm/ ears of corn/ horses/ catalpa. veins in my hands. I'm aware of growing older—getting stronger and closer to my body. loving it and using it to run, breathe as I turn from self to self to self. walking in the mountains last summer after I had lost so much love and could think only of my empty house I began to struggle into my body, to work with it and know that it would climb for me/ that it would love me and use me without telling lies; that the blood and the sun and the water of the clean even life would make my body fresh, and that something then would happen to the order everywhere that is always right. the unmatched shoes. the feet. the open mouth. the indian names of months: the moon of strong cold and the moon when ponies shed. the deer rutting moon and the drying grass moon. lately I've been seeing ghosts out of the corner of my eye. I don't know who they are, but they tell me that there's an underside of the world that bears knowing. in mexico in the cemetery outside of ensenada the word "perpetuidad" was written on almost every gravestone or wooden marker. the flowers were everywhere: real and plastic and paper. one man had built a mausoleum—bright blue cement—over the grave of his wife. he had scratched flowers on the side and painted "mi amor" in an arc over the doorway. inside was a bench with two small cushions on it—the cushions had ruffles around the edges and had been there for a long time. there were many graves of children. one for a little boy said, "he flew to heaven at the age of three years," and his picture was on the gravestone. death can't be a failure. but part of more. one phase of the moon. hidden resources. colors between dreams. to keep looking for small ways: the leaf frozen in the stone/ a few yellow pencils/ the wooden turtle whose legs move. when I think of my feet I feel the mexican shoes around them and have to wonder where I'll be the rest of the day. a bell in the air for the new month. wings.

THE TURTLE

one woman plays
hollow gourds with mallets
another
older
sings about snow
I hear the branches
break under winter

being alone leads you back
the water touches absences
cleans them to look at
I hold the idea of myself
as it is
everything alive
brushes my hair

FAMILY

juice runs to my wrist I love citrus the
clean white part under the skin
oranges have always been with me they tumble
through years their roundness all the women who held them out to me
every food a season you get back to it

I'm older and older I find what my mouth needs
children a man that strength of beginning
I live out the shape
my breast follows its own curve
marriage of two halves never straight ahead
I listen for what I remember what I don't
is there too
coming with whoever imagines this was next to me all the time

VISIT

I

marla gets off the plane and I see her walking fast, toward me, dressed in
white and purple. we hug: I can feel that she's taller than I am, and
I'm a little afraid of her. she's shouting that she can't believe she's in
los angeles and saying, "shit, baby, shit, I'm not really *here*." I've
dressed up, too, the way women do when they want to impress each
other—a long skirt, earrings—but I feel as if she's not looking at me.
a few people stare—she's waving her arms and her ass and I'm think-
ing about driving home on the long freeway with so much/ nothing to
say.

she likes my house. the wooden filing cabinet, the pink and green shawl
on the old chest, the cat, the quilt, the flowers I picked for her, the
windows, the lights outside on the hill. she's terribly tired and starts
to really talk. the purple comes off. her nightgown is long and she
tells me that her little boy didn't want her to come. "the first thing
I've done on my own—on my own—in ten years." I start to think of
the ocean/ picnics/ shopping/ going out with men like we were nine-
teen years old—laughing and fussing with our hair. once, when we
were in college, I stitched her into a dress—she was going to a dance
and the dress was new and too big in the waist. when she came back
to the room she was drunk, and I had to get the scissors and try to cut
the stitches while she stumbled around, feeling sick to her stomach.
we kept laughing and snipping and finally she threw up on her new
shoes.

II

I've been out of the city for a month. camping around the west—wyoming,
colorado, utah—outside of any life except my own moving. I got com-
fortable in rain: crouched in leaves, or close to a fire, or lying in the
back of the pick-up truck with a tarp pitched over me. I began to like
the smell of myself.

at first, the wind scared me at night. once I couldn't sleep much, and kept
waking up from a dream about climbing a ladder, carrying a pail of
water. a wooden indian at the top said hello in a mechanical voice. I
woke up, rolled over in my sleeping bag, and the dream changed: I
walked into a room full of plants and flowers, all marked and identi-
fied. I felt excited that I'd be able to know all of the plants of the
area—columbine, paint-brush, mariposa lily, all the sages—I wanted
to take a long time to look at everything. a woman was there as a
guide. she wore a beautiful, flowing dress, and the room had the light
of a greenhouse—generous, but filtered and shadowy. I began to ac-
cept the wind after that.

back in the city, I had to think about my car, insurance bills, my landlady.
I felt fat, after corn and potatoes for a month. staying inside made me
restless. when marla called and said she was coming, I couldn't stand
the thought of having her in the house that was already pushing in on
me. but she's an image of myself I sense in mirrors, pieces of glass,
clothes that fit even though we're not the same size, handwriting,
never thinking about it. I remember a coyote howl/ moan/ bark. I
heard the hollow of the roof of his mouth. bones in his neck. how his
paws felt on the rocks. I could have looked into his throat and seen
the shape of the enemy/ lover he was seeing.

III

I wake up in the middle of the night and marla's crying in her sleep. I know it's a bad dream, and I feel it moving into the room where I am, making the air stop and my shoulders cold. I get up—push myself out of my own sleep—and go into the bedroom. she doesn't wake up, but keeps making the sounds of trying to escape. I touch her face—it feels soft, like feathers or leaves, and she thanks me for coming in. "I've had this dream before."

in the morning I get up early and sit outside for awhile. it's going to be hot. the yard next door has just been watered and looks green, fresh. we'll drive to the ocean and let the tide get into us for the day. we can take some fruit/ climb around the rocks to a cove that might not be crowded. when I hear marla in the kitchen, I get up, but my foot's asleep and it hurts when I walk. she stops making coffee to lean down and rub my leg until I can stand on it.

—for Marla Lanagan

COUNTRY BANJO

the note before the next one
you don't know what you'll play
my own days of lying face down in the land
droughts
I know the way some years are sitting on the porch
an instrument like mistakes

those days you can take anything
chase/capture
a hand turns your dress the shape of hips
some days cars go by
you wonder who names the streets
a pile of letters in the back of a truck

it's not in planning the next move
an inch never equals twenty miles
I end up driving
just to feel the road slide

gaps
bass notes
I could learn to take pictures
crop out an awkward hand/ the extra branch
a camera seems easy
but you get what you see that way

MARLA: A TUMOR IN HER BREAST

circle of no pain just being told
to come back
to what it is   always one more more than one
worry   the ground moves up five women on your mother's side
you say you'll finish it yourself
pills   food of dying
I've seen too where that goes deep in my own
way at night   people you love
gone to other houses   rest   they don't think of
no future in more days just time

cold   the lights on for holidays
I want music out of drums   kids their noise
what I hear   my breath
afraid of how easy it is to lie down
snow would feel good all over my body
rabbits   bears close by to watch   then some river
making life   even in winter I go back
to when I put the plants in the garden
the color of the soil   manure and bark
worked in   raked to a mound
saved by what grows can be held   born
even now as it's dark outside no one coming to see me

it's not much I don't say that
I want to pierce my ears for gold rings
learn some song about making love with a stranger
call you
drunk midnight on new years

ANCESTORS THEIR HEAVY SHIRTS

unfinished women smell of
talk what they eat to make up for
sickness you can't name it
my grandmother wipes her mouth
my past
stuffs words down the throat they never came from

this house listens to its own stories
I feel space between walls
the weather isn't sure of itself I wonder
if one end will meet the other
my ribs my ceiling

what makes sense not what I see
some cactus gone for months without
water my own blood I wait for
how I am still female still planting

I start
I start to move it's time
I dream of the snake what I want
fear
his bite two holes I cut
my hand the sharp point even against my belly
poison splashes in the sink I enter
my own caves I pull

to wake up to go out I smell light
I'm real shaped as I always have been
still clumsy but traveling
I stand with my age these rooms
their clothing shed
I want feet then to rise the color
the wing that fast winter bird
loses everything carries it with him

FEASTS (1976)

this is about
what we carry. celebrations that we continue to believe.
and we turn through them, through the stories we've heard over and over,
to our own story of this time, this place. to say

        that we will see our faces change.
        we will become trees, or wagers
        that never make any money but can turn
        our gold into ordinary ground, the best
        possible solution.

to say
nothing holds on.

the right way to live held out by mothers and fathers in the shape of how
many rooms there were in our childhood houses. we move to a city; love the
wrong people; make more or less than we'd ever imagined. discover in the
middle of our lives that the first years had a thinness, an imitative quality.
we look back.
we peel off
an old wool sweater, find that a sheer blouse with buttons down the front is
what we want now. this is about

what might have gone on last night while four women talked about a quilt:

how it grows rather than being planned.
aletheia's hair piled on her head—the hair works
loose through the evening—one long strand of
it falls on her neck. they see it grow longer and
longer until it's the longest strand of hair in the
world. it reaches the floor, then through the
house, out of the back door, around the neigh-
borhood—playing with children, talking hope-
fully to old people and fences—moving on, still
attached to aletheia's head. the hair

and the quilt as the time that moves in front of us. streets and stores and traffic lights and the strangers that repeat every day, always and never the same.

this is about a woman who is to be the bones and the invention. something of her
history
as false as all of us telling what towns we come from when we introduce ourselves at parties. something of her present life, which is impossible because by the time it's written, it's done—has become some other way of walking around the neighborhood to see if last night's rain made any difference.

> when she was young, she always
> wanted to be named maria.
> this was men on horseback with
> fine saddles trimmed in silver.
> lace.
> but now she like plants, sees
> things happening more slowly.

most of her clothes are from a thrift shop and she doesn't think much about who might have worn them, only that they are close to what clothes should be. her name
is
short, easy to write. it has letters that can be moved around, so that halfway through this, the name can become some other name. or she can get back her real name without much trouble. this naming: what it covers/ what it exposes.

her name is clare.

II

yes, everyone will have a name. they will appear/ disappear:
some as they really are, some as they can't be except in
dreams, fantasies—
it is impossible to live with everyone, to be with them
at work/ in bed/ before or after they come into clare's life.
but that may happen, too.
the double, the triple.
what parts of ourselves surge forward, sit back.
clues.
how he breathes—the man who is bill who comes in twice and is never seen
again. how clare met him and knew immediately that he liked her that there
would be a moment when she would know that his breathing is too shallow,
too quick.

> some need in her for a dark man now, one with
> a rising face of angles and bones. he will begin
> to move under this without her knowing it—
> she's seen him many times, knows him from the
> neighborhood she lives in, has been avoiding
> him. but he is sitting at home now, talking on
> the phone to a friend from out of town and he's
> coming toward her without warning. or

> with all the warnings we give to each other and
> then we're surprised when we get what we want.

III

to feel the cloth take up dust, ease it from one life to another. clare carries the old house, the one from last week, out of herself into the yard to shake and rumble until there are clean floors everywhere. she protects, divides, loses the ends of days that were good in their own ways but have nothing to do with her green T-shirt how it smells under the arms after the sweeping the mopping.

her poor furniture and what is expected of it. places to sit, to find out how the room looks from all sides and there they are: the two grandmothers, a mother, clare as a child, clare as she was a month ago when she had her picture taken at the county fair. she rubs the old wooden chest, rubs the chairs, rubs the inside of her leg where it suddenly itches. she remembers a mexican serape that covered a table at home, when she was a kid. how gourds the family grew in the back yard looked on it.

> she watches for them.
> she thinks of their houses,
> of how they'll all leave
> about the same time,
> will start toward her.
> she'll be ready. she'll
> open the door and open and
> open the door.

IV

somewhere close to the beginning:
luis as she takes his picture—as if in the little frame of the camera his energy
holds still, just long enough. the flash bulb doesn't work. he laughs, says it's
his power, and clare remembers crows that flew across the new mexico sky
as she drove there once, their bodies gathering the hills. black, dark green,
purple—coats to be worn for special ceremonies. something straight inside
your back to lean against.

the camera as the simplest, the most ordinary way to capture, and it can
never carry the sound of an old blues singer on the record player or that it's
been a hot day, now
cooler:
they all feel like saying whatever they've saved all week, and the flash bulbs
scatter and interrupt but some need in clare to want the pictures that she'll
go to pick up and won't be able to wait—will pull over in the car and park
for a minute just to look at them quickly. a reflection, a name. to write the
date on the back and find them, in twenty years, under a pile of old letters or
insurance policies. to be surprised at how a face looked and
what is he thinking?

luis goes outside to wait for another friend who's having a hard time finding
clare's house, even though he's been here before. some days like that: direc-
tions you haven't followed for awhile, streets unfamiliar since you yourself
have moved—another way to drive. paul finds them. he wears white pants
that come close to the hot day, and clare looks—his white pants white shirt—
and sees him through an old book about bullfighting: a picture of the author
in an authentic spanish costume—sure of himself, but out of place with his
british nose.

paul's moustache.

how much he really knows about books. and once, someone said to him,
"you're so rational, you must be a mystic." under this, for clare, is his wife,
who is dead, whom they all knew, who is still somewhere in clare with ruth's
own dinners that came close to how we nurture with asking if anyone wants
more, saying don't move I'll get it. her death still pushes clare: at some
point she sees paul sit on the couch between two other men, and wonders
where ruth would be if she were here, how she would find her spot—the

43

place on the floor, on a pillow/ she'd hug her knees and sway back and forth. she'd start by asking, "and you know what *happened*?"

the women in the house now, everywhere, their special voices like water wheels like papaya or carrots. like breeze. they're in the bedroom, the kitchen, not to help or pretend to be outside of the men, but to be everywhere, to talk, and aletheia in an orange long blouse with intricate embroidery. at the end of the evening, clare will hug her, feel how small aletheia's body is, and hesitate for a minute, won't want to let go. she is apart/ away from her husband. the embroidery goes on and on around the sleeves. the same story, but changed in the way things turn out from minute to minute. they've looked at each other, these women, on some nights—wounded together by men who won't make up their minds, by aletheia's child upstairs in bed who needs everything at once, by their own opening and closing of events— where they want to be and how to walk there in a short skirt with legs free to move as fast as they want them to. when aletheia came today, both of them dressed up, they told each other how beautiful they looked, grabbed hands, circled the room a few times, skipping, before anyone else arrived. aletheia's shawl fell on the floor and they left it there until they were ready to sit down and talk.

OH, FOOD. EVERYONE HAS COME FOR FOOD:
SUDDENLY THEY ARE ALL IN IT—THEY CARRY IT
FROM THE TABLE TO THEIR MOUTHS TO THEIR
BELLIES—

the soup with lentils and sausage.
clare's been cooking thinking all week
and counting how many how much of each
thing. now the food does it by itself—
works and stretches until

	nate stands by the table and
they all have	says yes to everything and
what they want what they've been	says yes and eats more bread.
hungry for what they thought of earlier.	his new haircut with one curl
plates bowls spoons into the food	sticking out at the back of
all steaming all ready	his head is how he finally
they take it across the room around	recites his parody of "the
and through themselves.	raven" which goes on and on—
	the string of words and

44

how they love each other by eating it all
by eating to stay alive to add to
what they have brought here and
what clare has made.

it is so simple but not always like this
to be able to see everyone's hands,
throats, a whole chain of
how to chew swallow pick up taste

a fugue. a line that you read—
it stays with you until the words
change places/ you make your own
sentence/ live out one of the phrases
until you realize one day you haven't
worn a heavy pair of shoes for a long
time that there are several boxes
of books to give away.

foolishness make clare want
to give him more bread,
more
garlic bread, more garlic bread
with herbs mixed in, more
garlic bread that has been in the
oven/ is just cool enough to eat a
whole piece in three bites.

one of them says

that christmas is coming how good
it feels to wear a loose flowing
dress on christmas day so you can
eat as much as you want to eat
without feeling your clothes
tighten against you. cut off the
food, the enormous full feeling,
the eating

as much as you want to eat as much as

sarah is the one who finishes the
last piece of pie. she eats it
right out of the pieplate, the final
note, the crumbs, and did that slice
of apple know
it would be the last?

even though they've finished, they keep going back to the table, finding
what's left. a big bite of raisins with nuts mixed in. they continue and con-
tinue
and then
look up. find themselves laughing instead of eating. they laugh about cars
and how to say "touch-up paint" in spanish, about how they learned to drive.
trolley tracks. they laugh at themselves—tell about times they've been to-
gether—how legends go on until clare knows that each of them will be in
another story, years from now: they will each be the special one who did

something funny, could never get anywhere on time, didn't understand some word that led to all kinds of trouble. clare hears other talk, soft muttering of two friends near the plants and window. they say, "reproducing our reality," and "he's just leaving this body for another one." the other places we all go when no one is looking, the difference between how to pick up a glass and how to drop it. success in accidents in watching the background of a painting to see what moves first.

clare has her picture taken with her navel showing.
she says she wants bracelets from india for her ankles,
silver rings for at least three toes.
she's not drunk.
she's taken seriously, as she means to be, and bill tells her where
she might buy some.
she tucks her long skirt under her, ready to listen.

someone whispers, "the soup is even good cold." echoes of plates and voices. bill is the last to leave. the stranger. the one clare hasn't seen on different days, eaten other meals with. he moves like a bear who is full of ideas—a sudden paw reaches out. they spend some time weaving and stitching and checking the back of the material to see how it's coming along. she wonders how his face changes from noon to six p.m. she pictures how it was in mexico when he was there, as he talks about a plush hotel and then seeing a dead pig—a carcass in the street. mexico. a place like the parts of herself that are warm, dark, sometimes helpless or fertile or acted out with masks.

this exchange. a moment when it might turn into real trading, but clare yawns. a deep breath. she says goodnight, be careful driving. she waits. turns out the porch light.

> clare takes off her clothes/ takes off
> the evening/ comes back to it in
> dreaming
> that a great poet is dying, that she
> doesn't go in to see him. she walks
> farther and farther down the corridor
> and feels light, happy, because she
> knows how much distance there is
> between her and the door with his name
> on it in important gold letters.

a heart-shaped stone, wrapped in a note,
appears in clare's mailbox, not mailed.
put there.

> the woman who left it for clare is
> margaret
> who is new in this, but who has been
> here all the time. she's older than
> clare—not a mother—but a combination
> of women:
>
> one who is far away and lives in poems
> written on half-sheets of paper
>
> one who lives next door to daniel—
> her house filled with ferns and the
> shadow of a man whose beard has been
> a monk/ a village/ a mouthful of nails
>
> another who is known for a journal,
> volumes stacked in her basement, the
> superb collection of womb and paper
> and snow.

clare and margaret meet often. in their houses, in streets between the houses, in dreams when margaret tells clare, "your problem is that you always choose handsome men." or they don't meet. secrets between them that they write to each other, that they may refer to later, a word or two, but too private for much conversation. the stone. margaret writes, "there is a faint, pink groove on the surface, but it is still intact, whole." clare puts the dark red color to her face. invisible, as all colors are. but a guide of some kind. the pink groove runs through the stone, at the top, like a scar—something that hurt once, that has healed and has brought a sort of clarity: nothing is perfect, but everything happens as it does because we allow ourselves to become part of events, of other people. even, when we gather enough years to forgive, of ourselves.

on this particular day, clare feels pregnant, knows that she isn't really, but there's an urge in her body to nurture:

she looks back at the past few months as if they've
been eggs. next week she'll read a book about sorcery,
about becoming totally aware, and she'll want to be
as alert as possible, ready for anything. but now, with
apples baking in the oven, with those round gold ear-
rings that she always wears, with silence and the stone,
clare becomes the pregnant woman in all of us. some-
times things grow slowly.

she thinks back to november, december. times for people to gather.
her energy was like children themselves—
how they climb onto walls and don't worry about falling off.
it was as if everything started over. the men who stepped in and out.
their breath and deeper voices. daniel. holidays.

now, the sky has turned: those clouds
that take another shape when you look away/ then look back at them.

and when paul dropped by recently, he talked about a relationship
with a woman that's been going on for six months. has ruth been
dead that long? he says that he and the woman argue about
philosophy, psychology—but it's really an argument of

how do we see our faces?
are they histories, tigers or moths, the same or
the opposite of what we want them to be?

we never see them, of course.

clare hears again, "I'm tired of looking in the mirror." who said it?
all of us when we
need to remember our middle names, the ones we never use anymore,

the ones that have been misspelled with plans—single-spaced lists and no
room between appointments.

clare feels the couch under her—the ordinary, the deliberate. those
celebrations. she's been avoiding the excitement of searching/ of putting on
all her bracelets at once/ of looking for the new the complicated the unknown.
she reads a line or two about women—that their one power is to be
untouchable. she copies out the words. not true, quite, but she makes them

a way to get back, to turn toward herself. toward more reading: other women, biographies. she leans into wanting to find out whose breasts whose vision she has. she begins to feel her real mother in her own constantly cluttered drawers and short fingernails—not the grasping character of earlier dreams—but the mother who helps, teaches. clare still loves people without judging their disasters too much. her mother knew about that.
gave it, handed it to clare with

once, in kindergarten, clare came home late. she'd been kept after school for throwing handfuls of gravel at a little boy. she hated him. not for anything he'd done, but because he was weak. easy prey. she sobbed. she'd been caught. her mother fixed soup and said, "but you didn't mean to hurt him, did you? I know you didn't." the relief, and in it, clare still forgives as easily as assuming that nobody means to hurt anyone else. innocence of oatmeal. enriched milk.

her mother smelled of lilac cologne. there were lilacs that grew in the back yard. the back yard opened onto an alley, where clare would walk, up and down, looking at the weeds and flowers that grew between the two dirt tracks of the narrow road. she tried not to step on anything alive. every spring, her mother would pick up some baby sparrow that had fallen from a nest, nurse it with an eye-dropper, even though she knew it would die. all of the

sentimental. the true. the weepy, the full-bodied, the wise, the nostalgic, the

reason clare can never listen to scientific explanations, is more interested in how days, months change color. reverberations. the approaching noise of someone she's never known, or has lived with in ancient egypt/ the revolutionary war/ victorian england. large families. and she wonders

if she does want a child of her own. her family has been her writing, her plants. dreams. the sources of her own personal, hidden life as birth and re-birth. her bathtub. how she washes, prepare herself for every day as it comes—always the sweet oil, the powder—the body that continues as she continues, growing lighter, heavier, lighter. younger. older.

more in the mailbox. divorce papers. the final ones. she hasn't lived with that husband for almost four years/ did nothing about the divorce until a few months ago. now here it is. a long breath takes her into and out of: can men and women ever live together? differences. then how does a child occur?

how can any of us accumulate love and tenacity? stay next to each other?
she puts the papers in a folder with other necessary things—income tax, the
loan agreement for her car. dry proof of nothing she understands.

clare drives to margaret's house later in the day. there are no words to say
about the stone, but clare wants to talk anyway, to pick some of the dark
green chard that grows wild in margaret's back yard.

> they begin with a letter that margaret's
> just gotten from a friend in hawaii, who
> writes all over the envelope as well as the
> letter. margaret reads some parts to clare,
> tells about the way the friend used to en-
> tertain. no money, but canned cream of
> mushroom soup seemed like gourmet
> food because of the way the friend served
> it, gave it to people, accepted it herself.
> that leads them to
>
> the chard, how dark and full of iron it is.
> clare bends, chops, cuts it from clusters
> that grow as if they aren't food at all—
> weeds—the growth of what is never
> pruned/ shaped. clare realizes how stuffy
> she's gotten: thinking that only food from
> the grocery store really exists. she piles
> the chard in a huge brown paper bag—
> knows how it will cook down, how she
> needs a lot of it to make a meal. margaret
> says,
>
> "take all you want," and clare would like
> to stay in the yard the whole afternoon,
> stay with the chard
> feel
> her back move
> her hands grasp the leaves
> the scissors cut them
> dirt stick to her fingers
> the bag get fuller and fuller
> her hands/ the dirt/ the dark green
> she

50

misses the mountains. times she's back-
packed, listened to no noise, no noise.
freshly caught trout in a pan. an old man
who once said to her, " just keep walkin',
you'll make it." half-way up the steepest
trail she'd ever been on. to a few curving
days of the fish, the stream next to her
sleeping bag, a thin book she'd tucked in
her pack. dirty jeans. dandelion greens to
pick and cook. work and rest.

the chard will last. clare will make salads,
cook it to eat by itself, put leftover chard
in omelets in hamburger meals she stirs
up in the skillet in tortillas with cheese.
chard.
asparagus.
lentil soup. almond cheese cake.
it comes back to her: the pleasure of
food, of feeding, of what is natural,
of weak and strong, of

pregnancy. she goes into the house. they look at each other—clare reads in
margaret's face the round stomach, the easy clothes, the swelling breasts.
she had a child at thirty-nine. clare talks: her sense of wanting to be away
from men, but wanting a child. what's going on? margaret offers only a few
words—about women, about the safe places they look for in themselves, in
a family, in a house that keeps its own chronicle from year to year. the new-
born and the small. a nursery that tends seedlings or children or the spirit.
and healing. restoring. margaret says, "do you ever think that you might be
healing your mother? caring for her through yourself? her early death—of
cancer—that you may be answering some of her questions with your own
living?"

clare will save this. as she's saved a couple of handkerchiefs of her mother's/
a watch with a face so tiny she can hardly read the numbers. fabric and
time. and there is no answer to margaret's question except in clare's own
repeating it to herself, again and again.

they drink a couple glasses of wine. margaret tells clare about a movie she's
just seen—a comedy and at some point a woman singing, "ah, sweet mystery

of life," in a high falsetto voice. clare laughs at that, wants to hear more about the film. margaret gets up and does imitations of the characters. then clare talks about people she knows who are funny—who can turn a conversation around with a couple of words. clare and margaret laugh even harder. at monsters. at people who won't say anything over the telephone after they've called you/ at dirty words said in unexpected sentences. at how daniel looks when he's being very serious and talking about buddhist meditation. clare and margaret try to put his face into theirs, pretend to sit with their backs very straight, can't quite, but know what they mean. laugh at knowing what they mean.

louder and louder.

softer and softer.

one day. a few days. clare will look at children. "decisions only as what might take place." what she was thinking of as she headed toward november as she has kept the threads of all this—they combine/ attract the next events.

we do have masks, real faces, faces under the real faces.

her name

is clare.

her name

is more than it means/ less than the next season.
air
that expects us to be alive
tomorrow
and that book about sorcery.

a dream of women who made love to
her, kiss and hold her, and this is going on in every room of the hotel where she finds herself visiting.

it is her real name.

food strangers *tie everything* *the together* *womanhood*

two of them. two women. strangers. unknown details of houseslippers, tooth-brushes. two of them. coming, even now, on the plane. what to plan/ what to leave alone? three hours from minnesota to california for a writing con-ference clare's helped organize. strangers. flying. clare wants to compose the days they'll be here—every chord—so that nothing gets lost, everything flows, every

detail. eyebrows. the expressions on faces she's never seen. all the years these women have existed in the world at the same time as clare but they've never seen each other's

eyebrows. strangers. on their way. because

clare has invited them has invited through

letters, through knowing rosemary because of a magazine that rosemary has edited.

clare puts extra fruit and bread in the house. empties a drawer in the bed-room. can they both use one drawer? hangers in the closet. because she has invited. offered. said yes. even called rosemary once, long distance, about money and the airport and said yes, they can fit in her house, the smallest house, the house at the top of a house, the place that is so much clare's and she struggles with the clothes—old jackets and some odd-shaped skirt she made once—puts them in the closet behind the bedroom where there are already too many boxes, shoes, files.

because she has

invited. strangers.

she pictures them. rosemary will look like the blond princess of clare's child-hood: her handwriting is shaped like coins and slippers. she writes long letters, letters like castles–intricate. the other woman, helen, whom she's never seen or written to, will be quiet. inward. there will be problems of space and luggage. or arguments about "literature." —about symbols and metaphors and words clare never uses and won't discuss with anyone ex-cept luis. perhaps paul. only if they're eating and drinking at the same time. and rosemary and helen will find clare sloppy. or too rational. or tight with her money. or she spends too much on magazines. they'll either think that hollywood is decadent and see only the smog, or they'll want to meet movie stars. neither is the truth, neither is the way clare lives, and now, as these women are flying are on their way will be here in three hours—less than that—

"why?" clare says out loud. "why

have I invited them?"

53

V

the airport is like a plane itself. what doesn't stay on the ground for long. travelers, people who move and know languages. clare always wants to go somewhere herself when she's here, even though she fears getting lost, ending up in dallas instead of spain. she's not too early. not time to read or get coffee, just time enough to watch the gate, check the flight number too often, watch the gate again, look at a handsome man who's too young but handsome—does she always choose handsome men? was that dream about choices or about men? or about margaret herself, who's also waiting—for the old woman—the old woman, who, it turns out, rosemary and helen and margaret and clare will have in common through esther's years of writing. she's from minnesota, too, and they will spend time puzzling out this woman that no one calls a grandmother, who makes her own legend, builds it, and she is clare/ the others

forty years from now. what we begin to feel, shaking our backs our necks that ache after too many hours of sitting or working. closer and closer. out of snow. these women are coming out of clare's own years in seasons, out of someplace that clare understands, has forgotten, understands again in

the princess gets off the plane wearing jeans that don't quite fit—baggy—and she's thin—her collection of purse, tape recorder, books stick out from her like extra bones/ her long fingers. oh, rosemary, the end of winter and the leap into palm trees, leaving the windows open.

helen takes the shape of butter and melons and when clare hugs her, quickly, just trying it out, just to show that she meant the invitation, she is absorbed/ united. it is the bosom the wheat the five loaves of bread a day her aunt baked on a wood stove.

they have recognized each other at once.

there is no way to grow into it.

they start/ can't stop telling everything that comes to them: histories, moments, what to do next. they drive to clare's house, decide they'll go out again—to see some of the city—but they can't stop

talking. they talk about poets, cancer, politics, cats, diaries. they say, "yes, I know," and, "but maybe," and, "have you...?" and, "wait, I have to tell you..." as if clare has been born out of rosemary and helen, as if they are ancestors and vines that reach the present and the past.

now. in these few days. and rosemary and helen have come to clare for warmth. the amorality of california where the weather is the jasmine, the freedom, and how many lives you can have here, all at once.

they don't go out. they find their places: rosemary at the table, where she leans on her elbows, then throws her hands out in a way she has of saying, "this is what I mean/ there's even more to come." helen on the couch. she rests, smokes with real pleasure, exhales slowly, gradually says something else and something else until clare hears her own nebraska aunt who could predict the weather by watching the sky for awhile. clare sits in the chair across from them, laughs, pulls closer, interrupts, listens until

they go to sleep in clare's bed. clare sleeps on the couch. when the three of them get up in the morning, clare discovers that helen knows everything: the first thing anyone should ever do for the day is make coffee. it's the only time someone has been in clare's house and has gotten up ahead of her and made coffee. clare wants to cry. it's so little. has she been really lonely? she's never had sisters, has only lived with men in her adult life, has hated the idea of roommates and still does. this feeling of familiarity/ of family she has with rosemary and helen—they echo. they remind her. they all come out of the land in some way, out of knowing how to do things with their hands, to have opinions that are heard and important. women who haven't learned how to be pretty. women who make their lives out of what they have with them all the time. landscape. this is in their writing in their breathing in their eagerness to see:

the ocean.

the ocean on thursday	the ocean a week later
"there it is!" they talk of the lakes of minnesota of always being close to	daniel. eight o'clock in the morning and clare is still half in some wrinkle

but this is really

the ocean. the pacific the surf the gulls
the endless and the three of them take
off their shoes before anything else.
when they've touched it, made sure the
water is still cold, still salty, still the
ocean, they sit in the sand.
clare.
rosemary. helen.
each with a notebook that comes out
at the same time, how they reach for
pens as if they are all going to write
the same thing, but they can't/ they
don't and when clare happens to look
over rosemary's shoulder, she sees,
"clare. it's good to be in her house."
surprised. that rosemary should write
about her as clare writes about rose-
mary as helen has a notebook with
graph paper in it: all the tiny squares
she likes that would drive clare crazy—
clare uses only plain, unlined paper—
and rosemary is left-handed, which
changes every word and the way she
holds her pen.

clare writes: "birds. a circle of them that
grows wider and wider. and the noise
of water always unexpected—tumult,
then quiet—the quietest, as a man
down the beach bends over for a
minute to pick up

anything. how we all measure our feet
by the way we hold a small piece of
glass in our hands.

I sit with two women who are strang-
ers but have shared how I eat. we have

in her nightgown her feet curling into
each other and understanding that
there's no alarm clock that it's not a
work day that helen and rosemary
have gone home to minnesota that
there's nothing to do and

the phone. the phone rings like a plane
crash a sudden explosion.

daniel. clare's glad to hear his voice,
sorry he's called, doesn't want to de-
cide anything but he says, "do you want
to drive to the ocean?" mentions clear
weather, sun. his voice is the way he
always seems to be going upstairs—
taking two steps at a time.

why does she laugh? why does he
amuse her so much? she can be ironic
with him in ways that she can't be with
other people. he knows that we all
want someone to push into our houses
and change the furniture around. grab
our arms and send us flying. that the
best answers are sometimes the fastest
ones, not what we ponder and put into
our finest words. daniel makes clare a
dark lady with a quick tongue. he's a
trapeze, a threat. a still possible lover,
although that seems only
possible
and isn't said. there has been one real
scene of physical love between them
since january and early february. it was
good. it was on clare's couch, it was
slow and easier than daniel usually is,
and what was he finding out? clare
doesn't wonder about it. he'll find his
own way in this, as she finds hers by

made sounds with each other that match, collide, jump into pasts we barely know or know all of or can't imagine. we've pieced together something that is not ourselves and not anyone else—the fourth thing that happens when three people spend time talking, driving, watching an almost tangible place that is what we are now and will not be when the two of them leave or even when we see each other again. that place is

one of the birds who lands on the beach and folds one wing at a time. the waves come forward. the wind starts. I feel it through my jeans through my whole day of movement. there has been nowhere to sit down today, but something holds me, laps at my back, promising and changing and turning me through faces that grow more and more my own."

sea. source. late that night, clare will dream of herself standing in a doorway, looking into a room beyond the dream, thinking that she never wants to teach anything to anybody again. loosening. no need to instruct,
always wondering
if
the listener will smile. or if she'll be told that what she says is ignorant, foolish. the teacher as the critic as the judge as the person in herself who demands/ makes up answers.

silence. how easy it is to be silent with helen. with rosemary. in the center of

climbing into his big car which is close to a truck and she tells him, "I'd like to drive this all the way across the country." he would, too, so they talk about sleeping in the back, making money as they go from place to place, people they know that they could stay with. summer. too hot. the fall? too far away. but they keep it up—the talk—as if it has gone on inside of both of them: away, to be away, to be out of responsible thinking and into

one pair of levis/ no hot showers. the vision of movement. the masculine. the joy of hunting.

the ocean shines. stones have been washed up on the beach; clare picks one up. then another. they are those perfectly round, smooth stones that seem to have been put down on the sand very carefully. clare walks ahead, then daniel catches up and goes faster, beyond her. he doesn't look at the stones much—they seem small to him, just stones. clare has a pocketful and will take them home, wash the sand off, keep them on the table for a long time, thinking how the water shaped them. then let them go. the stone from margaret. "it is still intact, whole." clare has forgotten religion but knows something

about old hymns and the repeating sound of the waves.

daniel finds a long, thick piece of sea vegetable rubbery. a shaggy knob on

their talking is always silence. when they're at clare's house each of them simply goes away at different times. into the kitchen. to lie on the bed and read for awhile. out for a walk. they don't explain or ask if they can. how the real family works: each one is there, each one leaves, and when the house is old it still keeps them as they think of it, return to it just before falling asleep. nothing dies with people who are

willing to sit close to each other
near the ocean
willing to part freely
because they know that connections
have little to do with
sitting close to each other near the
ocean
on just one day.

the end of it. he holds it in front of him, between his legs, and runs along the sand—"my cock! my dick! my member! private members only! no one on the beach except private members!" there's no one to hear, but clare is suddenly embarrassed. some adolescent shyness. she only smiles a little at the shoreline, doesn't join daniel's running/ hopes he doesn't want to kiss her now. it is her body her vulnerable body her virginity that comes back for a moment. faced with the first hard-on the first tongue the first knowing that there is some power in men that is wonderful, vulgar, massive. what takes over. what doesn't stay.

they get back in the car. clare puts her hands in the pockets of her jacket. daniel goes into a store to buy something to drink—she doesn't want anything, but takes a sip of his seven-up. carbonated. tingling. he's thrust the can toward her and wants her to have some. what gift is this? when she hands it back, she looks at his face. nothing trembles, but looks away quickly, starts to drive. "yeah," he says, his eyes on the street. "if we want to go across the country, I guess we just have to do it."

it will never happen.

is it that we are always most comfortable with our own sex, with the similar organs, up-bringings, height, length of time, length of
each monthly cycle for clare is a life in itself. she recognizes the rising and falling—what drops inside of her, what lets go. she will have a day or two of

58

terrific energy: she bursts like a pod, like seed that flies through the air doesn't know where to land is picked up by the wind isn't ready to be planted yet. then the blood. the need to rest, stare for a long time at one page. once clare woke up in the middle of the night, menstruating, her stomach rushing with pain and release. she sat in bed the rest of the night with an article about raising chickens. every breed. the pictures of tall feathers, feet like little forks, tiny eyes. she discovered chickens in their variety but what they need to eat is usually the same. the constancy of her body. expectation. renewal. she knows that men feel this, too, but how? no one has ever talked about his own cycles to her. can she ask daniel about this? is it something men tell among themselves? luis. older. he told her once, "we've all been each other—men and women—at some time. otherwise, how could we get along at all?" his eyes are always womanly to clare—or is that simply experience, years, because she sees the same eyes in

> esther. the old woman. the myth of how to travel
> without money. how to stay in strange houses
> every night. buses/ portable typewriter. a couple
> of bags full of papers and woven blouses that
> unfold, cover esther's huge stomach—she sleeps
> in them, talks in them, the heavy fabric like the
> quilt the hair that began and grew longer and
> longer until it reached through the whole neigh-
> borhood. clare's photograph of her grand-
> mother: those beads swinging around her neck.
> pioneers.

margaret says, after esther has stayed at margaret's house, "you know, she sleeps in most of her clothes. she came into my room once, late, to see why the light was on. when she turned around to go back, her body was an el-ephant—the width, the skin. her feet! I've never seen such brown feet. I want to visit the women in minnesota and north dakota that she mentions so often. rivers of women."

there is some bitterness about esther that frightens clare. men as oppressors. poverty. bad teeth. years of politics that make a woman unacceptable to governments, to the suburbs. the constant travel: "I have no home," esther says. "I live in the woods." the woods may be margaret's house or someone's apartment in san francisco or the desert. rosemary tells clare that it's often the house of esther's daughter—a large, comfortable place. but for esther it

59

is the woods. the cabin. the shelter that is necessary so that she can sleep safely until the next day, when she will be on the bus again, on to the next place, the next person who may call her crazy, not listen to the words that leap that won't stay put in the books she's written. books out of print. little publicized. books that the women who come to the conference want. to buy, read, find in themselves/ in esther's cornfields, birth, rituals of beginning over and over.

over and over. what women do. not progress that leads to a place with more buildings, more money, more contracts and employment. over
and over. where are our homes? in our hands, in our actual nests? or the other side: clare when she earns her living. takes care of what is right in front of her, comes up with a solution. sees something through to the end. each person. male and female. but. clare comes back to the differences. each new combination of cheekbones.
clare turns suddenly. nothing there. but it's her own death. a ghost, a father. something of
ruth dies in clare's last few thoughts every day. what they have to do with each other isn't over, will never be finished, and ruth must be

> just as she was just as she wasn't.
> clare wishes for another funeral, to celebrate ruth's complete passing from one country to another. ruth wouldn't see them all, clustered around some end-of-winter fire, reciting whatever they've learned from her death. but they would all know something, would begin to trust their own shadows:

> never really the shape of the thing they reflect. they are their own. they depend on a real thing to give them life, but then they spread and contract and obey their own laws. light/ darkness. the internal and external family.

clare looks at rosemary and helen. they make her feel so much at home, even in her own place, what she thought was hers. they all share their writing—it helps them to compare, to exchange craft/ themes, their own second and third and fourth selves—the selves that make the writing, join them to language, whom that language touches. bitterness?

praise. clare hears that word. praise. it is what writing has become to her—
aimed upward in some way. shouts and blessings. it is what she basks in
with rosemary and helen. that they don't tear at each other's pages. and all
the women who come to the conference for two days, who cluster, tell their
names, give what they've written and found out: praise. it comes from un-
der the language. it is not just talking. it's poets, witches, troubadours, seers,
the woman with a face like a potato who comes up to clare during lunch:

"did you ever feel that your work was no good?" the woman looks at clare as
if clare can really answer.
"yes," clare says. "yes, often."
the woman waits a minute. then she says, "thanks. you've helped." walks
off, as if it's all right to be frightened. clare notices the woman that after-
noon, and the next day. she's in the workshops that go on. she doesn't speak
up, but isn't afraid to be there, to listen, to go home and write for herself, for
whoever has other questions to ask.

STARING AT THE AMERICAN BUFFALO (1976)

1

There were a few left when I was a kid in nebraska
I was afraid of the fence but not of them

2

tough and shiny/ these small eyes
not to be caught under
every time I look behind me
I gain and lose

I take the buffalo as saint
how it feels to weigh a thousand pounds
protector of blatant dreams

the buffalo
feminine
suck of
Buffalo

3

I paw the air. I wish for no enemies, but without them I would have noth-
ing to do. I come awake as the hump on my back gets meaner and meaner.
then there is the desire to huddle with others who are like me, who under-
stand the meaning of wariness/ of living in protection and lust/ of living
with footsteps that echo/ of living with every change that is not final can
never be final is hopelessly alive.

I throw the I ching: the wanderer takes my hair like a stiff wind. my
mother would buy me a new coat every other winter. I've been surrounded
by luck/ the circle of wagons. it's time to hear each sound with all my
ears. clouds move across the prairie, fast.

present tense

4

the sting of the bullet

the buffalo lingers over a stalk of grass, she catches the scent of something
hard, unwelcome. she begins to trot.

a necessary friend of mine is hunted. one of her breasts carries disease
carries a tumor carries a warning a crisis a blind rage. if I lose her as I've
lost three others, I will never look at the sky again/ never look at a place to
be safe under for a whole night.

I would dissolve her poison with my own milk
I would carry the burning teeth in my two good breasts
I would be this strong except that I am breaking/ I do not weigh as much
as I think

the buffalo and I rub against each other's legs to feel the connections of coarse, unraveled fur. she eats what is growing in front of her/ she has her calf in the spring/ she knows which direction the odor comes from. the buffalo settles into the undergrowth where she knows she can't be seen. she opens her mouth and snorts a trail of weeds that are yellow in the unmistakable shape of living as your hugest body tells you to live whether you can or not. buffalo skulls everywhere. yet she looks at me and says, "I'm as real as increasing numbers."

5
if you don't know me
you'll recognize the running
if you don't know your own animal
believe, anyway, that you are helped
feel the land turn as you go
the movement, in a tornado, of one house to another spot

6
I will never be rid of the dumb grunt that makes no words of itself. I dream of dying pigs. I dream of my nebraska yard, flooded. I remember the unbearable engine of the train that took me out of childhood, away from natural doubt and muscle. it is impossible to write the word "machine" without trembling. the buffalo drinks clean water and knows the difference.

7
some light spreads, though its shadows keep me alert. instinct. I gather the courage, again, of wanting too much. I grow a look that tells me in one breath whether I need to stand next to you or not.

a good man strides through the grass
I don't ask him a thing
he scratches his chin

I'm thankful for thunder in the afternoon
the buffalo growls, "come and try it"
she pulls out a heart as warm as sun through her deep brown hide
I can't get his yodeling out of my belly for days

8
prayer to the buffalo:

keep me chewing so that nothing gets lost by swallowing too fast
keep me alone but close to the herd

keep me ready for narrow escapes. I will close both eyes and squint hard
enough to see you as you lurch toward me. you will take me on your back/
I will take you into my shoulders. whatever we do will be full of communion
with whole trees/ with stampedes and whatever else is large enough to
stand our smell. the hook of my tongue will learn to eat from the ground.
we won't know the end of anything, but we'll never be finished with
orneriness and salt.

9
when you're a stranger, you look to what keeps its outlines steady
buffalo are not mistaken for rivers
each birth is how they will always look
my four legs rattle
my feet stitch themselves into hooves

PROSE POEMS AND A POEM
(1975-1977)

THE SPACE BETWEEN SAYING GOODNIGHT
AND ACTUALLY LEAVING

The temperature is just enough for something loose around my shoulders. A backyard is a summer is a retreat from neighbors is a way of spreading a cloth on the ground. One man talks of canoeing in Canada on a placid lake. The other man—I don't know him well—compliments me: the sort of sentence that rolls out of a mouth as if the tongue has been saving it for awhile. I see that he means what he says, and the knot in my shoulder, which has been tying me to irritable memories all day, eases. The woman that I know as a lover of unfinished buildings is passing more food. She's going on her first backpacking trip next week. As she describes her new hiking boots, she says, "a real commitment."

I would like to sleep in this yard tonight, stretched out against the moon at its peak. That moon: creamy yellow and I could dip my finger into it— come up with a taste like the cheesecake we're eating. A family recipe given as a wedding gift.

The man of the placid lake looks straight at me. I've known him for thirteen years, but he's been gone for ten of those. There's no reason why I look away from him, down at my hands which are folded in my lap like the daughters who have already gone into the house. This little nervousness pulls me into my shoulder again. Protection, and the opposite desire to get in the car, the four of us, and drive to the mountains. To start walking at midnight, without proper clothes. with only a flashlight, with only the food that's left from this picnic. How much we could find out, away from the rows of corn that grow only sweet, dependable ears. I pull my shawl around me more closely. It is not exactly what I want, and the wool slips down my arm, catching me in the dream I had recently of my hair constantly changing its length.

At the end of the evening we are all at home. I imagine that she's trying on her boots for the tenth time. I imagine that her husband, the man who's kind, reads something out loud to her that he wants to share before he forgets it. I imagine that the other man thinks of the woman who has left him to return to Canada. I imagine that I'm getting out of bed to sneak back to the yard. I realize the moon is changing her place in the sky, as she can't help doing, and the four of us pass some of her light between us before we decide to stay where we are for the rest of the night. As it turns out, we will not be together again.

TRAFFIC

I want pockets. my hands need to curl and lean. there have been strangers in the past few weeks: men who have that look of wondering about me. there are things I don't know how to tell—that I watch the mirror for the end of summer/ a return to warm clothes. why am I being held by someone's arm as I cross the street—an arm I've just met, that might either push or guide me?

I search the stores for pockets. some sweaters have them, just at the right length, close to the hips, so I can burrow my hands in them, feel the soft wool give a little. it's reachable pockets I want, without much in them. maybe one handkerchief, folded. or a piece of hard candy that I can take out, suck, put back in the wrapper/ in the pocket. something to last all day.

and there's been an argument with a friend who's a lover who's not a lover who might be and always has been and never was. it went on for a whole morning and afternoon, between our houses, over the phone, in his kitchen. both of us dressed up because other people were coming, and there was some need to hurry. it was settled with our holding each other for a minute, but that didn't make us forget how long we've known each other and not at all. arguments don't heal, even when they're about giving up something that's ready to be lost. it's been several days. I still turn him in my head like dice.

pockets are rooms. pockets should be of matching material. I fall asleep thinking of them: there are ways to make them and I wonder what's in my closet. extra cloth. I must ask someone I know who sews.

as I sleep, I dream that I'm a werewolf. I feel myself caught, going under, losing my senses. this is frightening, because I can kill someone, but pleasurable, too. a great fog in my body, a return to some deep state of aggression and submission. this stays in my stomach as I wake up. it's the middle of the night. I have never been the werewolf myself before.

it is always about who is hunted/ where we leave our trails. it is the story of trips from here to there and what we bring back is never the solution. I live in a combination of alleys, stairways, ripe flowers under a face that promises little, but I never know until I risk the open door the open legs the vision of shattering glass. that argument with my friend has the odor of what's been left too long, and its weight is too heavy to be balanced on either side. the men who look at me and wonder about me are my own curiosity. these strangers are accidents. they wait to happen, and they will.

finally, I do buy a jacket. something for fall, to wear as the days get colder. its pockets are valleys, the land between hills, the ability to see what's with me as I walk. pockets are not gamblers. no wheels to be caught under.

NO PLANS

there is some temptation to be normal, but it goes away. the wine ferments, loving itself from grape juice to drinking. I relish any process that takes time. not a simple book to read, but the pages do turn.

LUCK

Too many strawberries. Too many roses. All the blossoms turn into fruit before I have a chance to appreciate the gradual ripening. Too much sunlight every morning. And the moon is a cradle or a flag or a pot of jam or a painted toenail—never simply a source of tides and light. This is no fantasy, but a time of victory when everything I drink is a toast to health.

I close the door and tremble. Who deserves to pick all the food at once, and, suddenly, even more tomatoes appear on the vines? Who deserves to stay up all night as I've done for the first time in years, watching the sky fill again from the window of a man who holds me with laughter that settles in the rug and stays under my feet for days? Who deserves teeth that never ache, hands that can pick thorns without being stung? The strawberries push at me with a sweetness that runs through my veins, joins my blood, rises to my eyes where I can seduce anything that comes toward me looking edible or loving.

I hover in the smallest room in my house, thinking I'll hide until this abundance is over. I sit down to work, wearing the ugliest shirt I have. I listen to dissonant music, but it only makes me want to dance, and I get up, and I smell the profusion of flowers and curls in my hair. The phone rings. The door opens. The mailman brings a package of more seeds to plant. I hope that the serious guides of my life are still in their caves, enjoying some party of their own while they wait for me.

I decide to leave home, to go on a trip, and I'm relieved when my friend and I have car trouble. We stop in a flurry of exhaust fumes and jerking brakes. Then she says, "Did you bring the maps? Did you bring the wine? Did you bring money and phone numbers?" I answer yes to everything, and she says, "Oh, you're perfect!" I notice that there is lush scenery all around us. I pray out loud.

FEVER

Call it anything but a straight line. Call it a story that you can't find your way out of. Call it a woman you love and a man you love. Say that they might love each other. Say that she goes away. Make her beautiful, with dark eyes as sad as not knowing what to do. The man tells her goodbye and hopes that the distance is not too great. You stand in your backyard, watching the flowers, red ones, and you are pushed with a blood you recognize as loss before it even starts. So you make sure that it doesn't start, though you have a dream in which she comes home and puts one arm around you and one arm around him, saying all three of you can have each other with no one left out. Her eyes have turned to trust you can't understand. It is a dream that keeps you away until he suggests you visit. You do. When you visit him again, you can't quite breathe. And when you visit him after that, you actually touch his shoulder and can barely make it home. She returns; she has missed him but says she can't stay with him now. She talks to you for a long time. You do not hide things from yourselves, but there is some great secret that none of you knows. It is the secret of what will happen next. She is not as sure of her decision as she thinks. He is taking long walks in the early evening, when it is not as hot as it's been. His dog follows him. Your eyes follow her. Her back is graceful and quiet. Each of you turns in your separate neighborhoods, and it is not even a complete circle. The still air crumbles. Summer is deadly.

FOR THE SPIRIT

plums find themselves eaten
where has it gone
this fruit
the last song

———————————

water picks up the summer
a finger pressing the whole body
again, again until every inch is drained
I tell you this is slow crying
one finger
then the next

———————————

who calls out

mountain/ sky like a very old heaven
I want to put my feet on this background
no, the sand says, stay where you are
it's enough for now

———————————

in the wilderness
I step on thorns
I love their reminders/ I am not alone here
we will see each other when we both get back

INTERVIEW
WITH LELAND HICKMAN
(1978)

RAINBOWS CARNATIONS AMERICAN CORN
(an interview with Holly Prado)

May 29, 1978

Old Sol is benign this young afternoon of May 29, 1978. At the poet's freshly acquired apartment in Hollywood, within sight of the Griffith Observatory, Holly Prado sorts the two white and four tangerine-colored carnations into her decision about having received them, and then pours white wine for us. I ask her if she would mind consulting the I Ching during the interview. No, she says, she would not like to do that. Then, she has a question for me—: {Which is not recorded on tape: Will I give her my responses to her writing, my insights into her work? She needs, she says:}

I Ching

...Some help in starting to talk about the work, because I don't see it with any eye except the inner eye, and that eye gives me both courage and self-doubt.

Well, Holly, that's why I considered starting out the interview with a question for the I Ching. Whether or not you would want to ask a serious question publicly, and find yourself some sort of guideline—I don't know.

My sense of the I Ching is that I would have loved to have done that about three years ago.

Yes. I understand. There's no point in using the I Ching as some sort of game.

Well, it's hard for me to conceive of using it publicly. I think what the *I Ching* does for me is touch my own unconscious and the collective unconscious, and it usually takes me a long time to absorb what it has to say, and my suspicion is that if we asked it a serious question, both of us knowing that that serious question was going to get into print in a literary magazine, the I Ching would come up with something like "Youthful Folly"— in other words, "Keep your mouth shut. Don't ask me what you already know." *[Laughing]* What was the question that you had in mind?

If you feel so hesitant to do that, then that's not—auspicious.
What was the question?

The question? No, you would have to determine the question.
Oh, ho ho ho ho *ho*! Not only do I have to use the *I Ching* in public, I have

to determine the question!

No, we've already decided that we're not going to do that. But I will try to answer your question. I can't do it in great detail because it would take an awful lot. I respond to your work in such a way that I find myself somewhat in your position regarding your work. Not that I do not know that it's brilliant—and that's a tame word—and why I think so, and what I respond to—but I believe that most readers who find your work, and return to it, get into a relationship with your work that is as private to them as the I Ching *is to you. And I find myself having to admit to a certain amount of—what shall I say?— not vulnerability exactly, but that's there, too—not indecisiveness exactly because something you say in your work about "decisions as what might happen" sort of guides me—but the meanings in your work seem like such a vast subject to me. And it's so close to me. I think that as we go along—... But I don't think I can cover it in one interview, or one meeting, just as I don't think that you could ever say everything you have to say in one poem.... How did you first discover that you were a poet, Holly?*

I never did. I'm not sure that I know that about myself. I know that I write. I don't pretend that I don't get recognition for my writing. I know that I write poetry. I got into a poetry workshop about eight years ago with Alvaro Cardona-Hine in which for the first time in my life I was able to work with people who were taking their poetry seriously, and I found myself in a milieu of writers that just excited and frustrated and enlivened me to the point where I knew that writing was going to be a very major thing in my life. I don't think anybody ever *called* me a poet, but what started to happen was that people in the workshop began to encourage me. Alvaro set up a reading at the Venice Public Library, which was the first reading that I did, and that was probably about 1971. I was very excited about words. When I got up to read, I could hardly stop laughing, because I was nervous and because I was so excited about the notion of being able to almost *sing* those words that I had written. I don't know where those early poems are. At the moment I read, they seemed astonishing to me. It seemed astonishing that words had come to me and that someone was asking me to read them out loud. Then people in the workshop—like Rosella Pace, Barbara Hughes, Alvaro, Ameen Alwan, Georgia Alwan—began to encourage me to send my work out. I think it was through some public recognition that my writing was valid that I began to take myself seriously. And Alvaro had the great ability for a long time to see where I was going before I knew where I was going.

How do you mean?

He was always pushing me to do things I wasn't quite ready to do.

Do you mean certain areas, certain subjects or in terms of the craft?

I think more in terms of craft than in subject area. When I began to really write prose poems, when that started bursting open for me. Interestingly, after a long drive I'd taken to New Mexico, it was as if in the rhythm of driving the long line broke open for me—and I came home and started writing prose poems, and then gradually I got to the place where I was able to write something like *Feasts* [Momentum Press, Los Angeles, 1976], which is a long prose piece—autobiographical poetic fiction, I suppose. At that point, I really had to go it alone. I'd been in that workshop for several years and I was getting a lot of messages about trying to structure *Feasts*, and that was a kind of craft that I did not want to impose on that book.

Were you in a workshop while you were writing Feasts?

By that time, I was going off and on and I showed about the first twenty pages of the book to that workshop, and it was one of those moments when I realized that I had done the wrong thing by sharing something with people that wasn't finished.

What happened? Did it hurt your work?

No, it didn't hurt the work at all. I realized by the response I got that I was really into something and I realized that I couldn't bear to have anybody talk about it, positively or negatively, until it had completed itself.

In other words, you had progressed beyond the point where you needed outside reassurance?

No. No. I still very much need to share my work with other writers.

Is it in terms of reassurance still?

No, it's in terms, now, I think, of asking people to help me see what I'm doing. People can often point out things in my work that I haven't been aware of—every once in a while, of course—pick up a line that's awkward or pick up a confusion that I haven't noticed. I don't depend on criticism from other people—and I mean criticism in the literary way of really going through a piece of writing and talking about how it can be changed—I don't depend on that. But I do depend on other people to help me talk about and know what I'm doing. The students in my own writing workshops and my friends who are writers. But when I was writing *Feasts*, my feeling was something quite different. It was that for the first time in my life I was working on a very long project, for me. It took

79

me six months to basically write the book, and it wanted to be secret, it needed to be held in the vessel, as the alchemists would say. It needed to boil and bubble and smoke and take me to places where it was going. It needed that privacy to transform itself into writing. So it was not really that I didn't *need* criticism of it, it was that in some very inner way, the book couldn't stand the outside eye until it was finished. Then the minute it was finished, I started making xerox copies and giving it to some of the women in a Woman's Building workshop that I was teaching, and asking them to respond to it.

I noticed your most recent contribution to Bachy, *"15 Morning Love Stories," was in xeroxed form. Are you sending those poems around to friends for response?*

I share those with the workshops. I read them first to Harry Northup because they're about him and because they really are about our falling in love and because they feel so personal to me that if he had said he did not want them to be public, I would not have made them public. Because I do have an ethical sense about writing about other people. Because I'm involved in personal writing, I always write about the people who know me, and if I need to say something in covering an identity, I can do that, but in those pieces it would have been perfectly obvious, to anyone who knew me, who they were about. And when Harry had heard them and liked them and said do whatever you want to with them, then I started making xerox copies and passing them around, and reading them at poetry readings, and making them public.

As a first part of my answer to your question: Among the kinds of poems you write that absolutely astonish me are the love poems. I noticed this in your first book, Nothing Breaks Off at the Edge [New Rivers Books, New York 1976], *which, for me, has some of the most exciting and moving—touching—love poems I've ever read. Erotic poems. This is only a part of what, it seems to me, you can do with your instrument. You go so much deeper than the erotic when you write an erotic poem. You started writing* Nothing Breaks Off at the Edge *early?*

Early.

It took a long time to write, to compile?

No. By the time I was ready to collect the pieces in the book, I had two or three years' worth of work, and it fell into place very quickly. There were a few pieces at the end—I had started a new cycle of writing, and there were a few pieces at the end that were from that new cycle that didn't fit and those ultimately got left out. But for the most part, the organization of the book was fairly simple. Something had gathered in me—the book had gathered in me—and when I started shuffling the pieces, they fell into place fairly easily. I'm interested in what you say about eroticism, because I remember one time saying very, very blatantly that I wanted to write dirty poems! And the response I got to that was shock on the part of other poets, and I realized that what I wanted to do was really touch what goes on intimately in my life—and that doesn't mean just sexual things. It means the intimacy of life lived from day to day, with the people that I care about, with myself, with my own body, with the kinds of changes that I go through, with the darkness and the light. And I really wanted to move somewhere into the Nature of things in a deep way. I mean, Nature is obscene and ruthless and gutsy and impersonal and nurturing. I have an incredible sense of wanting to touch that in my work. A lot of the comes from a place in me that is _under_ consciousness. I don't want to say, unconscious—I have a very specific notion that the unconscious is my dream-life and a different kind of place from the place I write from. But I really see writing as discovery. I see it as the discovery of Nature as it moves through, onto the page. If I know what I'm going to write when I sit down to write, I usually won't write it; it bores me. I want to see those cycles. I want to see the ruthlessness of Nature and what she does with me to put the poem or the prose on the page. I work very intuitively, in that sense. Once I begin to see what's happening, once the images begin to come up—I just wrote a piece this week which is basically a letter for Harry, called "Climate," in which there is a moon, a long drive, fear, being together, loneliness, enormous love, and all of those things started to pop on the page, and they started to pop very quickly—I allow that writing to happen and then I go back to look at it to see what needs to be crafted. I have enormous respect for craft. I do recognize that some pieces are gifts that one doesn't have to do very much with, but I love also the act of rewriting, and a lot of pieces go through many, many, many drafts before I feel that I've fulfilled that original, raw message I've gotten.

Which is the reason for craft. In your poems, as distinguished from your prose—when I say this, I feel as though I'm making some sort of trivial distinction— [Holly laughs loudly] _—because you have managed, from my point of view, to make a prose which is fascinating to a poet—to say the least._

I've been saying for a long time that I don't see the difference between poetry and prose. Someone said that the only difference between poetry and prose is the line break, and that was such an easy definition that I have accepted it for a long time. I think there are differences. There are certainly differences in language. When I want a sentence, I want a sentence. Or when the *work* wants a sentence. I have the deep feeling that forms *are* organic, that they come with the work. When I sit down to write, it starts to come either in a line or in a sentence. I know almost immediately whether it's going to be prose or poetry.

What is it about the impulse that makes you feel you know what's going to happen?

Well, if I put a period at the end of the line, it wants to be a sentence. I don't know! Again, it's intuitive. I think a lot has to do with the rhythm of the story I want to tell. It has to do with the *push* with which something comes. I can almost always write prose. I can't always write poetry.

Do you find writing easy, does it come to you quickly?

I find writing the easiest and the most difficult thing I do. I find myself writing all the time. As you know, I keep an obsessive journal. I keep pieces of writing going all the time that I consider *writing-writing*—that may become public. I really love to write. If I didn't love to write, I wouldn't do it.

How many hours do you give yourself for writing?

I don't. I have no idea how many hours a week I spend writing. I know that sometimes I feel as if I'm writing and getting up and down to write four or five times a day. Sometimes I feel as if I'm not writing at all, and that usually means that I'm just paying attention to journal-writing, maybe in the morning and in the evening. Sometimes I'll spend several hours at a time at the typewriter—I like to write directly on the typewriter, as well as by hand.

Do you find that that affects the form of what you're writing—that there's a connection between the impulse and the way you choose to go about it mechanically?

Stuff goes real fast on my electric typewriter and my electric typewriter makes a lot of noise, which convinces me that I'm putting an enormous amount of energy into what I'm doing, and the writing is usually very energetic when I use the typewriter.

Do you have dry spells?

I have cycles. I don't have blocks in the sense that I hear people describing writing blocks in which they cannot write at all. I think those blocks are legitimate and I don't think that anybody can write at fever pace always, without slipping over into madness. It takes incredible energy. I do believe in the Muse and I think the Muse comes through and that the Muse is Nature and is sporadic and doesn't visit all the time. I think the creative process is a much different process than the process by which we think we live, which has some kind of continuity and rationality. I find myself in periods in which I feel highly frustrated—it's as if there's something I need to write and I can't write it, and I keep writing and writing and writing and writing and writing and ultimately out of these periods there may come pieces that I like, but I keep having the feeling that I'm not writing what I need to write. When the push is really *there*, and the Muse is *there*, and my hand is there, and the pen is there, or the typewriter is there, and we all know what we're up to at the same time, then I know *immediately* that I've written what I need to write.

That sense of synchronicity.

Yeah.

You say that you like the process of discovery and you feel that you'd be bored if you knew what you were going to write. Do you ever do any planning? For example, Feasts *is a long work. Was there any necessary planning that you had to consider?*

That book was written *as* I was living it, so all I did really was choose the things out of my life that I was going to write about and when I had the manuscript completed, I did go back to pay attention to the threads and to help make that book as whole as I could make it in terms of the threads that came up—the relationship with the man in the book, the dreams that filtered into the book.

They were ongoing as the work was being done?

I was writing that as I was living it, which is a very exciting and peculiar way to work. I don't think I would ever do it again.

Why not?

I think maybe the writing of the book interfered with some of the living of the life.

Not the other way around?

No.

Is it too difficult a subject to explore?

No, I'm just stopping to think, because my ideas about that are not very clear. I do write out of the immediate much of the time and that seems okay for short pieces, but to make fiction of one's life as it's happening is fraught with the danger of feeling that one can control the life one is living. Writing, after all, is a way of summarizing. Even if one has great questions about what one is going through, there's an enormous sense of

"If I can write about it, it is not so frightening, it is not so dangerous, it is not so risky, I can get it on the page and it can stand there as art." I think that during the writing of *Feasts*, I was really moving in my life and moving in relationships and that perhaps I should have been terrified enough to just have lived through it. The other side—and I do think that everything contains its opposite—is that I am *very* glad the book exists, and I still—when I go back to it—I still feel great life energy in it. No one was harmed by it. I wrote about many, many of my friends. I gave them all different names, with the exception of Aletheia, whose name is too wonderful to be changed. Everyone recognized herself or himself in the book and was delighted to be written about. I think it's a loving book.

I do, too.

If it were a harsh book or a book that was very dark or critical I might feel differently about it.

I don't think there's any—well, the question of what is or is not an accident seems to me unanswerable and I feel that Feasts, *coming as it does into the Los Angeles community—it comes into a wider community than Los Angeles, of course—but as it does appear, amongst us all as writers and poets, it stands as kind of a keystone—cornerstone— for a depth of feeling we all share. I don't think it's any accident that it was written in Los Angeles. But getting back to the idea of control: You mention somewhere in an essay about journal-writing [*New Magazine, May 1977*] that you have a Jungian analyst. And archetypes enter into your work. Now, do these archetypes come from some decision you make to use them, or does the archetype come into consciousness—well, I'm getting into a matter of semantics here—*

[*Laughing*] I have trouble with psychological language. I am now in analysis. I have read a great deal of Jung's work and Jungian psychoanalysts' work. I do use the words "archetype," "shadow," "animus," "anima," but I find them difficult because I don't understand fully the concepts behind them in a psychological way. I think that it's easy to fall into a psychological vocabulary and toss it around and not have much understanding of it. Maybe all I can say about your question in terms of archetypes is that I'm fascinated with symbology. I'm fascinated with *things*. I have a really primitive sense that everything has some kind of life that we as human beings invest in it psychically, and when a symbol is *attracted to me*, it stirs something in me that makes me feel very excited and then I want to write about it and I want to explore it and maybe then I want to do some reading about it. But I have the feeling that symbols come to me through what my eye notices, what my heart notices, what gets excited in me—I don't think that I especially choose what I'm attracted to. When that attraction is aroused, it's inevitable—it's like a love affair that has to be completed.

For instance, in your poem "This Is The Truth About An Old Woman," the old woman is a symbol in the work.

Sure.

At one point, in reading Jung, I noticed that he talks about the Old Man and the Old Woman, as symbols, saying that they could mean either that the person is attempting too much control over life, or needs a teacher. How do you respond to that in relation to the writing of that poem?

At the time I wrote that piece, I was ignorant of the idea that you've just suggested. I think that I have *always* been concerned about what it is to grow old. At that moment, I was seeing myself as a woman in her thirties becoming aware of being a woman and wondering what it was like to be an old woman. That piece is a combination of dreams, a combination of fantasy and a combination of people—old women that I actually saw on the street. In looking at that piece now, I have a great fondness for it, because it did stir up the notion of old women as more than simply grandmothers. And it may have stirred in me a need for the Old Woman in myself, who might be some kind of guide into my own old age, which is much more complex than I ever imagined. I didn't have any sense at the time I was writing the piece that I was writing an archetypal piece, or that I was writing out of some idea of trying to find the archetypal Old Woman. In fact, she seems to be many women, in that particular piece of writing. I am amazed at the muliplicity of the sexes.

Do you have a sense of going forward in time as an accumulation of complexities?

I don't know if I can stand much more complexity! *[Laughing.]* Oh, Lee, I don't know, I really don't know. My sense, now that I've just turned forty, is that I have no idea who I am. It really is as if I'm starting over in some way, though I do carry my past experience with me, but it's as if I've lived through the thirties and dealt with the problems of all of us in the thirties—*their* thirties—and that some of those things and the dealing with those problems have moved me into the forties, but I haven't solved all those problems, and now I'm saying, oh thank God, all the people who are in their thirties now can take care of those problems, I'm going to move on to the different problems. It's almost as if, as one moves through life, one faces the problems of a particular age and we all have to live through them and the next set of circumstances and difficulties and excitements. I don't know what the forties will be for me. I have the sense that I've been old for a long time. I have the sense that I'm just *being born*, that somehow the forties are a very ripe, fruitful time and that I'm beginning to feel some of that ripeness. Colors like amber are coming up in my writing lately. I also feel that it's a time I've never lived through before. I'm not familiar with what it is to be forty, or to be "in my forties," or to be a forty-year-old woman in a moment in history where that is not terribly old and yet we also have a youth culture that insists that forty *is* terribly old. I find myself with a lot of contradictions, and I do feel as if I'm beginning over again, in some way. And I'm looking, at the moment, at things around my house, at things in my new neighborhood, that are symbols of the middle. I'm interested in balance. I'm interested in the middle. I find cups, mugs, the Observatory—round things—coming into my writing.

You mean the Griffith Observatory?

I've been obsessed with the Griffith Observatory ever since I moved into this house, which is directly in line with the Observatory.

All you have to do is go out on the sidewalk and you can see it.

Yeah, and I have written one piece about the Observatory in which it becomes very feminine. It's a piece that *Chrysalis* magazine is going to publish. They're doing a piece around women's spirituality and got very interested in the Observatory piece—or I must say Deena Metzger [interviewed in *Bachy* 10] got interested in it and chose it as a piece to publish. I'm still writing about the Observatory, even though that piece may be finished and publishable. I'm still obsessed with the Observatory.

When do you think that piece is going to be published?

It should be in the next issue of *Chrysalis*, which may be out in June or July.

> *In your work there are lots of scenes which take place with you driving a car or a truck or something. And you mentioned earlier that you drove to New Mexico and that's when you began writing prose. What is the connection in your mind between driving and moving into the rhythms of prose?*

I hate machines. I never see myself as a driver. I rarely use car imagery, but I realize that that's a kind of blindness. Obviously, as a person living in Los Angeles, I drive all the time. Driving holds a real rhythm for me. My car comes up a lot in my dreams as a symbol of my energy. I'm either trying to maneuver around poles and park in a parking lot somewhere, or I'm pulling up the emergency brake and it keeps coming up and up and up and up and will never quite hold, or I'm driving at the edge of a cliff and the car falls over the cliff and lands on a road below. I've had a number of dreams in which my car really is my energy, so I have to admit that I am much more of a driver than I think. I think the rhythm of driving, to me, is very powerful. I'm terribly moved by music. As a kid, I took piano lessons. I was exposed to music. I've always been touched by music. I've always been touched by rhythm. As one of those middle-class Midwestern children, I also got dancing lessons as well as piano lessons, so I have a feeling in my body about rhythm, and when I drive—I have a standard shift on my Datsun—I love to shift gears! I get fascinated with the difference of speed and the way that one can move one's feet and hands in a particular rhythm to shift gears. I'm interested in slowing down and speeding up. I drive aggressively.

I've noticed that.

Have you? Yes, well, Harry says he's going to enter me in the Indianapolis 500. And I'm going to have a load of poetry books in the back of the car to sell when I win the race. *[Hilarity]*

Wouldn't hold you back any, would they?

So I think there is something going on with driving that I'm not totally conscious of, but it really is a rhythm for me.

Has it any connection with prose?

I think it has a connection with writing generally, both poetry and prose.

Really—because I was speaking to Bill Mohr [Los Angeles poet and playwright] the other day and he happened to mention that reading your poetry out loud—when he took some of your poems to New York to a reading—he found it very difficult to get with the rhythms. The rhythms in your verse are complex. I've noticed this myself. The rhythms of your verse are more varied than the rhythms of your prose. And I'm still back at the question of why some days you'll get up and write and you'll choose to hit the return key, whereas other days you won't.

I'm not sure. And I'm not sure that I can answer that question in a way that'll make sense to readers of this interview. I can only say that it has to come back to my body and that my body shifts a lot. Some days I feel very, very tired; some days I feel full of energy. I go through a lot of cycles about just how I feel physically. I think that influences the rhythms of my writing. I'm interested that Bill said that my rhythms were difficult for him to read, because they're so *easy* for me to read. They feel *so* familiar to me. They really do feel as if they have come *out* of my body. And I really don't have trouble reading my work out loud. I love to give poetry readings. I've had in the past few weeks the sense that I really want to *sing* the work, though I have no intention of setting it to music, but there is something in me that is pushing through that wants to sing in an even more rhythmic way. I'm really beginning to see my rhythms as much more musical than I've ever seen them. Maybe that's connected, too, with driving. Maybe it is connected with being more in touch with the rhythms of my own body. In a writing workshop several years ago, I was reading a piece of mine out loud to the group and a young man in the group was taking his pulse while I was reading, and at the end he said, "Your rhythms are just like my heartbeat." I don't think all of us have the same heartbeats, but it interested me that he connected the notion of rhythm with the inner rhythm. I do have some feeling that much of writing, for me, is connected with bodily rhythm which one is born with, and that's connected to sexual rhythm in a very large sense, it's connected with the notions of foreplay and orgasm, it's connected with the difference between sexuality in a masculine piece of writing and a feminine piece of writing—and I don't mean that men only write masculine pieces and women only write feminine pieces—but, I think, there are pieces in which there are multiple kinds of orgasms and pieces which build to one climax and then drop. And I'm interested in rhythm, I think, because of that early experience of mine with music and dance and somehow those were the ways I could be in touch with my own rhythms in a social situation in Nebraska in the '40s, when people did not talk about their bodies and didn't *use* their bodies very well. The arts early on for me were a way of being in touch with parts of myself that were not acceptable in my ordinary, outer world.

One of the very distinctive things about your work, Holly, that I personally find deeply inspiring, is your attention to the details of Nature. In fact, I think that you are writing the most important Nature poetry today, as well as other kinds of poetry.

I do love to put roots in the ground. I'm very much a city person, and then something comes up in me that really wants to dig in the dirt. One of the difficulties that I've had with this house that I've just moved into is that there's really no garden space. But I find myself always figuring out ways to garden in pots. And I bought a green pepper plant and a tomato plant yesterday, and some lettuce seed—vegetables are important to me. I like the earthy things. I like the things that are so ordinary they are easily overlooked. We eat a tomato and don't think much about it. It's a way for me to *ground* my life, to really physically plant things. And I do have the sense that there is a kind of perfection in plant life, in animal life, which works instinctually, that human beings are hungry for. We do occupy a very peculiar place in the universe. We are partly primitive and partly divine, and we have that odd way of knowing how imperfect we are. A plant just grows. I love to watch the birds on my patio because they move only out of instinct *[and they have been singing throughout this interview]*. How do they know what season to mate? We have many more complicated notions of that, and living in the city, for me, is very complicated. Living an *intellectual life* is very complicated. I think that I get back to a kind of instinctual side that feeds me. Feeds me literally. I hope I can eat the green peppers that grow and I hope I can eat the tomatoes that can grow. I find myself talking a lot about Nature—which I mean in a very large sense and I suppose that comes out of a reaction to thinking which becomes so cool that there is no passion or no surprise. I like thinking, and I admit that there is room in this world for many, many kinds of poetry. I tend to dislike East Coast poetry in a very vague, general sense— because of the coolness of it, or the lack of passion, or the craft before the feeling. I tend to like Los Angeles poetry because I feel that poets really are stretching and risking and exposing themselves. I like personal writing. I like it more than any other kind of writing. That's a prejudice of mine, because we are all tempted to think too much in this society.

The question will arise, then, of confessional poetry. I don't consider your work to be confessional in any way, but people do consider mostly personal work to be confessional. Another question is, How does one make art out of the personal? I remember, about a year so, you mentioning to me, just by the way, that you were thinking about that question—how does spontaneous writing become art? Or as Jung speaks of that very same problem, How does one make the suprapersonal out of the personal? Where are you on this question now?

In the past week I've been thinking a great deal about language. I've been to three poetry readings. And I love to go to poetry readings. I love it that people in Los Angeles who are writing poetry or experimental fiction, or whatever it is that we're hearing, are willing to be public and to give readings. What I've found is that I am not only hungry for those people's lives but I'm hungry for exciting language. I need a poet not only to confess but to lift the confession to art through language. And please don't ask me how it's done. I can tell you a lot of things that I believe about the image as opposed to the flat, general statement. I can tell you what I believe about use of metaphor. I can tell you things about poetic leaps, in which one puts on the page not conversation but the leaps of one's own mind. But I don't have very many answers about exactly what is art. I know it when I hear it. I know it when a poet is not only speaking passionately of a life but speaking in surprising language. I don't always need to understand the language, but I need to know that the poet has considered the language deeply and has a great range of choice about language.

You teach a lot of workshops. I know teaching workshops is very important to you. In a workshop situation, when you have the urge to help someone rise to an artistic presentation, you then tend to talk about their range of language—is that what you are saying?

Yes.

What are your feelings about teaching workshops?

It really is the work I've been given to do. I am blessed with the ability to help people write—*[A knock at the front door. It is Harry E. Northup beaming—fresh from reading an advance copy of Bachy 11, which contains my interview with him. He joins us at the dining-room table. Holly places cheese and homebaked bread on the table and pours wine for all of us.]*—I'm fortunate to be able to earn a living basically by doing that *[helping people to write]*. But my deepest feeling is that nobody teaches anybody to write; that maybe that use of language that we've been talking about comes out of doing an enormous amount of writing and taking one's own risks in the privacy of one's own life, and then one comes to other writers to hear—as I said earlier on in the interview—what one has done; that other people can help with that outer eye in talking about what's been written.

Do you tell students to read any particular books or writers on the subject of craft? Are there any influences of your own that you wish to pass on to others?

I pass on my prejudices every time I open my mouth. I hope mostly to resist that temptation. Many of the people who come to writing workshops are convinced that their writing is shit, because they have read so many wonderful experts on writing, and they're sure that they can never live up to what's been presented to them as standards for good writing. My sense is that people need to find other writers as influences in a way that they need to find their own writing—rather intuitively. They need to do a lot of writing and they need to hang around bookstores a lot and they need to read books that people loan to them at precisely the right moment. They need to shuffle through a lot of poets before they find somebody who might really mean something to them. As far as reading literary criticism is concerned, I think that that is, for most people, such an academic and intellectual pursuit that it gets very scary. One comes away from that kind of criticism feeling that one could never possibly be a writer; that the only great writers are Shakespeare and Blake. Certainly none of us is Shakespeare or Blake; we are our own people. I think that people need to feel confident about their writing before they turn to influences, even though we're influenced all the time by all the stuff around us. I do encourage people to go to poetry readings, simply because they get to see living people. They get to see something that is full of life, and it may be strong or it may be weak, but it's alive. Critics are either far away or dead and great writers are either far away or dead, but poets reading their own work out loud, and taking that risk, are alive. Then people can hear what's going on. I think it's important for people to realize that writing is alive.

With that statement kept in mind by the person who is starting to write, may I ask you what have been your own personal influences that helped you learn intuitively your own way?

Oh, Lee, I'm so tired of that question.

Okay, we won't ask it. If you don't want to answer it–really—we won't ask it. Unless you'd like to answer it.

I am *truly* influenced. I find it hard to make a list, because I know when I come back to this interview and read it, somebody will be left out.

All right, let's just skip that part. Unless you really feel like you want to go into it? Okay. Harry, you can make a comment whenever you feel like it, you know. Holly, we've concentrated on personal, inner life. We've talked of Nature. But Feasts *is a book that deals with relationship to the outer world more than any of your other writing, with the exception possibly of Novels About England and France. Do you feel that a poet's social or political convictions should have anything to do with what gets written, and did they figure in Feasts at all?*

I never consider myself a political or social person. I'm much more interested in my writing and what is simply going on in my life. People have described me sometimes as a woman's poet or a poet who writes about women. I never think I'm doing that.

I hasten to remark that I don't think you're doing only that, either.

I write from a woman's perspective because I'm a woman. But I think it gets much more complicated than that. I'm not interested in propaganda. I'm not interested in slogans and I'm not interested in convincing people. I think that when one begins to write out of a particular social perspective and a particular political perspective, people should write essays rather than poems. To me, poetry is just something very different from that. I do think that one's idealism and one's sense of ethic very deeply influence one's writing. I think that if one doesn't have a sense of ethic, the work gets very crude and strange and "off." And one begins to deal in an image that one would like to have as a poet rather than the writing itself. I'm interested in a woman I'm working with now, who has been very political and is now beginning to write a lot of autobiographical material about her life as a political person. It's exciting because she's coming to it from a personal perspective and I think that if ultimately she finishes the book that she's working on, the work will have a marvelous tension between the personal and the political. But that's because her life's been involved in it, not because she has a particular political axe to grind or because she wants to convince us all that we should live in a certain way. I am very hesitant to tell people they should live in a certain way. I do have a *rigorous* sense that each of us has a journey to fulfill. It's so much work to pay attention to your own journey that you better keep your nose out of other people's.

Who is this writer?

A woman named Susan Chacin.

She's a student of yours?

Yes.

The third book you published was Losses [The Laurel Press, Los Angeles, 1977], which is about all kinds of losses, revolving mainly around the death of your father. Death is a theme, though, that goes through all your work—and loss—something that you're constantly dealing with in different ways. What do you feel about poetry as a form of therapy?

There is a movement in the Los Angeles area called poetry therapy. It always makes me angry to hear that. I think it diminishes what poetry does. I do feel that poetry is cathartic and healing—I feel that about art.

The making of it?

The making of art. But I feel that the making of art is a larger kind of thing than the California therapies that we all hear about. Those therapies, whatever they do or don't do for people, are fads. And they come and go pretty quickly. And I don't have the sense that the making of art is a fad. It may be a very primitive kind of clay pot that someone needs to carry water in and decides to put a little decoration on; it may be a highly spiritual prophecy. But the making of art is something different, for me, from California fads. I'm annoyed when poetry is equated with one of those fads. I am not annoyed that people want to write. I think anybody who wants to write should be able to write. I think if everybody were writing, the world would be saved. I would love to see *anybody* come to a writing workshop of mine and try to explore writing as a way of getting in touch with themselves and making art, but I'm not interested in the idea that poetry is *only* therapy—I think when one calls it therapy it says it's only therapy, and it's much more than that to me.

The other night I was at a workshop and a poet read a poem in which he had the line, "I was startled to discover...." James Krusoe [Los Angeles poet] was there and said that he was glad to hear that particular poet having an element of discovery come into his work—of something leaping into the unknown. In your workshop teaching, how do you deal with helping the person approach writing with the point of view that what is being attempted is important to one's ongoing life?

If it weren't important to that life, the person wouldn't be in a writing workshop. I do spend a lot of time talking to people about giving their lives more importance, that's all. Particularly the individual life. I think what people are caught in is what they consider a lack of time. Women who are divorced, who are working full-time, who are raising children, are very, very busy. Men who are pursuing full-time careers, who may have families to support, are very, very busy. And frequently they feel that that busyness keeps them from writing. My notion is that it is their lack of respect for their own life that keeps them from writing. And that if people really do find their individual life and their individual art important, then what they need to deal with is how can they earn enough money to sustain themselves and have enough time to write. I think maybe the message that I try to give—though, again, I try to be respectful of people's lives and understand that I cannot interfere with those lives—the message that I try to give is, if the making of art from your own life is important to you, perhaps you need to change your life to make room for it. Virginia Woolf's notion of "a room of one's own" is absolutely true. She says that someone who needs to write needs a room alone and fifty pounds a year. I'm not sure what fifty pounds a year was in British currency at the moment she was writing, but it means that one needs to be able to survive and have privacy.

Before we started the interview, you said you'd come to the end of a series of readings. You've been giving a lot of readings lately, and you've been paid well for them. Is that a relatively recent development?

Yeah.

How does it feel?

It feels like I can pay the rent so that I can still have time to write.

But the readings are over now.

The readings were enjoyable. For me, there is nothing like getting some applause for what I do. My first experience with applause was when I was five years old and I got to conduct the rhythm band because I was the biggest kid in the kindergarten class and I was the only one that the conductor's cape fit. *[Laughter.]*

Marvelous series of coincidences.

And when I got to stand and conduct the rhythm band and the whole PTA applauded, I was hooked. I did a lot of acting when I was an elementary school kid, and in high school and in college, and I have a peculiar combination of things going on in me: I'm very outgoing and I'm also very shy. And the writing comes from a very, very private part of me. Then when I can give it out to people through a public reading, I feel very rewarded. To be able to read at colleges and universities where often the only contact that students *and* instructors have with poetry is through books, it's really wonderful to be alive and to be there and to get my own work out to them and to hear them respond to me. As you know, I'm sure, some readings go better than others. A lot depends on when you're reading, the environment, who sets it up, how many people are there. Generally, this spring has been enjoyable. Enjoyable.

As far as readings are concerned in the Los Angeles area, for the poets you know who give readings—and everyone wants to give readings— from your experience, and you've given a lot of readings and they have been very successful, can you give any advice to poets who have the problem of facing a reading?

[Laughter.] Well, of course, the other side of me that hates to interfere with anybody's life is the side that loves to give advice. Speak clearly and smile. How's that? I don't know, I think that when a poet stands up to read her or his own work, what needs to come into the work is that person's voice, that person's nervousness, that person's sense of life, that person's idea of what it is to share work. I think it's terribly individual. I love

hearing readings. I have heard a number of wonderful and horrible poetry readings in my life.

Why were they horrible?

Usually because the poet really did mumble or was ashamed, somehow, to be standing in front of an audience, or couldn't stop talking about how the whole thing made him or her feel. I just want to hear the work. I feel proud of people who are able to get up and simply read their work and let it stand. I think there is, as well as an enormous amount of good work going on in Los Angeles, an enormous amount of junk being written. And I'm not sure that anybody knows the difference. I think we live in a moment in Los Angeles when there's great excitement around writing, when people really are doing a lot of writing, when there *is* an opportunity for people to stand up and read and we are all so hungry for that, that we give a lot of credence to the work that's being done. I would certainly—as I think I said earlier—give credence to anybody who wants to write. I do think there is a great difference, for me, in language, and there's a great difference between what excites me and what doesn't excite me, and there's a great difference in a poet taking things seriously and not taking things seriously. There's a difference in the amount of time a poet has spent really suffering with the work, and a poet who feels that everything that falls onto the page is worth sharing. I think that a lot of what happens for me in Allen Ginsberg's work, which I like, is that he insists that everything that goes on in his mind is interesting to other people. I think that Ginsberg has an extraordinarily interesting mind. I'm not always interested in everything. I do believe in choice, and I must say that probably 90 percent of the things I write are never public.

Speaking of that, your journal is probably more than 90 percent private.

Yeah.

You once spoke to me about the dark side of Holly Prado, and how you tend to keep that part out of publication. Do you have anything to say about that?

It's been coming in a little bit more. I recently wrote a piece called "1965: What I Haven't Said About the House on Macbeth Street." And that piece came as a real surprise to me because it centered around darkness and drugs and magic and things that I had almost forgotten about that time. My social persona tends to be generous and blonde—

[Laughing.] True.

—My inner life tends to be much more mixed. And as I move along, one of the risks I need to take is at least to allow that opposite to come into the writing. But that's something that happens as I discover it. Again, I think one of the reasons I am so interested in Jungian analysis is that it helps me discover the sides that I have been blind to. Some of those dark sides are beginning to be allowed *in* me and perhaps they can begin to come onto the page. I'm not interested in living out those dark sides by actually doing a lot of drugs or leading a kind of street life or leading a dark life outwardly. I don't think that's necessary. And I think that people misinterpret what it is to live all of the sides of one's life. I think that that's a very inner process. That's one reason I'm grateful that I write. The Witch, The Destructive Hag, The Circe, and The Terrible Mother—all of those feminine characters who are in all women—can come forward for me from my dream-life and from my inner work, and perhaps I can make them poetry. That's a very, very fortunate thing and that helps me live them. It helps me recognize something that Jung did say about people who strive for perfection: He says, "Don't they realize? We cannot be one inch better or one inch worse than we really are."

How much does the journal-writing enter into your writing?

I find many, many things starting in my journal. My journal is a real conglomeration, and I don't make any rules about what can or can't be written there. A lot of it is kind of a day-to-day documentation of what happened; a lot of it is rambling around. Because I really love language, I play with words a lot in my journal, and I find myself playing with writing. I use plain, old, ordinary notebook paper so that I don't worry about wasting paper. If I'm using really fine paper, then I feel like I have to write really fine words. But when I'm writing in my journal, I don't have to *do* anything—I can write as large as I want to, I can use as much paper as I want to, and I write a whole lot of—exercises, basically—just things that I'm fooling around with. Sometimes I find that I'm sick of using the words I have been using and I make "A List of Words I Am Sick Of." *[Laughing.]* Then I make a list of words that I think I would like to use. Most of the time, I don't use those words, but somehow that playing around with lists interests me. I was interested in looking at an anthology of contemporary poetry recently, in which it seemed as if every poet represented was just writing *lists*. I *loved* that and I wondered if that were the editor of the analogy who loved lists or if poets really like lists, or if there was some connection with religious litanies in which one just names and names and names and names—I don't know, but I find a lot of what I do in my journal is a kind of listing that refreshes me. I don't know how other people deal with their inner lives, but there is so much going on with mine that if I don't get it out onto the page, I don't know what I'd do with it. I really *need* the written word. I really need a lot of paper. I really need a lot of place to play and fool around and see what I'm thinking about. Sometimes just have a good time.

Do you keep a record of all your dreams in your journal?
I do.

You use dreams a lot, of course, in your work. Do you have anything to say about that for anybody who's interested in using dreams?
What I usually tell people is just start by telling the story, that many dreams are incredible stories and all you have to do is tell them. I have come to a place in my own dream-life where I realize that I do have a sense that dreams are sacred. I work a lot with my dreams to understand what the images are. Again, it gets back to that notion of symbology. One reason I'm attracted to the Jungian mode is that Jung is so interested in symbols. He always insisted that he was a scientist, not an artist and not a theologian. But he was fascinated with symbols and what they meant in people's psyches. So I work a lot with my dreams, and what I find myself doing these days is never giving away a whole dream. When I use a dream in writing, there is a little something left out or a little something added. What I would suggest to people who are interested in using dreams is that they really keep track of their dreams for a while. Not to give away the dreams too quickly, but respect them as stories, respect them as the other side, the unconscious side, and see where it leads them. Again, I'm concerned about dreams becoming a California fad . . . . What is all that writing that you have there?

These are all notes on your writing that I've made over the last year.
[Laughing.] Oh, Jesus. I think you should just read your notes onto the tape recorder and you'd probably have a very interesting interview with me without ever coming to talk to me. You probably speak better of my work than I do.

I don't speak better of your work than you do. I praise your work to the skies to myself, though. [She laughs loudly.] How's the interview going? Is there something that you want to talk about that I haven't brought up?
Turn off the tape recorder for a minute. I want to go to the bathroom and think about it.

[When she returns, Holly says she wants to talk more about her journal and symbology and ritual and myth.] The experience of writing a

poem and of having insights come to you from the poem itself is fascinating to me right now. I'd like to talk about that. And I attended a seminar last October which you and Deena Metzger gave, where I learned about journal-writing—I started keeping a journal again—I learned about the use of ritual and myth from your point of view, and how effective they are in teaching and writing. I'd like you to talk about those things.

I read something recently, either by Charles Olson or Robert Duncan or Robert Creeley—

That's quite a spread. We'll call Creeley and say, did you write this, or—

Well, it was the idea that you start with a line in a poem and the next line has to be a fresh perception.

Each idea must immediately follow another, INSTANTER, as Olson said.

You know that one?

Yes. [The actual quotation, from "Projective Verse," is: "ONE PERCEPTION MUST IMMEDIATELY AND DIRECTLY LEAD TO A FURTHER PERCEPTION . . . . at all points, in any given poem always, always one perception must must must MOVE, INSTANTER, ON ANOTHER!"]

That idea both awes me and interests me as something that I really do try to do. I'm really interested in starting at one place and getting to another.

Does that mean to you that there can be no lapse of time between these perceptions?

No, I'm not real rigid about where my perceptions come from or the lapse of timing. I do tend to write in chunks, but I'm not fussy about from where or how they come. I do think that idea is exciting because it does reverberate with discovery. You don't know where the poem is going to end when you start writing. I had a dream one night in which another woman was following me to the rest room in some place where we were giving a poetry reading and she says, "How do you end a poem in which one stretches an image?" I was irritated with her in the dream. I didn't want to answer her questions. And suddenly in the dream, I turned around and grabbed her by the shoulders and shook her, and said, "The end of a poem like that comes from what you learn in the writing of the poem." And it was to me that sense that the poem moves—

What do you mean—"like that"—"stretching the image"?

I don't know! It was a dream! *[Laughing.]* But it seemed to me to impinge on the idea that you brought up—one perception leads to another leads to another leads to another until you just really stretch something beyond what its rational bounds might be. And then by the time you get to the end of the poem, you're practically lying on the floor exhausted and struck with how marvelous it is that the Imagination exists. Because it goes so much farther than anything we think we might want to write about.

In this context, can you talk about the word "fantasy" and what that means to you? Is there any difference in your mind between Imagination and fantasy?

I don't know. I think that's a question in semantics. I know that my mind or body or self functions in a lot of different ways. That there is the real perception I have that you and Harry and I are sitting at my table in this house that is fairly fresh to me and that it made me feel good to put actual bread and cheese on the table *[finally, I do notice her homebaked bread and cut a slice]*, and that you brought a bottle of wine and that I've opened another bottle of wine and that there are flowers here that you brought. That I have a sense of the human and the outer and the fact that we are really people living in a physical world. And then I have a perception that when I go to sleep tonight, something will emerge from my unconscious, in a dream, that I have ignored, that I don't know about, that I need to look at, that is coming form an *ir*rational world. And I have the sense that if you were to both go home at this point, and I were to sit down and write something, that I might touch on an area of fantasy in which you might become one of the birds who comes to my patio. And Harry might become a swan—which is an image that I really do have of Harry in some ways.

I noticed, I noticed.

In a kind of half-conscious or fantasy place, things can turn into other things, become other things, and I will not be dreaming, but I will be writing from some place in me that means more.

It seems to me what you're saying is that the distinction is that the Imagination is what leads the fantasy.

Gee, Lee, I don't know. I think that's an idea of yours that you ought to write an essay about.

Well, maybe I'll keep it in, maybe I won't, but it's fascinating to me at this point to figure out something about the Imagination.

I *will* say that over the past few years I've had a lot of experiences in doing dialogues with characters who have come up in dreams, or dialogues trying to find a character who represents a particular mood or feeling I'm having, which is a Jungian technique that Jungians call "Active Imagination," in which you *are* conscious, you *are* awake, but you move into a place that is a bit less than conscious and you try to make or objectify or bring forward characters or objects. They often seem like fairy tales to me. They often seem to come from that mythic place that people have had always, the place that makes myth, the place that makes the stories that we keep repeating to our children. That is a world that is familiar to me, and although I do not repeat those particular dialogues—I don't repeat them in my writing—a lot of my writing comes from a similar place. It comes from a place in which I move a little lower in myself.

This is an exercise that you use in your workshops, too?

I sometimes suggest it to people. I'm hesitant to thrust people into psychic worlds that may not be comfortable for them. I have a great respect for the fear that we all have of irrational worlds. I do think that people find those worlds if they need to, and I do think that there's an enormous need for those worlds.

For instance, in the interview with Deena Metzger [Bachy 10], she talks about how mad can we get. Do you feel that leaping off into the unknown is enough risk for a poet, or should one leap off into certain dark unknowns and irrationalities?

That depends on how much the individual poet's psyche can bear. There is a peculiar edge. We all know the stories of poets who are mad or alcoholic or suicidal. I do think that the unconscious really is the unconscious—it is what we are not aware of. When we start taking little steps into it, people can go mad or they can really fulfill themselves. I never know. I am not a psychiatrist; I am a writer. When people come to me in writing workshops, I hope to work with them both rationally and intuitively, but I do not want to push them to places where they can't bear to go. I think that people will find places for themselves—I have a great faith in the human ability to find its own riverbed.

Well, I understand your point of view and I hope that anyone who does not want to go off into some dangerous unknown will not—if you'll answer the next question—ignore the previous one.

[Laughing.] Ooooh! What's the next question???

Well, I don't really know what either therapy or poetry are all about— I am in therapy and I am writing poems, and I feel I want to leap off into the dangerous unknown—within the confines of a poem or the confines of a doctor's office.

—I think you do, I think you do—

—You said you wouldn't want to take on the responsibility of advising someone to go into the dangerous unknown. Would that be a categorical admonition?

No. There are some people I would *urge* to go into the dangerous unknown. But, again, I feel I don't have the right to make decisions for people. When I started to keep track of my dreams, it was because Ameen Alwan said, why don't you keep track of your dreams? He was involved in the Jungian process at the time; he had been in the workshop that I mentioned earlier, with Alvaro. When my second marriage broke up. Ameen came and helped me start a vegetable garden. He was a man who seemed to want to be a friend in many ways, and when he said, why don't you keep track of your dreams?, evidently it was the right time for me and I stumbled very blindly into keeping track of my dreams. I read a book about this whole process of Active Imagination and dialoguing with characters and I started doing it with no notion of the dangers. I think that one does go blindly and innocently into the things that are important to one, and I suspect that people will go blindly and innocently into whatever they need to do.

Good answer.

When I work with people in writing workshops, I hope I have some intuition about what they can or can't bear. But ultimately the answer is not mine, it's theirs. If they want to plunge into the dangerous unknown, I wish them well. If they want to stay on ground that seems firm to them, I also wish them well. What I try to do is give them some experience of my own process. I think that's mostly what writers *can* share—the process of writing—the creative process—which touches all the things that we've been talking about in terms of Nature and Jung and dreams and teaching and all the kinds of things that go on in one's life. The creative process.

I'd like to know more about your journal and about how the ideas of ritual and myth work into your creative process.

There's a line in some of the things I've been writing about in the Observatory piece, in which the Observatory says, "To observe means to celebrate a ritual." That's a dictionary definition. I just put those words in the Observatory's mouth—or she decided that she would say them to me. It seems to me that in looking closely at things in my life, I need to describe them in writing, transform them in language, and live them. The simplest ways that I have to live things is to lift them beyond routine. Because my house is a real symbol of my personal life for me, what I find myself doing is making up rituals that will remind me that life is important. I light candles a lot, and every time I light a candle, it is not only to give some illumination but to give some remembrance of fire, which is a basic element. When I dig in my pots of dirt, it's to remind me of earth, which is another basic element. When I open the windows, it is to let in air, and when I take a bath, it is really to be baptized. I keep reminding myself that life is important. I think because of the vastness of our contemporary life, and perhaps because of the media that we are bombarded with, we are convinced that to slow down and to observe rituals is foolish. I always need to come back to lighting a candle, digging in the dirt, taking a bath, to connect myself with those elements. Cooking, for me, is the greatest alchemy. To turn raw food into cooked food; to turn a whole carrot into a sliced carrot. There are transformations which go on in the kitchen for me that are just always magical. I need that as a way of enriching my living, just as I need writing as a way of enriching the ordinary life. Writing for me is a ritual. I have very little understanding physiologically of how hand and brain work, but I know that when my hand makes marks, I've performed a ritual, and that handwriting for me, or typing on that incredible machine that I don't understand at all—I'm always taking it into the Smith-Corona dealer and saying, "The ribbon won't go around! The 'm' popped off!"— but it is a system, it is a ritual in itself. To really be close to things in life is a ritual—

It's interesting–in the typescript of your poem, "15 Morning Love Stories," all the "n's" rise up.

That's right. The "n's" rise up. *[Harry is chuckling.]* What does it mean? *I wish I could print it that way. I was going to call you up and ask you if I could.*

Well?

It's too late now. I'm sorry, I cut you off.

No, you asked me to talk about ritual and I really got wound up about it. *What about the journal as ritual?*

The journal is the only place in my life where I have a relationship of myself to myself. It's a place where there's nobody else. As I think you perceive from the way I live, I'm very fond of the people in my life. I'm very fond of the people who come to me in writing workshops. I'm very fond of the poets that I know in Los Angeles. There are a few people that I love very, very much. When I work in analysis, I work with a man that I feel is the right person for me to be working with. But all of those things are really relationships with others, and when I come to my journal it really is a way of making a relationship only to myself. I can say things there that I can't say anyplace else, and I can see who I am in a very raw, unsocial, primitive way. I don't have to make sense. I don't have to make a relationship with someone else. It is the only truly private place that I have in my life and it's terribly important to me for that. I write about a hundred pages a month in my journal. I write about everything. Some of it is very very dull. I go back and reread my journals. Just after my birthday this year I went back and read from one birthday to another birthday. I read a whole year of my journals. And I made some notes about some things that I thought were going on. I made some notes about outer events and my inner life and my writing. I don't know that I saw any patterns particularly, but I got an enormous satisfaction from spending about four hours just obsessed with rereading my journal for the year. I felt truly rewarded that I had put all of the energy that I could into keeping that journal. I have a sense that journals are just as individual as the people who write them. Some people like to make little notes to themselves in offhand ways and stick them in a folder. Some people like bound books. I like a looseleaf notebook.

Did you have any premonition of this reward before you started making journals?

No. No. I didn't know what a journal was.

Why did you start?

I started because I felt I was very much out of touch with what I was feeling. At the time I started the journal, I was teaching high school full-time, my marriage had just broken up, I was starting to be seriously interested in writing again. It was as if there were some kind of process in my life—

Excuse me. You said "again." Did you write before?

I've written most of my life. Writing has just surfaced and gone underground, surfaced and gone underground. In the fourth grade I remember saying that my great desire was to write a play and direct it. It's been with me for a long time. When I came back to it, it was because I was at some enormous moment of transition. I started by keeping a tiny, tiny notebook in which I just jotted down a little bit about what I was feeling every day. That was something that I had never done before, except maybe in diaries in junior high school. Very gradually the journal took on more and more importance. I think that has a great deal to do with the fact that Anaïs Nin lived in Los Angeles for the last years of her life, and that the publication of her diaries dignified the journal form. In the course of my getting fully back into writing, I came in touch with some people who were really thinking about journals, and in 1975, when I first met Deena, she asked me if I would help organize a conference at the Woman's Building for women writers to come to—a weekend conference to which writers from all over the country would come—and a lot was talked about our own journals. And two women from St. Paul, Minnesota, stayed with me, women I did not know except through their writing, and we found ourselves late at night, after the days of the conference, taking time to each go into her journal. The experience of being in the house with people who were writing journals at the same time as I was writing journals really verified the fact the journal actually existed. I just continued to be very interested about documenting one's life. I think that there is that notion that is a particularly Oriental or Zen or Eastern notion, that one's art *is* one's life. I am too Western to not want a product. I want a product.

All the same, I feel you've been very influenced by Eastern philosophies. Is that true?

I would not like to say that. I feel myself *very* American! I would stand up for corn any day!

How high?

[Together:] As an elephant's eye!! *[Laughing]*

As an elephant's eye!!

Yep. I would stand up for corn as high as an elephant's eye. I don't think I can escape who I am. I think we are *so* fortunate to have so much stuff in print to read. I have been able to be exposed to the writings of Jung. I've been able to be exposed to the *I Ching*, I've been able to be exposed to writings from all over the world—*The Tibetan Book of the Dead*—I've been able to gain the benefit of *history* basically, just because books are so available. And how can I *not* be influenced? I think the Sixties in the United States, in which people really rebelled against the Fifties—we all rebelled against our parents, we all started to notice love and peace and flowers–I don't see how anyone can *not* be affected by that period in our history. Certainly I've been affected by philosophy that would have been impossible to me had I continued to stay in Nebraska or had I continued the kind of consciousness that I was raised with. I can't help but say that I'm influenced by all that.

May I title this interview, "American Corn"? I think corn is a category that we haven't really understood. There are two kinds, at least. There's the bad corn; then there's the kernel of corn, which has to do with the love of the things around us.

I got very excited about corn last fall, traveling in the Southwest. As I think you know from some of the things that came up in the workshop that you and I shared, the desert really affected me. I'm still not sure how, but it was a very powerful force. What I found myself noticing so much were the different colors of corn. I grew up with ordinary corn—corn-on-the-cob. You planted it in the garden, and it should be knee-high by the Fourth of July, and you ate it. And that got into me as a kind of symbol of the earth and survival and ordinariness. Then when I touched South-western Indian corn, which was a lot of different colors, where people did dances to the corn, and then in some reading I did I discovered that corn is the one plant that depends on man for its propagation—it's been culti-vated for so many centuries that it will not cultivate itself, it depends on man to plant the seed—I got very interested in corn as a symbol of a plant that does fulfill itself, but it also needs human help. I find myself making cornbread; I brought back some necklaces from the Southwest that are different colors of corn on strings, which I like to wear sometimes. Corn has come up in the pieces of writing about the Observatory. The Obser-vatory seems to get contrasted with the desert. The snake of the desert, the Ancient Man whose voice was the desert. The corn that indicates sur-vival. There seems to be something going on about corn that is very much my Midwestern self and also very much my mystical self–I'm not sure what corn will really be to me or how it might fulfill itself.

Can you talk about what you mean by your "mystical self?"

Oh, that side that does the writing; that side that knows there is One in all kinds of things; that side that believes that whatever attraction goes on between people, there is a third thing that is created out of two people coming together; the feeling I have that there is always the other side to anything. I just looked up *[at a wall poster]* and saw the title of Eloise *[Klein Healy]*'s new book, *A Packet Beating Like A Heart.* And maybe that is something of my own mystical side—that notion that there is a heartbeat that goes on under everything. It frightens me and elates me to be in touch with that after many, many years of doing, I think, what most of us do—which is rejecting religion and spirituality, rejecting whatever we are brought up with.

Rejecting the search for what you call "a justice you don't even know is there." Speaking of justice, what would you say about the city and the poets and the particular time into which you've—as Jean-Paul

Sartre might say—been thrown?

[Laughing.] When Harry and Deena and I were driving back from Riverside the other night, after Deena and I had given a reading, and Harry was bringing up a whole lot of interesting ideas about the personification of this country as feminine, and Deena and he were talking about that, I began to think how extraordinary it is that the people I know are all alive at the same time. I don't know *why* we are all here now. I only know that this particular life is the one I have to live with, and I am very grateful for the people who are in it, and that none of us will be alive in the same forms in a hundred years. There's an old Chinese curse that says, May you live in an interesting time. I think we live in an *interesting* time. I think it's confusing. I think it's horrifying. And I think it's a time of great possibility.

In "Sometime Later," a poem of yours in Losses, *you say, "I'm not told about the next trip I'm to make, but I'm shown certain oars, broad and well-balanced. I'm given a chart of the stars, which I can't decipher, but they tell me to lift it over my head and direct my thinking toward the big dipper, the holder of any water I'll have to cross." So, what's happening? What's in the future for your writing?*

I have no idea. Harry's always saying to me, "Where do you think poetry is going?" *[Laughing]* And I always say, "I dunno, I dunno, I dunno." I am not a good fortune-teller. I am intuitive sometimes on the spur of the moment, but not in terms of the future. I hope to keep writing. I guess the thread of my life has always been to make art. The first thing I ever did in kindergarten was a crayon-drawing of a rainbow. That rainbow has reappeared in dreams. That rainbow has come into my writing. I know that there is something in me that wants to make something shining. I don't feel that that will ever be divine, but I feel that it will be what I can do, and that the work of my life is really to make some kind of art. I don't know what that will be in terms of history; I don't know what that will be in terms of other people's response to it. I just want to keep working.

[I felt that the interview had come to a natural close, so I stopped the tape. But another question suddenly occurred to me:] I've never been very good at dancing, Holly, but in the weekend seminar I took with you and Deena, I had the revealing and somewhat uncanny experience, helpful to me in my writing on that day, of being taught how to invoke the Muse through dancing. Will you say something about that?

Dancing and Invoking the Muse, colon: The thing that I keep noticing is that something comes along if one gives energy to it. The thing that popped for me in getting the idea for all of us in the men's workshop that Deena and I led, to dance for the Muse, was simply that we should give out a little physical energy to get some creative energy. I find myself dancing around my house a lot. I think that dancing is a very primitive kind of way of incanting something. The notion that the Muse was originally incanted by people going into a trance, and that those trance things were probably the origins of poetry, interests me. I think that one thing that everybody really *likes* to do is dance. I think that we're all pretty hesitant about it because we're all pretty awkward with our bodies. But dancing really will stir energy. There is a really direct connection, for me, between the physical and the spiritual. You stir energy in dancing, you stir it in lovemaking, you stir it in cooking, you stir it in talking with other people— putting out energy, giving energy to something, will make it alive, will make it real. Extended into psychic research, people can move things around—tables—with their minds. We don't have to do that. But I think we need to realize that we have the ability to dance something into life.

[For two more hours or so, as evening fell, Holly, Harry and I—over our second bottle of white wine, bread, cheese, brandy—discussed the "interactive interview form" as opposed to the unrecorded hence unpublishable freeflowing conviviality of the "interactive post-interview form." And on the following night at Papa Bach's Books, the publication party for Bachy 11, Holly wore one bright tangerine colored carnation in her honey-colored hair.]

—Leland Hickman

INTRODUCTIONS:
15 MORNING LOVE STORIES
(1977-1978)

1.

I know you I start at your face
quickly
what is your face
shifts I see you so clearly
then it's my own mouth comes closer
how we love whom we love as
ourselves
the care of my eyes as I see you
what
did you say
say it again
quickly your mouth in my mouth
the mouth of my eyes
all I can see

2

how it happened: I was obsessed with rivers and couldn't say why.
helpless, but more confident than last year. pages of rivers. cities of
rivers. my eyes put rivers in the middle of rooms where people gath-
ered only to talk. it finally rained.

I'm awake, not understanding how the summer turned to this—we
are learning to sleep in each other without solving the question of
whose dreams come first. you moved toward me somewhere in the
night last night, and your hand found my dream of someone I didn't
want to be with. I'm awake, remembering the strength of your breath-
ing to rub through an angry dream—not to change the dream, but to
make it liveable.

it rained in early august and the next week you came to visit me and it was no visit but what I had prepared for in my staring at rivers. now, I protect any dreams you're having only by following this farther into the countryside. aphrodite whispers, "arousal and patience— that's all you need to hear."

3

slender mornings the grace of french swans
I saw them last year I saw them
dive without effort simply long necks
france the only country where it could happen
white swans again and again

you sleep while I remember the necks of birds
then you reach you wake up
"it's nice weather" you say you are easy
in putting on clothes such arms
you are not a swan but
"I had this incredible dream" you say

I know without effort with all effort
of travel of memory
of this very moment when we begin to talk
there are so many real things
whether I dream them or hold you whether
it is light or the actual warmth between hands
I am glad for the swans diving as
we are in france we are not there we are
at home here
rising

4

I will never I said I will never
fall in love again I will never
the falling who could imagine

a woman old enough to be alone
a woman I will never

I took my body as its own tree rooted
the leaves turned red mature
I said I will never fall in love again
glad
no womb but such
bright leaves

where did you come from
I never I will never
all you did was send a gift meet me we met
the park was full of oaks but we
lay on the ground
eager
each blessing of skin the red becomes vintage blood
lifts me farther than falling
I have not had such freshness
I cannot finish what I meant to say

5

"the flower himself"—a friend says it. she means it as a joke. you will
be embarrassed that I mention it. I can't help it I didn't plant you I
have no control over flowers I tease you with her words the joke as
you grow shy in your doorway. you do not know how much sweet-
ness there is in your body rising tall pushes me into that bloom. I

have watched gardens for a long time. we have met and the way we met was that I was shy myself. you sent flowers. when our friend asked if you'd sent any more, I said you were with me, so she said, "ah, the flower himself." those large bronze chrysanthemums flooded my head with their odor of horses and autumn with their ability to stay new for so many days: the vitality of your height and you are not shy and you know it, but I tease you. this is a pungent season.

6

these hands of not too early in the morning
we talk form and content you say they are
one in the other I take them your hands
open to me this is the real story we promise we won't
repeat what we say here won't tell
the secret I don't know what it is
yet later we eat
not wasting food but until we are filled

7

it's more fun to cook for you than for anyone else because you always say, "that was the best breakfast I've ever eaten." I'm so used to qualifying things. now I don't even ask for specific examples.

8

we dance at a party. we have not danced together before. you say that I'm a good dancer and you're a fair dancer. I only think I love dancing more than you do. I like to show off, and everyone here is a friend, though you're wearing your black shirt like the stranger who's just hit town. when I look at you, you begin to smile. you're smiling because I'm looking, but you aren't smiling at me. you are smiling, I think, at dancing. you say, "I don't like to dance in front of people I know," but we're dancing and we know these people. we are, as it turns out, the last ones to leave the party. the next day we say what a good time we had, over and over, though we mention mostly who was there. I'm wearing red a lot of the time. I wore it at the party. I will wear it today because you like it. you are a better than fair dancer.

9

TRIES ON HIS COWBOY HAT ONE MORNING

you're
the whole
damn
rodeo
baby

10

AUGUST

how I do nothing but bathe
I sit in the tub how
you adore my legs I think

I will never be cold again
not here in this soaking
we both smell of water of what can occur
it runs over my head down your back through my legs
I do nothing but lie in the tub lie
in the clean bed
your arms
all the springs all the wells

LATER THAN SUMMER

the jacaranda tree is not in bloom
I have bathed early I have left my voice
in water
in purple flowers that are not this season

you smoothe my arm as you pass me
perhaps you have something else to do today
but I don't think so
you ease into your own bath
as the tree a fan opens with air

promises: the more I am silent the more there are
I watch the tree not in bloom the kindness
between things: cups   eyes   leaves
sleep and freshening
you come back
we let out our breath in the same room
no other sound

11

you say, "I hope I don't drive you crazy." I don't fear that. I fear one unexpected word. I tiptoe to keep the room from blurting out some thick argument about truth or why I make so much noise when I get up early. we talk of the edge between love and hate, but it doesn't help. we do not say the word. maybe we will never say it, but I stay afraid. sometimes it's a good fear that's willing to shudder, to take what comes with the faith that explosions make entrances. but I do not invite that side of the fire. I touch you, hesitantly. my own hand, which I trust, could curl into a fist before I have time to warn it. your shoulder moves your arm now to hold me. it could shrug. it could break down a door.

12

doves and pigeons come to the roof outside my window. I do not remember how it began, but I buy bird seed as I buy plants for the season or fresh candles. they are aphrodite's birds, doves and pigeons, though I did not know that until lately.

I rub your back. I've put oil on my hands. I try to feel how it is when someone does it for me: the knots of muscle that want to be released; the tense skin of the lower back that simply needs to be touched; pressure points along the spine. I rub you and I have wanted to do this. it has occurred to me some nights when we've been apart, when I've fallen asleep, alone. I've wished for your back—to lie against it and let my breasts stir with your breathing. you started this today by rubbing my back a little, which gave me the courage to approach yours. I move my fingers as if I'm learning a new island.

the birds perch outside the window to eat. I can't see them from the bed, but I hear them pecking through the grain. the bear is also aphrodite's animal and I understand that love is larger than I am. I do what I can. I make offerings.

the oil is simple vegetable oil, though I've put in a few drops of frank-incense, which warms to the skin and means "pure incense" in old french. you say to me, "you have the touch." I can only think how long it is taking me to believe that I deserve you, how many tight words I've said about men about women about this time we all live in, how I've suffered from the absence of nearly every feeling yet now there are so many lives in me that I shake—I can't write letters or read a book all the way through. I say something to you about heal-ing. I am not cured, but am truly in the beginning of sacrifices and invitations, truly in the middle of the bed, truly in the birth of seeds and our two backs.

13

meaning, dear one, is the papaya and the mango. you ask me which I like best. I say papaya, because mangoes have such big pits. and you say that papayas are better for the long haul because they aren't too sweet. this is another breakfast. you're about to go home—it's a wel-come gray morning, just right for walking. I told you secrets last night, close to the pillows. you listened. we know what we hear of each other, and there's no reason to mention these things more than once. we've been laughing about meaning all weekend. I threaten to leave notes for you that say, "meaning is the sum of all its parts," or, "a meaning saved is a meaning earned." now you look at the papaya and talk about its color—the beauty of the half that's in front of you, waiting to be eaten. what is outside of us and inside of us: that's the great mystery. we eat, not knowing what we'll do today, each of us alone, knowing enough to take us there.

14

the streets darken with october

between us
the thinnest air in fact
nothing at all
you are not in me but farther
we have held so many of these mornings
please be as safe as
fine air reduced to no space between us

here in this house
we are all the cold we've lived through separately
then that discovery of food of fuel the whole body
some years ahead of us
whole
please

there is so much
chance of accident when there is so much fertile rain

15

the deep ocean. a palm tree in my mind, even as you turn to me. you
say, "I love california." it's a pure morning, the water itself, and I'm
refreshed, though there's been too little rest. the sun opens the room.
I watch as you speak. I watch every face of yours that I know: the
hero, the brother, the trout, the desperado, the victorian house, the
monk, the tuxedo, this palm tree. the arousal this is your half-smile.
all of these faces, touched with light, with the simple blood that cre-
ates us all. I come close to your hair. I say, "stay alive."

three months ago, in the first dream I have of you, I go into another
room for a minute. when I come back, I know you're waiting in the

hallway to surprise me. you do jump out, just to tease me, but it's a shock—I tremble through my whole body of ankles, belly, neck, thumbs, veins. you take me in your arms.

aphrodite says, "you are in this and he is in this. you will stand here, in the ocean, your feet like churches, praying, forever. what questions do you want to ask? you know that you have none."

there aren't any predictions now except coffee and music. we yawn. "I love california," you say again. we are not going back to sleep.

—*for Harry E. Northup*

POEMS AND PROSE POEMS
(1977-1979)

HOW IT DOES HAPPEN

one spring when I was learning to drive
when I was half awake to leaving home forever
a girl more than a girl but without a sex of her own
all tears
only learning
to drive to look out for things
one spring
I took the car the gray chevrolet
away from the afternoon away from school
into some part of town
I forget I have forgotten so much
those years are still salt running to my tongue
I took the car, shifting gears
learning
and then stopped

it was someone's swampy place with trees
all I remember is moisture, the sponge of moss pressed under my feet
did I take off my shoes
wherever I was I was alone
violets grew under the trees in great clumps
in great purple clots they were more blood than I had ever felt from
the paws of boys from the thumbs of my own tears
violets as moist as I hoped I would be sometime
wet lavender the odor of surrender

I had been trained to know verbs
but not how to act from my heart
and here were violets
I picked them, my hands shuddering
I picked more than I could carry
more than was fair
I picked them and dropped them and held them until I could sing
all the way back
violets wilting on the seat next to me

123

listeners
to the popular song to the growth of new crying
I suddenly knew that nature can be counted on
if we are really lost
what I stole and killed in that afternoon
came into the stem of what I would be able to give later
what would feel like the reason
what I would not cry about
all the petals of blood living their lives through me

I lie next to you now
it's late at night we're happy we can't sleep
you ask me what the world is
I tell you a funny list of things
the last event is your mouth
in the darkness I do not mention violets
but I lift myself on one elbow
and lean to your face
my breast against your arm
so that I can say your mouth my mouth
moist
after all these years

CLIMATE: A LETTER FOR HARRY, 1978

The long drive. The long evening. A car, a moon, this coming home to go to bed without washing my face. Summer. No socks. Your tall body around me as the moon approves. You want to talk and talk. There's a moment when either of us might get up to eat something or to drink one more glass of wine. That becomes staying where we are. Your mouth passes into my mouth into every mouth into the rhythm of the freeway that we've just abandoned. To be home. To have turned off the headlights. And now you say that sometimes you only talk about things because you're afraid. As we turn our mouths to each other, we share all danger: the sudden deaths of cats not fast enough to get out of the way of the traffic; the vicious intruder who might hold a knife to our throats while he takes what he wants. We give ourselves up to fear and kiss it into even more risk. We enter the first full summer we'll spend together. Drownings could occur. But the moon controls the tides, and there's more grace in her than we realize. Her rising first quarter tonight has been as honest as my bare feet, as honest as your whispering to me, "Don't go to sleep yet. I'm lonely." I'll never know how we can be lonely when there's so much love, but I'm lonely, too, thinking of the few more years before I lose my fertility completely.

A long drive and its ending, its way of stopping in front of the house. I delight in this bed. I choose the color of the sheets to please you. We wrap ourselves in them and we whisper and we make love in the sound of the wordless moon. How have we learned the courage to feel under the wheels of the car, to feel into each other's bodies? How have we gained the power to say, "I'm afraid. I talk of things because I'm afraid."? Suddenly, we begin to laugh at how happy we are, and you get up, then come back, and half-sit in bed while I put my head on your belly and really do fall asleep.

Tonight, there is so much gusty wind that it sounds like gunshots. Tomorrow morning, the first thing we hear will be a man in the neighborhood, who's crazy, shouting, "So you lost our three dollars! So you lost your three dollars!" We'll make love again, then, to help the early hours ease into the room along the bamboo shades that anyone might see through if he tried to look between the slats. We'll taste the same mouths we had last night, remembering that we didn't die on the freeway. Summer. Open shirts. The ocean comes, with its knowledge of how months roll to one side, then to the other. Oh, Harry, let us always be afraid. There's so much to live for when we know the possibilities.

—for Harry E. Northup

MY LOVE, WHO IS A POET, TOO, AWAKE

his son and I in slow beds
my ankles circle in a dream of opera

he worries his rooms
he walks what it is that he has said
about himself about his work about the people who may read what
                                            he has said
who may
he thinks
kill him
he does not mean guns he means the soul and I can only whisper
"there are seasons of this"

his son is struggling to tie shoes
I am beginning to loosen the boundaries of my own house
he pulls our shadows into his spine
he holds us and worries
he holds himself and worries

it is my job to write the dreams
I wait for the next unseen character to sing or howl
I wait more than I walk
my deepest voices never know the end

yesterday his boy said "no more sunset" as we drove here
I said "we just get one a day"
it made us laugh
three of us going to the same place to spend the night
so much man woman child
so much worry and dreaming
shoes and food
of course I'm not asleep anymore
and in the morning the boy will remember something we did together
months ago
I was sure he was too young to go that far back

I am willing to be exhausted
willing to stare at my own beasts who rise from the music
turmoil takes its time
it takes nights like this
it takes the fish we ate at the ocean and the sun going down
one sunset every day
for some reason we've been given to each other
to listen to confess

these seasons
he worries
I wait
his son frowns over unspelled words
our power is not what we solve
but what we try so hard to notice in the dark

—*for Harry E. Northup*

THIS IS HOW I NEVER

green shirt green day
this summer I attract
music
light
and friends
boats comfort the lake
yet
I find my hand breaking twigs

to sit with this pulse
green park green july
why do I love one man's shoulders under
the green shirt
why am I afraid to die
why does music play for us

I do not see
the gods

I see green
the boats are not adrift
some balance holds even a holiday
light turns my legs more bare
green turns the sky
hopeful

july
but my fingers take up another twig
someone says
it was a good movie
yes
I've seen it too

I try but I can't forget
that there is never enough for me

that green might become
a real god
trembling
as he steps from one of the boats
as she leans to kiss us
as we
rise
to our real lives
the ones we pretend we don't have

the distant water shakes my eyes
I know music
will I ever touch its face
I know his shoulders
will I ever see how muscles think
summer
I want as much as I deserve

such arrogance
I can't even
make the twigs themselves again

still
to reach for someone else's voice
and really mean
I must have the whole body
green shadow green lake
so fertile
but look
the sun
the sun breaks away from us again
before I can weave any name
the light might come back to

CURES

having no idea. looking at stars above the house. a voice points them out to me. my friend: an older woman who has learned the constellations. I try to see what she tells me. scorpio, hercules. having no idea. I lean against myself, damp with summer, and understand that I've lost the power to memorize anything. my friend says she doesn't worry as she used to about small pains in her body. she's getting closer to death, and those hints don't matter much one way or the other. more stars come forward. it's a rare night when so many leap like this above the city. she gives me more and more names I can't remember.

DAYS OF SWIMMING

1

this entrance is colder than you've ever wanted it to be
as if you've fallen
not chosen
the first few minutes in which you learn the noise of your head
wet
all over
in the element that takes the shape of everything
water always makes room for you

I swim with friends
the teasing is to come on in just plunge don't wait
the ones who hesitate know
they are getting into more than a hot afternoon

2

someone asks what I'd do if I didn't live with words
"swim the channel" I say without thinking/without ability
only the vision of arms large and oiled
huge with practice

he says "it's a solitary occupation"
but so is anything
most of us grow alone in the womb
you train your ribs to breathe against the current
perhaps there's someone in a boat with food to pass over the side
but the kicking is yours
you search the territory as a child throws every spoon out of a drawer
looking for nothing
he finds perhaps one clue then goes on to the next drawer

3

today at the neighborhood pool
we are all in the way
a kid jumps from the side/that's against the rules
I push toward an open space
immediately filled in front of me with others tangling in the chance
nothing is allowed here except the water
we want it enough to pay for it
to splash into how we are undressed
awkward in these strokes of sex without mating
the rush to the belly in public/we do it/we want it/we swim

4

young boys come reckless on surfboards on shoulders of water
I envy the way they go out again and again
obsessed

I'm so white
not nursed in sun
not used to this weight of heat in my legs
the ocean is longer than I can bear
I never really swim here
but squat in the surf watching not turning my back
white

sand washes under my feet/ I collapse against a short wave
I reach for anything familiar yet want to close both eyes
this heavy mother
her pull is what I feel in depression
something whispers sleep
it would be perfect to go deeper to go home
but the pulse stays ignorant
I lift my neck to a building with gray paint steady on its walls
I have exercised just enough

5

in half a dream you see the island in the distance
where you will climb to the shore
proud of your lungs
where you will writhe for a moment in dry air
not ready to walk
as if salt is the only thing to eat
as if we were made from whales/ they still hold our layers of fat
under the skin
what keeps us warm in the tides

6

water is everything I own this year
I have a lot to learn/ I never dive
once as a child I ducked under two feet of a shallow pool
then couldn't raise my head again
but I did
the months before this summer have been like that
nothing safe
I'm damaged by dead friends/ false starts

if I don't swim I won't find the center of the lake
every time now
I become my body swallowing
I take the flood
to be healed in cold and pleasure
healed in muscle
healed in fear

AT NINETY: THE WOMAN NEAR THE DOOR

folds of skin
gather
she carries each day as a coat

quiet is what she wants
to listen to
death/ her great-grandchildren
in dreams of saving each tomato plant
there has never been any waste
there won't be/ she goes deaf

someone brings a camellia
red
flecked with an accident of white
she smiles
says
"I don't like to wear cut flowers/ your body
changes them so quickly"

ABOUT WRITING POEMS

any woman
lifts a child carefully
shifts her weight to provide
balance/ she knows it is odd to be taken
upward from the ground

we sit in each other's arms
whatever words we exchange are not promises
only the hushing: it's all right
to be here, above the sidewalk
to be held and to hold on
we'll do this with grace/ with the look of an old painting
yet the child grows taller, takes over the sky
the mother wilts, tenderly

there is no blood tie that does not change
there is no way to stop this

WHAT IS IN US THAT ALMOST SEES ITSELF: A SERENADE FOR CAT

1

Um, no one around. Cat goes ahead with its plans. Everything in blood-rise and noise as seasonal as the population that won't stop growing. Just what we like: to know we're alive. Cat for witches, cat for neighbors, cat for windowsills, cat for the roofs of cars, cat from ancient Egypt where it got a gold ring in its ear. If you won't let cat in, there's always the other door. A smile like a leaf you thought you saw fall, but you aren't sure.

2

One's a mother. One's a cross-eyed stray who finds more years than he thought he would have when he lived from the scraps of take-out stands. One's addicted to catnip. Four are new-born kittens. The others are strangers, but the same ones.

3

The old legend: Cat will smother a baby by lying on the baby's face. This isn't true, but we hear the howl before mating; we understand that he has barbs on his penis which hurt her as he leaves; we watch her fight with the kittens to make their legs work. Perhaps babies don't know how to struggle enough, soon enough. Perhaps cat is teaching us to breathe. We all believe we've left home, but cat, on top of the trash can, hisses. We know nothing about finding a new place to live without promising to be good.

4

Full moon and summer solstice are on us at the same time. Everyone tears the bark from trees; everyone prowls in the street; everyone can

137

see in the dark. Just what we like: enough danger to keep us stalking the neighborhood. Enough grace to be admired. Enough instinct to save us from ourselves. Enough power to be both male and female. Enough muscle to destroy furniture. Cat: always black and white.

Cat puts its eyes close to mine. Looks in. Similarities and differences which can never be explained, but which are more reliable than checklists.

5

Cat returns from singing, says it's tired of being a symbol. Speaks so clearly that I'm shocked into enough strength to follow. I find myself in front of mouseholes, waiting. I can't turn away.

6

Down in the darkness. Cat screeches. Assistant at spells and cauldrons of brew. Tortured as a demon, a backward prayer. Who hasn't seen cat perform magic? Who hasn't seen cat appear from nowhere, then disappear just as fast? Who hasn't wondered where cat came from, and being told North Africa thousands of years ago doesn't answer the question. Cat persists—as Jews persist; as Women and Men persist; as Moon persists; as Orpheus sings anywhere he can find listeners; as Diana knows the forest by its odor of mulch underfoot; as Eve is curious, continually curious; as the Magician comes in a dream to say that things are going well in the other world, if only we weren't so stubborn.

A child crouches to pet cat, and cat allows this with a look of recognition.

Then runs. Has some vision in its head—a head of underground passageways, a head of vital organs, a head of spine and the resilient whiskers that catch a breath of the next corner. Runs like a fire you didn't mean to start with just one match. Runs like water when the faucet is turned on too quickly. Leaps to a halt and has found whatever it is that I can't see on the sidewalk.

7

A bite, a wavering kiss, a promise of chaos after I pile up everything I own. A lunge into the water and knocks over a whole bowl of fish. Someone asks me, "Are you all right?" I stay alone, walk the alleys, dream that I'm being given what I can't believe I deserve: how to use hands and feet to push farther up the tree. Endless fascination with what comes next. Cat watches as I offer chocolate milk, chunks of meat, a mysterious plan to gather food from places other than the supermarket. Somehow, we come and go together.

Enough instinct to save us from ourselves: We are all creatures of warm boxes and fading memories. We are all geniuses with our gift of scent. We are all furred in our wanting to be held, comforted, then dropped so we can chase whatever obsesses us. The leaves blow through the neighborhood as if they carry the messages we need to go on. Cat hears them and lays that smile at our feet.

Cat preens. Yum, yum—the taste of mouse on a dirty paw.

THE WORLD SERIES IS ABOUT
WRITING POEMS

For Eloise, who told me why baseball players' bodies
look the way they do

there's so much to remember
it's all in this pitch these legs that may
or may not
push to any base
someone wipes his mouth
there is so much spitting there is
wind you never count on
nothing's really a home game
is it

———

how a ball
the most important player
becomes a souvenir
fast so fast

———

no wonder there are so many italians and blacks
you have to have grown up in a tough neighborhood

———

can't get it can't get it
it's gone the crowd
goes wild

at least half of them hate you
you're stuck with your glove
in all that sun

―――――

pride
has nothing to do with it
one day you are suddenly obsessed with
velocity, failure, and being called
part of something larger than yourself
you will do anything to play
no matter how tired you are
all you want to do is connect all you want to do
is connect all
you want to do is connect

―――――

nobody told me
how a bruise sticks to the knee for a long time
how even sliding into home can
crack a bone
or the whole skull

―――――

the worst is that every play is shown
over and over
and you do watch it

—For Eloise Klein Healy

141

The 1980s

HOW THE CREATIVE LOOKS TODAY (1980)

I see that her face is almost transparent, and that she is very nervous—she's so eager to tell me what she wants that I never do understand what she wants. I suggest shorter sentences; she defends what she calls "flow." How thin her hair has gotten—a sort of city-pigeon nest without much strength against the wind. I love her stained teeth, and her desire to get a part-time job for the sake of her mental health. I see under her face to the bones, to the electrical throbbing of brain, brain, brain. Not with horror. Her weakest reasons are the most believable, and when she puts on her jacket and smiles with relief and says how helpful I've been, I want to take back all the advice about periods and commas.

5/15/80

Egyptian, and holds two cakes from the bakery. Pays with food stamps. Many cold canned drinks and I believe a birthday, though she asks directions from someone which makes me think, "From out of town?" It's her profile that I fall for: a sphinx, a crocodile, a princess, a lotus. And wearing shorts so I can see how long her legs make her and the cakes the best possible accompaniment. She feels me watching, and I am. She turns and smiles and what a large mouth I have never seen such a large mouth on a story.

5/16/80

Is not calling me up to go for a walk in the park which we have promised each other. But I haven't been home all the time either. Maybe she's washing her hair. Yes, I think of curling how it curls all of it from one end of the street to the other, and how the park is another kind of curl: up the trail then down to the dark spot where the smell is of hermits. I read "The Song of Solomon" and believe all over again in the coming and going of passion. When the trail stretches up, to the farthest top of it, my breath always falters. But I do go there. Almost a vine, that trail, almost a full head of hair and anytime will do. Is waiting to call me up. Is waiting to be called.

5/16/80

Perhaps it is encouraging to feel so tired, so suspended, so hungry. Everything forgotten, and to sink down, into the spine of what I've called my own. Carnations are the homeliest, freshest flowers. Write about the opposite: strong sunlight, when it is almost a thunderstorm. The embarrassment of hunger, when everyone else wants to be thin. I wasn't born an artist. I haven't had the nerve to forget carnations. But here in my spine, where I lie down, it is easy to say "bone." To say, "Don't make me laugh."

5/21/80

Four children walk fast on the sidewalk, going to school. Two of them carry flowers that they've just stolen from a nearby yard. They walk fast to escape their stealing. In another block, the flowers will belong to them because no one will have seen where those flowers came from. The children will have forgotten their fright at seeing me, an adult, walking toward them just as they picked the flowers. They will have forgotten the few petals scattered on the sidewalk as witnesses to the rough jerking of stems. They will have forgotten everything except the flowers themselves, which they wanted because flowers make school a little pinker, a little more fragrant than usual. The flowers will die by afternoon, and the children will forget that, too.

5/23/80

She performs. It's her favorite act: the free spirit. She hands out paper cups. Disposable: oh, she loves to move into a house and never quite get settled. Her boxes of magazines, her suitcases of dried ferns, her many ideas for social reform which always turn on the philosophy of free food for everyone: all these are never fully unpacked, but the paper cups are reachable, convenient, and are passed out with such generosity that no one seems to notice how poorly she remembers names.

5/26/80

She's been clapping to the music all morning and now touches me with huge, dry hands. In this face is the face of what I might be if I'd been born black, been born ten years earlier than I was, been born to applaud singing and preaching and all the young women in the church who have had babies recently. It isn't even her history that makes her wonderful, but her hands, so large and so eager to touch me without knowing anything about what she's touching. I look like a strange, half-wilted lilac in my cotton dress, a dress I enjoy because it is something of Easter, though today is not Easter at all. But it is Sunday, and it is her hands and their reaching into my pale color and her mouth which moves to say something I don't quite hear. Later, my friends tell me that was the moment when the minister asked everyone to turn to a neighbor and say, "I love you."

5/26/80

And aren't we all strangers? This one comes down the street swinging an old walking stick, looking perfectly free. A troubadour? I envy the anonymity of poets who followed their songs from one city to the next and left nothing in writing for anyone to praise or damn. I envy the stranger, with his helpless limp and his face as wrinkled as any face that has lived with itself for hundreds of years. And aren't we all walking? And isn't every city an alien place, where we don't know whether or not we'll get food and shelter? And isn't every day a stranger to us, in which we meet our own stranger in the mirror and in the clothes we wear and in the things we hear ourselves saying to others? And isn't being a stranger a protection against being caught in what might become a comfortable home? I envy the stranger, and I hide from him as he comes closer. There is so much danger in his crippled leg, in his clear voice.

5/26/80

In the park, in the park, and I'm getting all dusty. Birds say this and that. Utterly green my hills yes mine they belong to me when I'm here and the birds, too, but suddenly a snake—long enough to be absolutely sure in its dull gold with blue-black lace—how silent it is around the snake how suddenly silent.

Does not belong to me, even the dust I bring home on my shoes.

6/6/80

The usual people do not come and so she stands naked in her bathroom, drying her body after a bath, and sees in the mirror that no one can tell what she's thinking. She does have to talk when there are those other people, those who trust her, those who are suspicious of her, those who wonder about her, those who appreciate her sense of humor. But she is naked and no one is here as she looks at her face just washed and remembers that no one can tell what she's thinking and that today she does not have to talk so that anyone will think that what she says is what she's thinking. No, it is not complicated at all. It is the way the yellow towel moves up and down her legs, doing its job.

6/17/80

She leaves a message for me. I leave a message for her. She asks if I will; I tell her I will. Two days pass. I begin to worry. I call her and she's not home so I leave a message. "Did you hear me tell you that I will? Did you hear me say yes? Did you hear me answer your question? Did you hear me say that we still know each other though not as we did even two days ago? Did you hear me leave it all on your door?" She is one person I always have to break into, as one breaks into a coconut with a hammer and then something sharp with which to dig out the meat. Even drinking the milk isn't easy. A mutual acquaintance says he thinks she'd remember his name, having met him several times, if he wrestled her to the ground. Oh, delicate and thick-husked muse, must we always try so hard, when really what we say is, "Yes. I will. Yes. I have answered your question. Yes. We know each other."

6/17/80

Dust in the corners. I crawl to parts of this house that I've never seen before. A few leaves. A few feathers from the young bird the cat killed yesterday. A few snatches of loose carpeting. Collections, collections. In the bright air of summer, I throw away what I haven't noticed. I look at it carefully before it goes.

6/20/80

She decides that everything occurs through action, so drives her car at the maximum speed limit. She sees that the sky is moving, too, with its many clouds like soft feet after days of unbreatheable weather. Prose, she thinks, is always like driving. Prose, she thinks, is what starts and keeps going. What's the very end of everything? She does think of death. She does touch her breasts, testing for lumps. She is as soft as the clouds and as busy as feet today. Fifty-five miles an hour and no cancer. "Prose," she thinks, "will save me. If I can just keep explaining and explaining the end will not be an accident."

6/30/80

He gives me what I want, which is encouragement. Yesterday, the two of us saw many people playing baseball. "I like it," I said, "when everybody gets to play." Almost all the players hit the ball and at least two got to first base. One boy made a home run with a hit that didn't leave the infield. We all need the encouragement of the other ones. Today, I remember that he said, "I don't want anybody to analyze my poems. I want people to read them."

6/30/80

POEMS AND PROSE POEMS
(early-mid 1980s)

THE HOPI POTTER, IMPRESSIONIST ART,
A DELICATESSEN

her large hand trained to intricate design
what works its way from her broad face
through her arm refines itself as it goes
a dream finally shaped as a multitude of people of windows

———————————

in a tropical canoe
out there on water in
water the slap-slap of paint on canvas
sees color that is all there at once
then
separate as the eye just before it combines itself

a slow ride surrounded by islands
adventure but a net too
to capture the whole

———————————

the purest eye makes half a pickle holy
can lift pastrami to how we eat are
hungry for color "beautiful"
"wonderful" the people in the museum keep saying
and they mean it

———————————

lunch then after lunch
somebody has taken time to translate
photographs onto this wall to push

the camera away from the faces
to actually paint a cheek a
pair of rough wool trousers from 1890

I still can't believe how large her hand is
how delicate the brushwork how natural it
seems to hear her say that she simply sits
outside in a field until the right idea comes to her

---

everybody wants a closer look at the goldfish
orange that is better than orange
is
French I tried to get to Paris in my sleep
last night even before I saw this

---

always with us

boats pools reflections in
moonlit rooms a man in pajamas
a woman whose skin is a different cloud
the question of what are they talking about

---

this city its charities and luggage shops
the mural the sandwich
our minds such rich variety
someone wants less red
let her turn then to the self-portrait of the artist
serious brown and then to nude women
who touch each others' legs and then to
the exit where a new building is going up
right here in the future of what we did to pay for it

the large-handed dreamer dissatisfied
with what her mother and grandmother taught her
so her own training the fine brush as quick as
the right idea to catch
color to eat the camera and let the eye
do it as we are all our own artists
goldfish guide us
through the afternoon here at home soft traffic
and invisible birds but I think I know
how to paint their beaks with songs coming out of them

to practice water for years and never get enough of it

WORD RITUALS

WORD RITUALS (1)

The word in the middle of the body.
The word in the closing eye.
The word in the road, almost stepped on, but seen at the last
    minute, picked up, put in the pocket like a fallen leaf.
The word in the ankle.
The word in the song that everyone forgets.
The word in the bed that is always there, that is lain on for
    years, with every sleep, with every lovemaking.
The word in the dust behind the furniture, behind the unused pots
    and pans, behind the stove, behind the wall, behind the
    night.
The word in the collar of the man in the black suit in the dream
    of coughing.
The word in the lock on the bathroom door.
The word in the bark of the two dogs I never see, but they always
    bark.
The word in the photograph which never moves.
The word in the backyard of my childhood house where I buried an
    egg to see if it would grow.
The word in the speechmaking that is the silence after the
    speech.

The words in the book: victory and consummation.
The words in the other book: teaching and nature.
The words in the third book: blindness and imagination.

WORD RITUALS (2)

The word in the silence in a long lunch with the woman I do not call mother, yet she is something older, and I've known her long enough to ask what is the best and worst: that word, without social necessity, but only to ask who is this woman in the silence, in the turning of her head a little away from me until she can answer. The worst is her own mother who has lived too long. The best is a journey into country powered with vines, with age, with nudity, with covering nudity, with my saying, "You need your own life," and she nods, and there is the sudden death from a fall. The word between us in the silence which helps us fall, hurt ourselves, talk of how we don't know the purpose, talk of the final silence. The word in her hair, in my hair: We do not have long hair but hair that fits our heads, and there is no way to cover the nakedness of lines through our faces—those lines that are vineyards, are all the stories of what takes a long time to ferment. She nods. There is no word for the time we spend away from each other, thinking about the past, thinking of the man, now dead, who introduced us to each other. We lean across the table to think into her talk of land, my talk of imagination. Thinking, and talking, and not saying the word that draws us to each other, though there is no reason for us to be eating now, no reason for us to know each other longer than we knew my father, her husband. Her mouth tries to remember something, and I see it move, and we decide to say, "children, mortgages, map." My mouth tastes the wine, the fish, the bread, and though I do not look away or down, I feel the fall in the unspoken word, into the one desire we both have to continue meeting like this, unable to speak everything, yet hoping, yet silent. The single word. It is not how I kiss her goodbye and smell her bedroom, her ear, her name, my name. It is not our names, certainly, but a word that doesn't rise except to say that something is not dead, something is shameless and open and nodding as we nod to one another through the whole lunch. The word "mystery" means "close-mouthed," and perhaps that is all I can say, all I need to know. Perhaps we can never tell what the mystery is between us—why we like the same fish cooked different ways, why I share her love of solid ground and she does read my imagination, why we are so at odds with each other, yet we both laugh at the same time. Two women in the silence of laughing. That will have to be enough as I kiss her and thank her. As she says, "We'll do it again, soon."

WORD RITUALS (3)

The word in the ice in the glass of water.
The word in the stain that appears on a white dress in a dream
    of burning.
The word in the temperature dropping twenty degrees after the
    sun sets.
The word in the belly of the cat, a stranger, who comes to eat
    food outside the house.
The word between the toes.
The word that runs along the border between countries.
The word that tastes of two things at once.
The word that sits in the wine as the wine grows older and older,
    darker and darker.
The word that is the color between the tongue and the mouth.
The word that apologizes to the dead flowers.
The word that opens the gate when I'm nowhere near the gate.
The word that remembers everything, all the time.
The word that turns my head so I miss the most important moment.

WORD RITUALS (4)

The word in the meadow, though there's no meadow here, only ocean and the smoke of last night's fireworks—how sudden, those bursts, and the ocean with its moon on its back. The word in the meadow, though, the place where I go to lie down, as I did lie, once, as far away from houses as I could run. And still, so far away, searching by closing my eyes. I do not see easy cotton aprons, but insects, and the grass like fire against my legs. My meadow is in a dream: medieval, filled with marriages of heat to glass, silver type to its printing machine, food to ripping clothes, lack of money to an oven carved in a wall. The word in the meadow with my eyes closed is so far from aprons that I fear it, fear the word that might keep me with its beauty from the ordinary day, the actual temperature of things. The word away from the meadow was written in another dream, in a letter that was a recipe that spoke of how to live, and the joy was the joy of simple patterns. Please. Let me know the actual, the normal, the edible food. Please. Keep me from beauty. I fear the meadow, the source of so much desire, the source of being alive—not kept in loving words, but kept in the beauty of anything-can-happen, anything might be printed with those silver letters that the young woman is placing so carefully into the printing press while I stare at the flame under the glass. There's no ocean in my meadow, and the fireworks do not land safely on the water. Moon, moon, you have always been a sign to me, but not now, not as the tiger crouches in front of me in the grass and says, "You didn't think I'd leave you, did you?"

WORD RITUALS (5)

A man memorizes the word, the sacred word, the word that has lasted for a long time. The man takes the word from its ancient page and says the word as he lies on his bed, as he drives through the city, as he watches his son, as he drinks a toast, as he helps a friend carry a rug, as he shaves the beard he's been growing. The man repeats, loses, repeats, stutters, repeats, forgets, repeats, understands, repeats, hunts, repeats, starts from the beginning, repeats. The man remembers. The man says the word to others—he wears a gray wool suit and a purple velvet necktie and stands in front of poets and even in front of the woman who brought the word to him in his own language. The man says the word that has lasted for a long time, and there is the silence of people listening to what he has learned. The man does not know what any of these people hear. He will never know.

—For Harry E. Northup

WORD RITUALS (6)

The word beyond the rhythm of the clock.

I sit across from a woman who is dressed in blue, who settles her hands in her lap to listen to me. I am not quite ready to tell her my story which is too old, too stale, too much of what I've told over and over so often that I wish it weren't mine anymore. I look at the blue, the color of small wildflowers near my house that bloom through the overgrown ivy. I look up from the blue to the woman's face. She is looking at me, and there is a moment full of looking, full of recognition. The looking is the word beyond the seasons, and when I do tell my story, the story unwinds into a river that carries away all the fallen branches, all the mud, all the discarded bottles and cans, all the dead fish.

WORD RITUALS (7)

The word moves from my memory of a cousin on the farm who taught
    me folk songs toward the poems I write now—a constant
    desire to sing those songs, though I've forgotten all the
    verses.
The word moves from the simple prayer, "I pray the Lord my soul
    to keep," to the knowledge that there are many spirits in
    every body.
The word moves from the lips of the man who tells me a secret he
    has never told before to my own mouth which takes the
    secret.

The word moves as the pulse moves, moves as the swimming of blood,
as the repetitive heart-pound, as the feeling of any pure, lively thing:
I hear a child in the neighborhood call out now in the early evening,
"Hey, John! Hey, John! Hey, John!" to an older child, his calling an
echo of what beats in him to be comforted as the day grows darker
and darker. The word moves as my stomach moves against the note-
book I hold in my lap, as I wait for my dinner to cook, as I feel the
dark behind me. I'm pleased to see my breath move, to see my hand
move as it holds the pen. My other hand comes to the notebook to
hold the page steady as it has so many times in the past, as it will
again because my heart will continue to pound in sleep and in wak-
ing up, in feeling the word as this breathing, as the movement of what
I do every day, as the privilege of having some years yet to listen to
what is said in the neighborhood by children, and by the young man
and woman upstairs who stand outside and talk too loudly too late at
night. She says, "Love is being completely vulnerable," and he says,
"Well, I don't know." They go in, finally, together, and come down-
stairs the next day, together. I see them; I hear them; I understand
that they are alive because they are alive in their bodies and voices.
The word moves as the pulse moves, moves as the rush of the risk of
saying what is in us: need and fear and hesitancy. The dark is behind
me, outside the window, but as I turn to look at it, I can still see the
outlines of things. I can smell my food cooking here in the house,
cooking to keep the word moving. The child has stopped calling for
John.

The word moves from the one secret never told before to all the secrets that may someday leap from the body, from the old songs, from the closed lips.

WORD RITUALS (8)

The word beyond decay in every inch of the floor where I walk, where I pick up the word on the bottoms of my feet, where I carry it from room to room, where it moves through my body but doesn't say itself—yet is returned to me by the man who walks through the house, too, who meets me, who recognizes the word and kisses me.

Plants rot. I drag the old leaves of the lilies from their stems—tough brown arms, these leaves, and I set my teeth together and pull. Then I cut the stems down to the few inches they need to grow again. I do this all morning. I do this and hate to see such blood. I feel death in my hands as the torn arms of the lilies. I can't avoid touching these arms, but I hurry to throw them away, to concentrate on how clean and satisfied the short, rooted stems look in the ground, in the promise that next year there will be white blooms as tall as above my knees.

The word beyond decay beyond power beyond enemies beyond rejection beyond regret beyond what we try to make of ourselves.

The uncontrollable word that we walk on, that we feel pushing through our bodies until there is nothing to do but kiss with our whole mouths.

WORD RITUALS (9)

Every word an animal its blood climbing its hair growing all over our bodies. Every word a howl as wolves howl for others to come. Every word a snake which folds and unfolds without question. Every word its own jungle—its SSSsssSSS its oahoahoah its rrrrrr—the foliage, the night, a sudden death or the long pregnancy of the elephant. Every word mixed with ribs and tails, clawing its way up the tree, slithering its way down the tree, hooting its hyena hoot across the stiff grasses. Every word hatches its eggs to keep itself alive in the world that more and more does not want words, wants dead animals wants fur coats wants snake skin shoes rather than the companionship of another wolf howling back, finding its way to the den where everything can be told lying belly to belly and snorting grunting nuzzling with the sounds that make us all forest all jungle all living blood.

WORD RITUALS (10)

If we could remember our arguments. If we could remember what whips us until we scream, what drags us through all the human history of clubs, knives, razors, guns until we fight with someone we love, who loves us, until it is no longer love but the igniting of words, of bombs, until it is murder, until we can't take back anything, until we lose all love in cruelty. If we could remember.

WORD RITUALS (11)

The truest word: It is never said. It hums behind me as I watch myself speak, staying as honest as I can but never saying the word that would open everything. Words as I know them make sense. I ask them to explain love, boredom, loss, pleasure, work, greed, fear. But the one unsaid word explains nothing, simply opens so suddenly that it has to be entered. And then everything is gone. Everything is fresh. Imagine. To look at the cut on my finger and to see that it is pulling apart even as it heals. To look at my collection of stones of pens of candles of shoes and to see the planet Venus twenty-six million miles away. To look at the papers in the trash and to see gold fish circling their pond. To look at the mask of a vampire on my wall and to see a sister.

WORD RITUALS (12)

The word begins in the dark of the body, begins in the first one who ever spoke. The word begins in stooped weather thousands of years ago, the tongue crashing itself against teeth. The word begins in the ancestors who all talk at once in our dreams, who carry language from one country to another. It is cold and many freeze to death, but those who survive, who have the steadiest blood, who have the strongest tongues, carry the word into what they have never seen before, and the word describes, records, worships the new country, the breaking of boundaries.

The word begins in standing on green grass—it is a summer evening it is just getting dark and the word finds its way out of baby talk into a real word and the mother hugs the child and the father nods and urges the child to say it again and the child feels its feet on the grass feels the mother and father loving it feels what it has done is beautiful—as beautiful as the dog with its fursilk its legrush that the child still sees in the yard and has called by its name.

The word begins in our shoulders hunched over the first book: a story of an egg falling from a wall a story of a stolen pig a story of the leap over the candlestick the birds flying out of the pie the silver bells and cockle shells. Later, we discover longer stories of people who move just as our family moves out there in the kitchen calling us to come to dinner as we sit hunched over the growing knowledge that there is more than one world. We will never again look at any quiet street and believe it's quiet, that there isn't a gnome an ogre a wicked queen just behind that shadowy tree, that there isn't a hero a fairy godmother a talking horse just behind the fence behind the shadowy tree. The word begins in what has gathered in the soul of the world long before we were born, and in what is urging us into the next chapter. The word begins in the imagination that hunches over the book and hears the voice of our mothers calling us to come and eat—the imagination which understands dinner will be no more real than the Pawnee Indian we are following on our ponies across the Plains.

The word begins in wind that rises and speaks through the trees in front of our cave until there is nothing to do but answer. We cannot see who speaks, what face the wind has beyond our fires, our cooking pots, our bone cups, our children huddling in our long arms. We cannot see wind, yet it has the voice of someone who wants us to listen. It does not tell us facts about hunting or planting but tells us how many things in our daily work cannot talk about themselves yet cooperate with us if we understand their nature—an invisible nature that the wind shows us with a push into the cave, a push which upsets the pots, the cups—that makes the children cry, that makes us look at the one person among us who is listening harder than the others, who seems to hear the word that begins with the wind, who stares into the shattered pots, answers the wind saying, "We will honor these broken pieces and the voices of all that we do not believe we hear. We will give ourselves secret names that can answer you, Wind, and you, Trees, and you, Snow, and you, River, and the ones who have died—those we feel around us when we are quiet. We will be afraid of the voices and will also know they belong to us, since they come to us, since you, Wind, still blow, since you make the trees shriek, since you make us other than we were before we heard you."

The word begins in the dream I have even now, even this long way from the wind in the cave. My dead grandmother gives me a book of her poems—poems I know she did not write when she was alive. She does not speak to me as I know speaking, but still urges me, loudly, to continue to live in awe of language.

WORD RITUALS (13)

The word grows in its own belly, fertilized by itself.
The word, mother and father, son and daughter, is what we wish,
    always, to return to or move toward.

No wonder we talk so much, write so much, care so much, ask so much, dream so much. No wonder we search, exhausted, talking to our friends so late at night that we forget all the work we have to do the next day. No wonder we shake at the fate we live: to know the sex we are and to know the sex we are not and to know that the word is both tender and unforgiving, is both milk and responsibility, is both receptive and stern, is both sanctified and obscene, is both ritual and surprise, is both animal and meditation. No wonder we fall down, drunk with worship, when our friends finally leave us, when we have failed again, hoped again, seen again all the impossible and ever-present mating: muscle and kindness, weight and flight, sperm and the tiny opening in the cervix through which sperm travels with its amazing speed.

A moth circles the room, not knowing anything, but living this, too, without even the promise of how to say it.

So the word, our birthright, blesses us. So we are saved by our duality to know what we miss. So we are saved from pride, from blind instinct. So we are saved to cry out, to have no wings, to search, to risk ourselves. Sometimes, at the height and depth of orgasm, the fruit.

WORD RITUALS (14)

Every word is as ripe as pears that yellow in the sun until they
     are irresistible, must be thrust into the mouth bite by bite
     until all the body knows is pear—until the shape of
     everything is a sound louder than any single season.
Every word sacrifices itself every time it is spoken, written,
     sung, read, noticed, performed, chanted, pronounced, shouted,
     printed.
Every word needs help.
No word is a definition.

WORD RITUALS (15)

The word folds its arms around a crippled dream.
The word does not cry.
The word says, "There isn't much time."
The word is awake now, at this very moment.

DREAM COMBINATIONS

DAISIES BEFORE SPRING

a whiff of.   bunches grow the grocery store.

fly with yellow and the creamy wind.   march in the middle of itself.
just a whiff of.
comes with daisies when I've been thinking death freak skeleton:
all the disgusting odors.

now yellow eyes fly in the middle.
butter pollen.
milk pollen.   cream breath against suffocation.
all day all body is death freak bone stink.
the skeleton breathes shit hate.

suddenly.   bunches and all friends of mine.
quick green under the flying.
vines.

I drink three glasses of red wine after a movie.
about a young girl.   about a grandmother.
a field where the first blood drops.   gathering a field.
I bring home daisies.
I drink three glasses of blood.

a whiff of.
the spine disappears.

CRACKS AS AN EGGSHELL CRACKS

oh, the soft field.
spring mother.   hoof weight into the mud.
food grass.   mud is no sin.   toe hooves.
all our weight.   sinks.   into.

cow patience.   a woman friend in her own house.
works bread.   dreams juice.   kitchen earth.
sits in a breast and moos.
a woman friend when I fell to the ground.
big blood.   some die young.
heat makes a child.
not in cans but in living globs.
when I can't put up with it anymore.
bread on the doorstep.   baby breast.

long fingers one man.
you have long fingers.   my man.
muscle touch.   rapture.   my puritan outlaw.
long.   prophecy within the flesh.
again.   intrigued with again.
wing fold.   eye spark.
no bad-guy-with-shotgun dreams.
throat star.

birth temperature.   shaky new tree legs.
sweat marriage.   the result.
how wild and tender every newborn eye is.
give us the nuzzling next to the tired mother.
a nipple doesn't care how good or bad we are.
hatched in the roses.

THE GREAT MEAT

teeth under the mask.   one more prayer bite.
I sleep against the ground.   unholy cold feet.
one more summer to face the crops: ever rising in spite of me.
a big glass of water next to the bed.

breasts pull through my shirt.   don't die.   I want to get out
    of these clothes.
it's a big hill.   the heavy accent I marry, unloving.
even the stalled car.

I apologize.   I owe a lot of money.
one woman's husband brings her packages of food when she menstruates.
christ is a rough street guy who gets the car radio working.

farm the earthquakes.
pin me to the altar.   but the grass escapes, unbuttoned.
all over the body: bites.
the heart, seeded and slain.

but it's time: don't break the closed petals.

someone slumps in the back seat, exhausted.
this piece of dirt.   weeds.
as I dig, there's one white radish.   grown alone.   grown edible.
the woman gets up from my body and kisses the black dress.

stand quietly.   I've only cleaned one window.   one sin.

but in the center I haven't touched.   that fuzzy dark.
the circle of seeds.   opens on its own.   that handful.
the cloud and water hand.

I can see.   I can see across the river.
a few women try to mend a broken plate.
a load off my back even against the lump of floor, crying.

GENERATIONS

black grape skin covers ribs beneath my dress.
covers breast loaves. covers breast horns.

little girl dolls. their arms and legs and heads make a stew.
one a squawking duck mouth.
one a rubber map of lumps. the most crooked nose.

without a mother I eat the child.
black juice, gradually, under the dress.

half mad eater of dolls. lover of dolls. tear them.

even to bone the yearning when I wake up.
the house where I kill to make blood flow.
crippled walking. major resurrection.
obscene and worn out thrift shop clothes ready for another color.
rose occurs and occurs. even limping, I eat.

one a butterfly with plastic cheeks.

it takes so much sex to grow fat on myself.
lip force. flesh knock. the juice ferments.
break up housekeeping: half mad guilt in the lap of leafy faith.
I carry it everywhere with me. I watch the colors change.
I bury what's left.

OUT OF THE HOTEL WHERE SECRETS BREED

my tight coffin.   this one wants me to lie down.
box of memory bones.

I recognize courage and walk.
raw.
yet warm insanity.   the broken code.

she guards each window.
walk.
the weather smacks at itself.
fresh air into nothing I see in front of me.
these pilgrims.   nothing but feet into strong herbs.
don't feed the ones who can't eat.

box of curtains the strength of lead.
box of ash laws.   box of barren shoulders even richly dressed.
let the saintly truck dump it.
let her see the escape.

walk these gifts of absence.
courage.   with a real erection.
with a bunch of roses the shape of wine.

BROOMS

ordinary soap.   childhood vagina.   stone bud.
the house when everyone's gone.
my own gift.   no visitors.

dead grandma.   she won't talk.
under my panties.   ritual lips.

dead grandma I want your eggs.   freckled.
the good advice.   your map.   tell me your chin.
wind blows your flowers off the china plates.
I keep a juicy orange.
hot old grandma.   blood calendar.   earth furnace.

come on.   our names.   eggs.
talk to me in the living room.   we both love cats.

you a funeral but a big meadow and even more wheat.
me a lamb kiss.   moist stone.   lonely.

ONE MEMORY WHEEL

ragged heart bread. I escape but still look back.
his puckered lips. all that sunburn.
once he kept me waiting. I waited. he married webs.
I was the seed of a knuckle.
ragged scrap. the fist.

when I had pulse luck.
fast medicine. that star moon skirt.
could be a snake on my head. all those roses on the shoes.
this skirt flames down my legs.

ragged spark. at least my own forest without puckering.

hermit mouth into the distance.
bare hands and vinegar and sugar. fist rose.

APPLE, OLD FAVORITE

good teeth, ready. no cooking.
not pared. not cored.

every lunch. teeth shape the rooms.
thieves, bums, junkies, farmers, tricksters, ghosts.
always in bloom. fits the mouth.
repent. get your teeth out where I can see them.

a park full of motorcycles. not pared. not cored.
fruit seeds everywhere we spit.

red mystery, polished. red weight, chewed.
white lily flesh, salted.

AUTUMN LUCK

cemetery.　almost rain.
almost rain but not yet.

a string of chilis.　hot on the tongue of the moon.
heat up the gospels.

christ smells of piñon incense.　a cement angel.
our moist breath, hidden in chilis.

moon gospel above the graves.
the church across the street isn't there.

the new cat nibbles the house for the first time.
opens into a garden.

ACAPPELLA

black girls' tight pants.   rock and roll.   how I stand right up there.
me, faint white thing.
scar laugh.   moon slam.
cuts the ice.
cuts the sweet desserts somebody who hates me wants me to eat.

later, the pond under the waterfall.
big rainbow flesh.   skinny root knees.
oh, yes, I sing.   am singing.

once, we were all in jail.
now, we drive everywhere at night, even to the street where I
    used to live, where I've left my good recipes.
fast gravy.   our skirts are hives.

black lady of more mail than I can possibly sort out.
black lady of the window I try to unbolt.
black lady when I say, "pray for it," to the young girl with
    blond breasts who asks for a neckline that plunges.

stand right up there.
'faint white thing.   I've never had much vocal range.   spend it.
release the blind one who's been lost in her room.
where darkness isn't flesh.
where the pond festers, bolted shut.

a pair of tight purple pants.   a skirt that buzzes.
keep coming, keep coming.   that awesome silver glow
                            around the mouth.

ARIADNE SPEAKS OF DIONYSUS,
OF LIFE BEYOND THE OLD STORY

This morning, the sandalwood incense of grain. When rain joins
wheat, I know he is moving there, is the wheat, wet with high
bird song, the grain's yellow struck with sun, with water, until
it is all his white music.

He has come from years of wanting me.
We are real women here,
rising from generations of fear of women,
lifted out of the lie of subservience.
My eyes are as wide as the mouths of the people outside,
shouting to welcome him. I rush, I hear

The freedom we will have with each other. His white hair is
my cotton robe, soaked with years of waiting; we are wet then
burning I am

The bird

While heads of grain burst as if it is spring, not late summer.
Seeds open to sky and
we kneel.

The maze solved, our animals befriend and surround us. My hands
are sheep's wool, goat's milk. Their language is mine, all
secrets drop

Red, on the sheets, and I swear that the sheep sing.

The promise I make, married, is to neglect nothing, to be
entered by every season, to grow old in praise of this blood,
loosened from mountains, which pushes toward language that has
always been used, forgotten, recaptured in

The animal that I am, the woman who will bear his vines, tangling
and untangling in his rich shadow, made true to myself.

Would you resist a feast?   Lungs whole in animal breathing
over and over
the god of virgins   young mothers   wrinkled bellies.
Mother and father, this quick-hoofed,
clean bed.

Earth!   Look at what I become:
white flowers, white breasts, their red nipples the perfect center.

And in spring, every moment a labor—to bring forth one leaf
is to birth a child.   I am the pregnancy.   My husband writhes,
groaning, the force behind the inevitable pain.   And our wild laughter
when anything green does live: olive trees, grapes.   Calves, fish,
new birds.   Men are not ignored when children are nursed but are
ripe with milk themselves, fertile men with their poems and art,
their way of talking so that words set next to other words are
cells of the body, fresh

Food.   Rain channeled into streams, crops tended, nourishment
given to

Edible knowledge.

You think there must be terror in this, that a story is foolish
if it tells only joy, but I am the string-breaker, the refusal to
perpetuate obedience by fear.

Monsters: the grotesque lines of our own faces in water,
rippling, subsiding.
The hateful, weary of itself.

We do not sacrifice pigs or cows or children.
We do not commit suicide.   We do not ask others to kill themselves.

Snarling mouths have nothing left to teach us.

Women, penetrated, enriched, dance from the spine, are the axis
of the world.   Everything spins from our thighs, the willingness
to love what can return our own harmony to us, to increase what
is already present.   This
is peace, friend.   This is the future.

Faces carved above doorways can leave their stone if they wish.
Any art, touched by spirit, comes alive.

As string-breaker, I bring you new weather.   My husband's inspiration,
my freedom

Fertilized with images that lift themselves from earth's mud,
good sleep, the silken-eared ability to listen to what moves
through us, always:

Seeds planted in birth-labor, melody and pause, not a mystery
but breath,
natural,
high-pitched
excitement, then a throat filled with
the exchange of hurried youth for telling time by the ocean's moon.

Our animals write our hymns.   The women chant; the men add flutes
and horns.   Children with their small drums join us.   No one
excluded, nothing invisible in this place of

Image: the immediate, many-voiced prophecy.   We are not drugged.
We are

This island of bloom and art.   Our images spread like coins,

all wealth at once,
tossed onto your floors to be spent.
All stories are made of one thing becoming another,
every moment the same moment and all moments. Not time passing,
but your last night's dream, mine.

These new images:

The snake is the bowl in which you will gather herbs.
The umbrella of Hades is his desire to shelter his wife in
the time she is with him. When she returns from his world,
she is the healed cat.

Worlds mingle, combine themselves, never as distant from marriage
as you think. Grapes robust as cheese. Melons hatching as honeyed
cakes.

Breast, hoof, palm, beak, udder:
After a lifetime of waiting, a lifetime of passion,
given to renewal. Images, not philosophy,
create us.

Mate with what frees you.

My broken sister, the Ariadne of the wrong time, could only fall,
turn her bones in her hands until she rotted into this new island.

To trust heroics is to forget that war does not love us. The
rising life is this god, this equal. The goats prophesied
many children, and I have given them, in my sister's name: the
health of strong wings, the old story now a bright star, light

within the labyrinth.   My sons and daughters shine as the next
chance.

We begin again, every morning.
One daughter's braid has grown as long as her spine.
I am proud of what I see in her that is in me.
Daughter, the bird who has cracked its shell, who dances her
wings along the grass.
"Mother," she calls to me, "he will come today," and she means

Dionysus who is her father and her husband and
her brother, her children.
Spring, coming and coming; whatever season blows in the trees,
the green effort bursts
not just once
but every morning.

In whiteness, I am my daughter,
as she is
the son who remembers our history in his poems.
We worship what we are meant to find.

Cool soil after ecstatic mouthfuls.

LUNA'S POEMS

THIS PRESENCE

the blue of it   her
generous eye
our eyes look to the lake of her face
we meet
sky
the history of water
she gathers us   we become moon
for this brief time

we are not what we think we are but what
we hope to be in the looking
the full
body
changing
into one unchanged

IT WAS

the moon in the ground black and tortured
nothing to breathe

I had put on strict clothes
a spore who held itself until I was dead enough
to break   then could feed moon's multiple
cats   wolves   rabbits
tend her
fire
the smoke of burial clearing

claws in the bark of the tree
fur lifted by wind
her healing a lavish animal when the shell burns away

OUT OF A LONG SILVER WIND

a rare occurrence that happens
over and over   blood streams
across her body   will it flood her
no   it leaves room for light

the first poem I wrote
was the moon in the center of the day
mystery made visible when we least expect it
the poem
lost
the moon blazes then
is tongueless   a chilled face against glass

but in moon's own time I'm given money
to trace the path of her mouth
to find and name the creation of blood
beating
through silver through sleep
through the hatching of afternoon

A CIRCLE OF STONES

with incense with
the seashell he found
moonshell
woman   man   tonight
in quiet tones he sees
wings then
words streaks of words
she lets my hair escape
we say "oh lady" and eat fish for dinner
her ocean   and make love
her light   this morning my hair is damp
she has been sleeping her water with us

how little time there is
our incense gone to ash
but the moon
not exactly full anymore
is somewhere where
stones give us the words of ourselves
turning

THE YOUNG MOON

her clouds her brothers slide across her dance
three girls just about her age on the sidewalk   I pretend
I don't even see them so they can push through these clouds
be the first ones ever to feel her take them in their high heels
to the forest of park where she brings out the deer
I try to look innocent so she will make my old shoes
get latin on my feet   open this man and me to laughing
all the way home   after a night like this
there are always empty wine bottles under the trees

GOLD

from poverty to the sure way he spoke to me on the phone
telling me he likes the one thing I've been able to write

about spring   the moon an owl   it's warm enough
we turn into eggs with eyes then feathers then
beaks certain of food

what I wrote was about things barely
moving after
a winter of debt

WE ARE SO MUCH

water so much the month changing its days
these houses won't last much longer
but their shadows will be new voices
broaching the air   that's how the dog barks
that's how the leaves gather in the street
green then yellow then
brown each phase a beautiful color
we should weep more often
make use of so much water the moon
swimming her memories until they find
a freshened country   the dog's silence   the next child

UNCHANGED

for thousands of
millions of

how many mysteries has she traveled
and me
here
bits of hair and bone
loving
history what I
always

understand as any of us
who is born from
water   came from
up there someplace

SIX A.M.

mark it
the one full-again moment this month
she'll be gone in an hour

water in the cup I drink some
and leave some outside
for her
all day

EVERY SPRING

EVERY SPRING

1. *Persphone's Entrance*

the golden skyward songs
they praise whole fields they glorify conceited light
while my child is the thread of shadow between furrows

to see me
close your eyes
when you do I am black I am unadorned surrender
welcomed by those who might
be forgiven if they empty their hearts

they pretend to sacrifice
but their incense smells of cheap hope
I know too much for optimistic names
to please me
never sing my return
add nothing to what I tell you of a slower world
where loss is untangled from brilliance
a clean blank wall a home for seeds

2. Hades' Loneliness

it is our bargain but I miss her
not the virgin's fragrant white narcissus skin
but wife
my soul-root

when we lie together we produce ripe apples autumn pears
the mating of one full life with another and it smells
not of blooming but of the season her mother hates in me
never decorated never danced

I am completely myself
the king
when I'm naked
embedded in sorrow her knowledge
fertilized by shadow

3. Demeter's Welcome

his silence wounds me
her eyes are not the color that they were

I am the oldest field
the freshly bursting grain
the one who finds
somehow
strength
what I desire isn't a fool's joy
she should see that in my own fierce eyes
I raise my voice above the crowd to sing
that all seasons can become a single beauty
the final ecstasy
if she would listen
is her dormancy as it enters my green stem as
equally mature love
this mother
bows to death the husband of us all
yet still sustains a great and unforgotten music

beyond shadow above loss
the true season
which has no history might arrive

embrace me
let it be this year

CONTINUALLY

COMPASSION

Not creation, but what happens later, after the world is made, when we're older. These clear pictures: black, tough-bodied birds, unmistakable. Branches, relieved of summer. Not the beginning and not the end, but eucalyptus pods that smell of medicine.

In this city of distractions, I often look up, at night, into black which is not simply a background for stars, but itself, a guardian. "And then, and then..." the story goes. When black shines in the ravens' feathers, it isn't the fear of being lost. I find a necklace of black links placed around my throat, a promise to wear the story carefully clasped, and also as an unending circle. My loved cat has died, his noisy hunger gone into mystery. But, in his own realm, he's alive, unburied by the grace of a birds's blood dropping on the soil of his grave. In the cat's redemption, he's mated with a female he couldn't have when he was nothing more than a foolish hunter.

I plant, now, iris and tulips in what was his death. On the ground nearby, the eucalyptus, language of continuance in the odor of time-honored remedies. Here in the middle, between sunset and rain, the speech of the dark assures me that the made jar of the worlds does hold, is clean. Let the bulbs grow wings.

TRAVEL

The sun, a constantly shifting bloom of persimmon and coral as it falls. One more day. Seagulls, flocks of them, quiet on the sand—a congregation, transfixed, to watch this passage as religiously as we do.

Home, that line carved in blood on the flesh, is always only repeated tides, rising to great waves now, this winter, when sun, moon and earth place themselves with more than their usual force. To pull us—where?

The question, even as I wrap myself into the arms of the man I've loved for years. We watch, amazed, the fiery change and balance, history as this passion of light and cloud that takes our eyes away, then gives them back to us at the final moment, the end of sun, to turn us in another direction. The gulls, released from prayer, spiral, up, above the sea. When the sun leaves, the ocean surges: twins in our bodies, heat and water, rhythmic, working their way toward our own deaths and what might happen after that.

Human lovers, human strangers, we button our jackets to hold gravity even as it holds us, even while we die. We carry the weight of what we understand, and of what can only be known by more than what we see—by what hides behind repeated time. Our feet through thick sand, we do go toward something with the ability, at least, to make guesses from our salty blood.

—For Harry E. Northup

PERMANENCY

It will rain again, anyway. One storm has already soaked into the dry, winter soil, giving the plants what I can give only half as well as rain that knows how to fertilize—mountains, streets, childhood and cypress trees—completely.

"Cypress": that hiss of syllables, the rough "s" of tongue to teeth, the whistled pleasure of rain sinking past the skin of the California landscape into the roots, our ancestors. An inheritance of my mother's crystal bowls and glasses, which I was given only recently, too late for sentimentality but at the right moment to say, "So be it," which repeats itself in the cypress, the sloshing traffic, the mountains too far away for me to hear, but I understand: My work is to believe in all the water that we need for this season, removed from personal decision.

The man I live my life with drinks from one of the glasses. The wine is alive in our kitchen, as we are. I can't protect the glass from lips against the rim, our slippery hands. If it's lasted this long, it will hold until it has to break. Why hide faith behind us in the cupboard, in the pretense that there's no future? The mountains, rich with rain turned into snow—turning into what we'll drink next spring.

HISTORY

January rose, meticulous white, on a bush too far away for me to pick it. Wind slices through assumptions of fate as sweet delight, although wild air may give a new design to the palm tree, bent and cracking.

Keep the root in mind, that ugliness, appearing hopeless but still a step beyond vulnerable seed. "You won't live through the night," a solemn teller-of-fortunes warns me. I do live, as if fate can lie, or just doesn't know, itself, what's going on. Rubbery aloe vera leaves expand toward an unheard-of flower like a disabled star. And the odd dog who wears a blue coat trots past, nobody holding him on a leash, as if he's dressed himself, can make it out and home again whether or not anyone comes with him.

Yet, I'm afraid, in these times when no one knows anything, when it's the end of work that only adds up to an empty box, the last page finished. Of course, it's death, and of course there will be death, someday, that's the real end of breathing. This isn't it. Lopsided, wind-cut, and let that be hope. But the rose not forgotten—even if it's too precise and far away—in case the truth is that we create our own destinies: imperfect roots but loyal to white that could meet us when the wind, fully released, having tested every stem, quiets itself and says, "It's your turn now. Tell yourself what you deserve."

THE WHOLE

Sand, lifted to stone—walls that hold everything I don't know. Windows, pure rectangles, outlined in black: the certainty of completion. My hard-blown, conflicted desert brought to geometry that never errs. Sunlight, then, soaks the walls, as water might, changing the shape. It's time to leave, to worry again about clothes, to be impure in my city of flawed music; to go home, having seen this largest possibility, visible but not to be lived in.

Consider it the union of noon with its most constant self, but we have to fall downward, past the joined hands of the clock, into the next hour, down to the orchids that are about to bloom just outside my front door. Surely, they're a wonder, but, on this earth, no more than a jungle's weeds, involved in their particular struggle—snails that eat the buds. I'm still the child of ignorance, the tension of waiting for these weeds to win or lose. Absolute completion can't make use of me.

KNOWLEDGE

Bach, in which the pulse comes out of sleep entangled in dying, but, at the same moment, wakes to breasts under flannel pajamas, to sun that exposes a woman as a lifted, curvaceous step into a bath of morning sound. Bach, tearing off his buttoned suit; his sparkling blood never afraid to shout our virtues. This water against my spine: undressed rosary. Bach, reciting churches as spirit made flesh. If we have enough faith to suffer, we have enough faith to praise.

REQUIEM

Take him, then, since you already have, without asking. Rip the note from my calendar that says, "Write to Jim." Crush the gift other friends were bringing him—to hold you off, to imagine we could dissuade you.

Death, are you ever peace?
Perhaps, once we've spit on enough candles.

After our stained faces soften, when he can listen without our bitterness, give him the litany of your true names, the ones you hide from us. Let him sing what we can't hear as you take him toward your unimaginable home. And, if you have anything like arms, or wear something like a coat, warm him, as we wanted to. At least that, now that he's yours.

—For Jim Elrod

GUIDANCE

The planet Mercury, a crescent at this season, its shimmering edges the atmosphere of our own earth. Even a tiny child is held up to the great eye of the telescope, to the orange wings on the feet of the messenger. His heels lead us toward everything that glitters.

In the night air, another walk around the pleasure of seeing so far away. Is our house the very one we notice among thousands of other lights? Yes and no. When we aren't there, it takes the shape of this changing time, a crescent: cradle or scimitar. How can we imagine what it does when we don't fill it with ourselves?

I look into more stairs to climb. I move forward, up, although the tricky ladder would tempt me back. But, step by step. I do lose the past. The stairs take me to music, to an uneven number, to amazement that I've come all this way. I know so much. And yet, what songs does the house croon, alone? What will Mercury, the gate-turner, do with me next? There's never just one key to the night sky.

We sneak up on the house as if it might burst, split apart by the sword, or has grown larger than it is, plump with new children. Odd that the furniture is still in place. Odd, too, that one thing has fallen from a shelf without my touching it.

ART

We devote ourselves to this mountain, to rock that inspires us, although it has no advice about the way its hymns are to be sung. We carve for years, making nothing but walls. Then, when we've used every blindness, when the heart is as sensitive as a knife that understands, suddenly, the difference between crime and heaven, a great, dark eye appears from under our work. Beyond the mute altar, the eyes we call ours and the eyes of the Master embrace.

THE CURTAIN

THE CURTAIN

1. *Four Grapefruit*

Just off the tree, ripe, tinged with red, to be given to my elderly Armenian neighbors, but I resist offering even these few to the man and woman who garden here, behind the house I live in. They garden in smog, in noise, in corners of this city property that would otherwise be barren. They whisper that aloe vera must be prepared in a way only they know before it can heal any cut or bruise.

This winter season of citrus: Who is the god of giving freely? To hold on too long to the fresh gifts will rot them. I praise the fat grapefruit but want to keep them, kill their ripe moment because there is a god who tricks me into believing that I deserve these juicy, shining things, that I've earned them, yet the grapefruit tree has appeared suddenly where nothing has been before. I haven't planted it.

The fruit is in my hands. Is any gift truly received? Is giving even valuable? The largest one, the one most weighted with desire—am I to have nothing at all to hold? The truth is that I'm afraid to be empty. The seeds might be saved and fertilized, but that would go on in the invisible garden of spirit, where I never predict what will grow. Or won't. The god of uncertainty, as unsure as I am: This god urges me to give over what I cling to so that the new year can come without making promises.

Take these, then. The tart fruit, daylight and blood. Let them feed you, god of the unknown, until I can meet the neighbors who do not speak my language in one of those corners where it seems that nothing will thrive, where I can wait without glowing faith, simply wait to see what will happen.

2. Mud

Weren't there things I was sure of, that we all knew, that kept the houses in their places and helped the seasons turn from mud to seeds to wheat?

A woman has prepared the house for Christmas, every gift beautifully wrapped. She guides a grandmother's hand as tags for the gifts are written. The whole family is happy to be here, but the woman, the one who is me, is not a mother or a daughter or an aunt. There's nothing she can call herself, even if she is loved. Wonderfully, a bird, outside, sings. An angel? Is it? If so, what does it sing?

And why is it Christmas only in this moment? The next season leaps to the city where I live now, where someone has abandoned an apartment. A promise has taken all its furniture. Then I leave, too; I say goodbye to a man who was kind—goodbye forever—but he returns quickly, in the next fast turning of houses, younger than yesterday, close to me again. Still, no name for myself. I hear birds as I sit, trying to remember what time of year it really is. Angels. Or fragments of what was once whole. Listening without seeing them, I can't make out which are the blue jays and which are the mourning doves, or are they ravens?

A bowl of food to be mixed until it's just right, but it's not right, never finished. Green vegetables, but isn't this the season of mud? The grandmother's hand shakes, but at least she knows who the tags belong to, although all my grandmothers are dead. I am the center of something that warms me, then decays, that moves until it is only a glimpse of feathers behind a bush. The landlady has hung a sheer curtain where a wall should be.

3. The Crossing

The wall which is not a wall but simply a curtain. Small sprouts poke through at the edges of the sink, where enough moisture has collected to attract them. Water and dirt. Crumbs and grease. The transformation of what was once on the dinner plates into bits of earth. Where did any seed come from, inside the house? A thing that might be fed, brought to life by the little edge of death around the sink? No walls here, and when I think how I might build one to separate the trees from the bedroom, a seed plants itself in my grandmother's belly. In her eighties, she would really be my mother. She is carrying a child where there are no solid years, no past, only the present. Ancestral pregnancy, the strange growth at the farthest edges.

4. Middle Age

Oh, my Japanese warrior, his hair as arched as all the courage it takes to face the enemy. Fierce head, proud with shining lacquer, but it droops now, and the wig, matted, falls until I see the foundation is only a shredded piece of gray cloth. Why have I wanted to live my father's life? Whenever I think of Dad, I see him in a suit, smiling bravely, extending his hand to a customer, sure of the sale.

Give back the wish to locate the treasure in the castle on the mountain after the long hike. The slender women, muscular, climb steadily, even though it's treacherously rocky up there. From the field below, I watch them, shading my eyes, remembering the time I swore I'd never fall in love again: I would be as courageous as art, that armor which makes strength out of slippery stone.

Words, slivered and pared, written over and over until there's nothing left of them. The birds, the fruit, the angelic gifts. Give them back. My leg hurts if I try to stand up. My foot has been wounded since I was a child, when something told me that the real treasure is the constant blood of love's confusion.

At last, a bedroom, and, in my arms, a Japanese woman, as round as I am. We are sleeping; we're breathing away what is too stalwart in us. A man enters—the one I've come to love for his tenderness, not his costume. When I can move, I walk with him through a temple of four curving sides, both of us circling this religion of blood and breath, leaning on each other. I look behind me every step of the way, until I know there is nothing following me with a weapon, with a mountain.

—For Harry E. Northup

5. All I've Got Is the Weather

Never finished. Never fully prepared. Not as greedy and not as empty. If fear is taken into the heart, mixed with today I said, "I love you," but my money was stolen anyway, there's still a medieval wedding ceremony with a juggler catching it all. The one I love has washed a new cooking pot, a perfect circle of heat. God of the elusive! Creamed onions and nothing but instinct, which turns the other way, its head an owl's, totally flexible, and, with practice, balances every tree in just two hands.

6. An Exchange of Rings

A silver and glass bracelet from the other side of the family, months ago, before I thought I needed it. Amulet of turning and turning. Young girls have magical coins in their hands to protect them from me. No one should know what she can't live yet. I don't know it all myself, and the silver is engraved with tiny flowers I can barely see. Persephone, not innocent, a woman my age, keeps a few plants, even in winter, whose roots are steady in this night soil. No exotic perfume, but, "There's plenty of wine," she says. Even without gold, I'm to give birth to fruit that's been crushed, fermented, enlivened.

One day I feel the excitement of what I have to live yet. The next, I wake up, panicked, imagining myself as a poverty-stricken old woman without friends. The fear is helplessness; the pleasure is the same thing—a crossing into the realm where I don't make decisions from sheer will but from fate, the voice that comes from somewhere next to me, telling me I'll be safe, although a disaster has occurred. I bring out my few toys at dinner: a witch nose, whistling plastic teeth, shoes that walk by themselves, the book that—if you flip it quickly— makes all the photos of a woman dance. My wine-red scarf slips to the bottom of the bag; I think I have it; it disappears. Persephone whispers: "There will be more to find," and I believe her, and I believe, too, that stepping out of my favorite strengths is dangerous. Sometimes, the fruit turns to a lump of clay that may be dead matter. Or the beginning of everything. The bracelet, as much as I depend on it to take me through this year, is invisible.

7. The Lump of Clay

Strange growth at the farthest edges. The god of giving freely. Incomplete sentences. Food—eaten, divided between nourishment and waste—this cycle holds us every day of our lives. Once, in my living room, the most powerful symbols of all: peacock, lion, black dog. What did the bird sing in the angelic moment of Christmas? It sang pregnancy, although I will never have a physical child, although I'll never again live with the certainty and good nature and faith of my father or of my young self who could manage, she thought, a lifetime of undaunted enthusiasm.

I sleep with the man I love and I dream of marriages, separations, more marriages. Who is ever complete? All I ask is to be less frightened of myself and of the aging spirits who promise both dying and perpetual myth, the making of our stories: repetitions and renewals, clear patterns and reversals. The fragrant citrus. The gladioli on the dining room table, turning black, ready to be buried. The empty house of my childhood which sits just one dirt road away from a cemetery, and yet gave me many, many flowers. The blessings of animals that I don't understand but worship. Here, part of the way through the garden, I still can't say my inner name, but I can move, even limping. What will thrive? The mysterious gardeners themselves.

POEMS
(late 1980s)

ISLAND

Santa Barbara Island was named on December 4, 1602, Saint Barbara's Day,
by Sebastian Vizcaino. It's the smallest of the Channel Islands off the coast of
Southern California, and the least-visited. Steeply cliffed, it includes two
peaks; the whole of the island was formed by an ancient volcano. Vegetation is
sparse; attempts to farm or raise crops have failed. There's no fresh water.

Saint Barbara was locked in a tower when she refused to marry a pagan cho-
sen for her by her father, Dioscorus. Unable to shake her Christian piety, he
beheaded her. (Some say she was tortured beforehand and that her breasts
were cut off.) Dioscorus, after killing his daughter, was immediately killed by
a flash of lightening. Barbara is invoked against explosion and sudden death;
she's the patron saint of gunners and miners.

1.

this ocean repeated
repeats
into itself the self who believes
nothing exists but its own pulse
a sleep gone so far down that no one
can find its heart

a law against touch
unless drowning's an act of good will

not our mother
we breathers and lovers of eyesight
of nasturtiums   the city's fistfuls of orange
how
somehow
we grew hands

as much water as we are
we prefer to mate with skin

2.

the ocean moves and we
prejudiced against silence
move against it   sun in our eyes or
not
not here at all

we suck at our stories of whales
their warm blood
like us they even sing

but would we be the species we aren't
would we ask for a body of two thousand pounds

when the boat pushed away from shore
we all put on jackets
closed our lungs in our chests to protect them

3.

the truth of indifference
which refuses to explain us to ourselves
or to illuminate the dense gray of its fish

I said yes to this
to an island I've never seen
the boat a way there   of course I knew it meant
water
out of sight of home

and someone is sick
who believed more than the stomach could hold
of course I expected the blue prettiness of imagination
the mother we do call the sea

4.

love
when we met
I thought you'd keep watch
but you aren't with me to put
both hands on the railing

you—
human goodness—
don't know where I am

5.

the island itself
a volcanic event
where a great waste of sun is so old
that it's blind is
bound by rock heavier even
than its tonnage of light

nothing like wind
or sister   brother
hello hello

lot's wife turns to salt
tribe after tribe of gulls
exactly alike

6.

rock as hard as the rest of what dreams are

too real
so real that I think I am never sincere

7.

if I could bring cactus
awake
could teach dust

saint barbara
locked in her tower
dry
not from lack of passion but from
refusing love in this world

can she pull up her own dress
feel through to the cracks in the rock

loved one at home
when we met
the rain we don't have in august
poured toward us

oh loved one

8.

when you and I met it was
orange   gold   the superb leaves
and edible

loved one
look at the worn-out gulls

I'm not these birds
or a cliff

am I?

9.

and there is
to the north
a freed arm of rock in its own place

but
no

it's still only
a saint whose name means stranger
tearless
faithful to not being saved from herself

10.

but we did rise out of the sea
used our new throats to say
we wouldn't be fish
we made ourselves into legs into thumbs

I blow on these skimpy bits of plant
inspired toward praise toward
the strength it takes to
thrust
up
out of stone which is water which is stone

the flower I put in my hair
when I thought I was young and
woman the hand that drops below eaten fruit
to catch the pit she can plant as seed

love
think about
music as intricate miracle
think about marrying me

but when I look up
there's not even a tree

11.

starlessness looks like this
like solid proof

I can have only
the food I've carried myself

cheese: that can be said
and tea without sugar—
the limits proper to one body

12.

gradually the saint as
a decent pilgrim but
less too than that
less and less

one true thing:
I wish I were somewhere else

this is the time I spend
willing or unwilling
with facts—
how to never be grateful
how to follow
like a blank fist and speak plain english

watch her
she braids her salt-white hair
quickly
efficiently
she refuses
to give up her lonely god

13.

no love or injury
or pleasure
cares when
the question is
thousands of years

a two-inch figure against
absolute sky could try to
believe
that the ocean below this rock
might be
an eye which moves
which isn't stupid

14.

might and might not

this is too large
and tiring and
what good is mercy anyway

whether we're accidental
or divinely planted
we won't be saved

we are held though

by gravity
by vertebrae
or barbara's christ the kind of god
who makes his camp away from others
and all he says is "faith"

valley
shadow
oil

shepherd
island

15.

there is wind here sometimes
loaded with pollen   measurable
and so not affected by hope but
there are reported days when
the coreopsis bloom such yellow
that they can be seen for miles

just not today

16.

land I'll go on seeing
eyes closed
even making love
even after autumn comes
weeks from now

even at a wedding
not mine

the husband leans to kiss
to meet her while
my new fall garden sprouts oregano and sage

but the island hasn't moved
it occurs just once
it's the rest of us who breathe

who marries whom?

17.

are we greed or
sacrament or dead
with our gold on our fingers?

the long braid unravels
untortured
across the saint's beloved's
shoulder and equally
the island has a night in which
all the hair is cut

these two or more meanings

and a final singularity
not yet mine
in which no one ever argues

18.

I've been a good child
but that's gone too
I dream of sizes   tightness
buttons

of giving the devil his due

it was love that
could be bought with itself

but it can't
although money hidden in a pocket
when you take it out
looks willing to be spent

it's beyond us
it's just beyond us
and not one cent more

loved one
we mate for life
and we don't

19.

I touched nothing
as we were told not to
not to disturb the gulls
or sea lions or walk off the trails

when a virgin does give up to love
there's another girl just like her
willing to obey so much long history of herself

in the boat's noise of going home
I kept myself on deck
colder and colder toward shore
and dinner and rest

20.

to think of belonging somewhere
to someone
to think about lungs when
it won't rain until september
not the month we met
but we are here
are lovers
and the afternoon before it does rain
I say I won't sleep tonight

unless I see
actually
see the ocean again

we drive there together and look at it
and look at it

21.

saint barbara never
probably
never existed

faith is what never happened
but we take it as creation

we're better acquainted
love
than we were before
and changed

22.

sun has no gender and whales are not
human although mammals

but without our myths
mostly
it's terror
all by ourselves and
death as somewhere else all by ourselves

we do not know:
that's the island's fatal word

23.

two months past the island
this morning's yellow city-lilies
spattered with orange in such a way
that I can't not believe

not in civilization but in
a fist through glass
the broken spell

nothing rises from contentment
not one stalk of anything

24.

no magnificence asks
yet
for my death

barbara perhaps
gave too much to
the christ who only wants new children
or daily prayer   plain loneliness
relieves history

take us where we can think straight for once

the saint of explosions
she
of all people
should tell the truth
should live a little longer

25.

eclipse of the moon
and an illness

it hurts
to let myself go
to confess both the closed
tight
mouth and the
need to crawl toward an open door

26.

one passage made ends nothing:
incarnation is not simply
a layer of fabric across a bare arm

my hand goes to my eyes
shades the brightness of martyrs and finds
a new wilderness

these deer-forests
these buffalo-plains
the twittering birds
the loose edges

27.

now
there's a river
and another chance

the island
a lesson in one god's facts
in the orphan's stubborn law
stays in place

now there can be winter and more

one month after another
each with its own dialect

28.

self-contained we're
self and the other language too

loved one we both
not accidentally
wear blue shirts today

the real place
has a wide variety of species
and alone or abundantly together
they do
make a new thing

INTELLIGENCE

it comes back
washed
thinner than it was
so that its good bones show

it has its own sweater
and doesn't need food

why not believe that a white falcon
inhabits this neighborhood
and that the friend I depended on
for the planets the secrets
the one who's gone
has entered me as a clearly-muscled wrist

maybe I wasn't born in spring
but now
in the cool season of messages in white bowls
the clay shaped for useful harvest
the falcon saying hello in lucid english

THE POWER OF THE NEXT
WONDERFUL MOMENT

something is loving our clothes as we die
something croons in an upper register that even
the dogs can't come home to

fibers and atoms
and secret forgiveness
one end of one day leads to
this music I can't reason with

my accumulation of paper
all blank
the way we suffer what we can never accomplish
the way something doesn't care and is
the soothing unheard far far away but diligent
voice of our undone things
happy to be left alone

A WIDER AND MORE INTRICATE CIRCLE

unexpectedly   my favorite dog and I take each other
up a stairway to god or to childhood or are they the same?
I cross into

wigs who recognizes me although he's dead but this is
the version in which god created the world for his dog
who wanted   wants   company   it's possible that
I'm the dead   that he creates my food and water   I call
"wigs"   name what likes to come with me   or he
calls me to himself

long ago   the first climb was stone after stone
the obstacles of my tough self   and at the end of it
god said "I don't know"   so I fell again   into seven more
years of drought   the dog left me then to my own burned feet
cooling only now
even more years later
in this easier   faster ascent to the house above the stairway
to at least several large windows   the unwished wish
come true   good dog   brisk divinity
his fine tongue and short legs and we make it
we're offered something to drink   we've been so thirsty

The 1990s

SPECIFIC MYSTERIES (1990)

LATER A PURPLE IRIS
YOUNG AND OUT OF SEASON

the gun some offering
heavy as law
falls
I was not meant to kill my enemies
but to enrich them with a winter of dreams

magic has nothing to do with power has everything to do with
the results of the gun turned to natural metal in sleep
what can be called gold
as long as a stranger is willing to take empty hands

THE FACE IT WILL HAVE LATER

spring fills the bulbs
I plant them my hands in soil
how long it takes

tonight
I want him so much that I can't say it
I can never say it
I move to him and wait
we're as blind as the rains
everything happens without sun until leaves appear
to feel him rise is the most exciting

dormancy then first breath
where all things begin nobody asks why

it's still winter
but something is inside the hyacinth
something is under the way the sky covers itself
whispering "stay where you are and don't look up"

HERE IS MY STORY A WOMAN REACHES FORTY

ragged my sweater too old everything some days is too old
yet geraniums
such spice in what produces leaves
the ragged body

he says
"we'll just make the best of who we are"

a woman reaches forty presses against it
the wall is no wall but something to steady the emptiness
I complain of weakness a vulnerable day
but breakfast is right here on the table

he and I make love
I'm not perfect
and the small tin birds that I pin to my sweater later
are all I can afford
we take a walk and stumble
"when I die" he says "I hope I'm listening to music"
"when I die" that awkward agreement to stay alive
the geranium is stubborn
I touch the two tin birds
it's sunny

I became forty so that I would know what stops
a glimpse of myself at fifty is
a woman who describes her garden without adjectives
it's just not how it was I'm sorry
I've counted on omens a tree larger than most
some stranger speaking to me anything
to keep myself from the real shape of a hand
it looks just like a hand today

one life at a time
this one
when I see a spoon or fork I can pick it up
I can rub the birds
make the rough gesture of a sweater pushed above my elbows
a thing is a thing I'm going to die I'm sorry
ragged body that still produces leaves

the emptiness
like a good night's rest or a pair of shoes to be fixed

if the other hand is still a mystery at least it's with me
and the dream woman last night her shining hair
I couldn't see a face but she looked at the distance
I look at spoons
and dying is the making love to what exists
the kindness of stumbling of music

NOTHING IS CLOSED EXCEPT ALL THE DOORS

the oldest woman finds every color
her grapes her orchard
and begs for less beauty
all instinct is to act without waste
when there is too much of anything something says
go to nature see what lives see what is killed

those of us who survive know
our fruit and worms the rapture
we will beg for age
our emptiness our permanent vines

—for the poems of H. D.

SHELL

everyone cancels plans it's april
I break the egg to eat the shape and tomatoes
those plum tomatoes all the oval promises

spring a city patio my bare feet
I'm up too early
knowing I've lost friends
the woman who doesn't visit anymore
the man who wants to know what is unknowable
and I can't tell him
every day I eat something that might have grown

who chooses what exists
a knife a gentle morning
a patio fertile with hyacinths and herbs
and trees I stare up
it could be any day in any april when the plans have changed
the woman stays in her family to take care of
with nothing left for those who do not look like her
it's not her fault
we're never any stronger than we are

spring mystifies
and is no cure but an inevitable hatching
the man so worried who thinks I might explain
doesn't see me now more human than I've been
less reasonable more hurt
the egg tomato bread will not come back
but they nourish me
as the morning grows a little older
its burden of silence its possibilities
if everything has changed then everything will change again
this is what april is
accidents and miracles the choices I do not make

an opening
perhaps to bone
and no apology

THE WIND THE QUESTION
OF WHAT IT WILL DO NEXT

let it take the last gesture of perfection

my language flattens as I saw a friend
flatten cloves of garlic with the side of a knife
to make them workable
rhythm comes and goes and laughs to see us search for it
when we are breathing all the time

through every window
restless damage and reeking of what is ready to be used

SKY

it is all string and grass in the beak
then flies so far away that I can't name the color
this ends with promises
I love him

just let me wipe the hair out of my eyes

I cook asparagus but only in may then move on
to summer squash to corn to pumpkin
suddenly it's winter here is soup
always a different set of clues

no wonder my friend who's crazy pretends she can't read
total failure is such relief

I tell him to stop asking me what I think
I think the speckled neck on one dove silly and lively
how can a home be a migration
yet there is something in feathers this quick pulse
there's no choice
I'm not alone anymore
my friend walks the same few shaky blocks
every day every day
twenty years of this for her and more to come
untouched

all right
I can eat these meals this noise as large as the whole yard
let us amaze the people who fold their arms and dare us
he and I look at each other
we've learned nests
flying
hunger

rocks against the tree
let us have no peace then
the promises begin to work in us

balanced on telephone wires landing on fences circling the seed
it's the right weather it's forever the right weather

—for Harry E. Northup

WHETHER OR NOT WE HAVE FAILED

is of no consequence
the leaves are huge
the only lotus we have
blooming out of
he was fully open this morning

yellow centers invisible now
"maybe someone picked them" he says
or they closed themselves when evening came
we take a long time
what difference does that make
we're fed
certainly clean enough
once a year we come to these booths of samoan
filipino chinese food

all the gods

we walk quickly looking for yellow to open
to close how many times
failing or not doesn't matter
it matters that we look
and then walk all the way around
everything again

SUMMER SOLSTICE ONE EYE CLOSED

full
sun the emphasis on light
I think of it without courage

god can be anything
a pigeon crushed to the sidewalk
a cat between wheels such a busy street
god can see anything on a long long day

half the birthdays gone
the balance splits
I go on buying things
a clock a picture frame
a skirt that reminds me of years ago
when I knew nothing when I lived nowhere

not quite fear
but solemn absence of control
not quite worship
although I clip my fingernails
then smoothe them

but another bird drops to my house
and later I'll burn myself
one arm accidentally in the path of heat

RISES IN THE EVENING MORE DAYLIGHT

the room fills with
a weaving from peru its natural dyes its lavenders
uneven and beautiful
which is my planning the last letter I'll ever write
then my hand to my face to remind me of stubbornness
this face
it is a visit from a stranger a visit from a sister
I give up the story that I was a happy child

black wool diamond in the center
with a stripe through it like sudden rain
pure grace
but paid for over and over if anything is to be whole
is to be colors purged from insects squeezed from plants
applied to thread combined with other thread
worked then finished

hour after hour
shape and weight and length
the handfuls of what I might have lived
what I do live
when someone says you're so serious
I think "not serious enough"
there are so many imitations

HOW WORDS ARE SAID

ferns the earliest yet did not shrink to fossils
the excellence of string quartets
old wounds even the scars I touch
hurt
even friendship I have given wounds myself
cello the ferns so much my language

eons
the earth in layers each scar another seed
on and on the music on and on
my hands I do not want them any softer
every pulse the memory of every other pulse

HARVEST

water begins in the mountains as snow
I did know how thirsty I was but didn't expect
this season ahead of a season
pouring into my mouth
a single leaf out of the desert
or a lake I saw once in the mountains in fog
it was this world I walked right up to it
it wasn't this world
someone held my mouth to it and said "drink
just drink"

FOLK TALE

nothing has ever belonged to me
but what I've called loss returns as souls
october teaches me its first day
in the death of my young friend
five years ago her tumored hands
failing shaking
when we talked we talked of breath
deeply more deeply breathe more deeply
then breath was gone but not her myth of cures

october
someone has planted zinnias in a bathtub in a parking lot
someone has learned the exquisite hardship of sanity

spirits everywhere not waiting for spring
here they come unmasked
I read a russian woman's life
her friends memorized her poems when
it was too dangerous to write them down
my own nordic ancestors set harps in their graves
ladders to the next world
the first day of october I follow the twigs cracking
laying their patterns right under my feet

a friend tells me she has a good idea
a friend tells me she's found one laugh in the middle
of an argument a friend tells me he has lived through
a meaningless war a friend
tells me a child has been born at home
another friend tells me nothing
but just hearing her voice convinces me to
give up hunching my shoulders for the relief of saying
all the poets all the friends all the dead

who are not the withered dead but
new
they forgive death they know they have helped
deeply more deeply breathe more deeply
the endless exchange the endless inheritance

take a risk
nuts split their meat falls in its pieces
small lamps from the bonfire where the masks are burned

FOR POETS IN AUTUMN

roses become their concentrated shells
carriers of seed

lorca neruda akhmatova
the dead we see the dead who see us
in this country where nothing ends

the birthmark on all our mouths
the slow mirror a bond

why go on except for such a family

THE SPILLED WATER OF CHILDREN'S VOICES

our hottest afternoons worn away
in this return to autumn

coming toward hallowe'en
my costume nothing like a blouse or skirt
but what is put on in utter gratitude
for all I was taught to sing as a child myself

my mother
I wish she were alive this year

her songs always lifted against decaying fruit
toward christmas that turns us
immortal
I give myself to october as it
rushes to wash my shoulders
as I go down long stairs to the illuminated heart
to the everlasting marigold-clothes
singing what continues

here pumpkins are emptied of burdens to receive light
our inherited faces melt
re-form themselves into seed

THESE DAILY ARTS

a new cup its initiation
a woman who says she won't hurt me
she asks me to believe her

wind makes a decent home
and shaggy white flowers like sleeves
no
like whiskers no
nothing I've seen before

starts from birth
starts from purpose and serves distance
wind not the steadiness of prayer but
perhaps a winter with candles

no angels today
just wind and
white on the rim of the cup where I put my mouth

WE MUST DISCOVER TOGETHER
ALL THAT GROWS HERE

wakening in a bed of leaves
musical yet strong feet these ancestors
here in the forest here
where it is a privilege to be born
my name your name sap in the tree
a new country a common dream
each one who has come before us spells the name
in crossing ocean after ocean
crossing that blood and that blood and this blood

tribal odor my ancestors say go on with it
the sap moves hard from root to branch
crossing continents crossing all our dreams
within the pioneer the old egyptian boat
within the boat is mexico and there on shore
the dancer the first feet of traveling
the privilege of all these maps

how to say thank you
for dangerous passage

THE GATE

wolf a companion
solemn between trees
in daylight not cursing any moon
not disappearing
I'm able to think when she's here

wolf whose education is silence
and the instinct to do things well
what is called winter any winter
stones in the ground cold yellow sun
yet my shadow with its feet at my feet
no need to fight over food

the wolf and I don't tame one another
but we both know the word "north"
the fertility of an old woman
her whitest hair not a boundary but a reward and
the future is each track in fresh snow

AMERICAN POETRY
(mid-1990s)

CITY/PRAIRIE

1. Sage, freshly cut, smells the same as horses

a prairie that only exists in pots out in front
of my house in Los Angeles—herb-thinking;
plant-dreaming. Sidney has brought me her
sunflower seeds, the "dark-headed ones" that
I'll plant in the spring, early spring, in an echo:

My uncle had wheat, field by field.
My aunt's garden held to the farmhouse, gave off its
peas, beans, corn and tomatoes as if it were easy to
summon all Nature, to trust

that we'd live through the winters when antibiotics were
nowhere in sight yet, and two cousins' mother had died
from a simple strep throat.

I plant rosemary, basil, lavender, sage;
there are nutmeg geranium, thyme and oregano growing.
Precautions, medicinal prayers. I've never cured one
single thing in this life; I doubt that I will.
I'm not a do-gooder. I plant for the magic:
mirroring The Mother Who Plants when Her seeds fly out of pods
or get shit onto mulch; spread through the world
by their own push and grunt. To farm is to worship Her body.

I turn the corner of a dream: Nebraska, birthplace,
gives its prehistoric, straight horizon to an air
which smells as moist as seed, the earliest
imagining, tucked into a pod or fruit, hidden
and yet teeming with bacteria, precision, knowledge

of a final shape. The dream: I move into a lake that isn't
even there, and yet I swim, and so do pigs. Our lovely shapes:
the forms we're given by The Maker of the Mud—our rising

from spring days the way my mother had her birthday
right before my own. Pigs are sacred to The Mother.

Pre-history: the clumbered air. I smell all water's charity
dropped on the seeds, our feet, the layering inside the earth
so it will be exactly where our bodies can take root.

We have what we emerge from.
White child, but I know I'm the buffalo,
could be Lakota chief when I grow up.
Belief in our exactness—red-blond braids,
tallest in my fourth grade class—
but also multiplied—just like America—
the hope of union, all the sexes, races,
states together, faces toward the schoolroom flag.
Give us liberty,

set loose those buffalo carousing through the grass;
let us be each other's truth and family. Let us
have America as miracle, uncynical, untreacherous.

I am the child; I am the animal: my shaggy little tail,
my angry, little eyes. An urgency:

2. *To break into a litany*

To worship old angels, their knowledge compounded
by years; whether dead or alive:

Who tease out visions from my grandmother's wild throat—

Who will not turn their wings to distant gold.
Who will not separate their days from ours.

Who give us warnings: It is necessary to speak up.
It is necessary to perform the visions,

I Pledge Allegiance To

Prairie women, crazed by wind,
by dust, by chicken ignorance.

Who did my mother talk to?
She, alone at the end of our street,
only a vacant lot between her and
Wyuka Cemetery. She was younger when she died
than I am now. Now:
I turn off kitchen lights. It's early;
it's still dark, and I am her, the first one out of bed,
winter breakfasts, winter lunches, winter soup.
And who could save her?
Not a child. Not me.

I talk and talk and talk.
I make a life of talk to make my mother's
voice. If I have never had a child, it's been
because I've had to love my mother out of death.
Give birth to this good leaf I found
when I went out to walk today,
the kitchen left behind me:

A leaf that's turning autumn orange and
red and yellow, and then a formal strip of green
mirroring itself on both sides. Subtly ruffled edges.

To pick up a leaf. To make much of it. To adore
this world: October 29, 1994, a Saturday, a very few days
before the anniversary of my mother's death:
November 1, 1954. Time enough to make a language.

I plan to go back,
to visit what I know loved me:
not even family, but the soaking light—
spring rain or frozen snow made heated with light's
clarity. The pure: to watch the world perform,
to wake up everyone at dawn so we could see

the Northern Lights which shown beyond our porch,
in sky that cared. Such personal commitment to belief.

To witness
is believing. I believe. I do, and yet
there's nothing there. What porch?
What dawn? And yet in memory, great movement of the dead.
They put their arms around my shoulders,
tell me what Aurora Borealis means:

O, luminous beginning.

I plan to just get on a plane.
See if Kay Turner Dewey and her husband Ted
remember me. Two names who'd be alive.
I plan to fly to Lincoln, rent a car, stay three days
or so. Of course go back to "S" Street, our old house.
Of course it isn't ours. Of course it might be gone.
Of course I haven't been there since the 50s.
I plan and then don't go. I'm so afraid to have my childhood
ended from the window of a rented car, my looking out

at where I lived instead of living there.

Ah, but still The Litany—

Old, compounded knowledge that we need, each year
an added book, my grandma humming through her priestesses,
the angels:

This one today, creeping to the swimming pool for exercise.
Her back diseased, so bent she is the height of children,
speaks to them, the little, agile swimmers as if
she isn't frightening. "Hello, hello!" and ever smiling.
Her fuchsia-flowered bathing suit.
Her shapeless thighs, their loosely-swaying flesh which,
when she touches it to soothe it, presses in, a dough

without its yeast. She is not scented bread, does not attract
the workmen who are fixing lights above the pool.
They turn their heads and shoulders
all the way away from her. And yet

she will not disappear. She will not turn away, herself,
just because she isn't what we want. She is, in fact, America,

the largest Mother Buffalo.

The largest Mother who will take our prayers.
She is not yours, or mine, but ours.

62% of the children in the city of Los Angeles are on welfare.

3. *The Indians*

Raise me.

I beg my mother for a costume with fringe,
and then for that feathered headband, and also
those beads to wrap and wrap around my neck.

I close my bedroom door. I enter the plains.
I practice walking noiselessly:

If I had moccasins,
if I had an Indian
to show me how.

Would an Indian even tell me?
If I'm not an Indian,
could I even walk

that way? Without a sound.
No deer or buffalo would bolt
as I approached.

To be an Indian, follow
hoofprint trails

so quietly
no twig would break.

Then it appears, the buffalo:
huge-headed, white horns curving to its head.

I love
to look at animals,
to not be noticed.
(Smart girls, good reader, growing up!
Play piano now for Aunt Jeannette!
Do I have legs to be a ballerina?
Big girl, ahead of her age.)

Here, I'm the invisible child who lies in tall grass,
looks and looks, wants to learn through silence.
I am the grasses. I'm the swollen chant,
the murdered buffalo. The horns become
a headdress, teeth a necklace.
Buffalo death, its sacrifice, ritual
apology and making use of every bone.

On the plains in my bedroom,
a child can know death.
My shaggy little tail.
My angry little eyes.
My hideous, glorious bulk.

What chant? What language? I'll never be an Indian.

How long is childhood?
The length of death.

4. *To want to be America*

Walt Whitman: "... exalt the present
and the real." At least, he knows what's real,
while we, here in the 1990s, sit stunned
in pornographic staring—celebrity replaces ancestors.
We need Whitman's

bright chest in America's face; his flap,
flap of wings (Adhesive Angel), those wings stretched
out so we become bodies of none other than ourselves—
good chins and educated hands: my grandma's wish
to paint her family china, paint a rim of gold along
the edge of every plate and cup. Brisk, artist's wind.
Her jumbled hair; her beads slide on her nobly wrinkled throat.

Someone tells me to be clear.
He relishes the provable.
I do not disagree, but there is more:
living in the bellies of the facts are wonders,
are the bodies of our bodies, are worships that America
cries out to: Make holy what performs in spirit, just as
Whitman praises what he sees and hears that is not there,
but witnessed, anyway—

This poem's goal: to be the buffalo,
to be America. The women at the swimming pool:
The day before Thanksgiving one of these
old angels tells me this:

"My favorite part of Thanksgiving is when it's over,
when they all go home. Then I rip off a piece of turkey
for myself, sit down and eat it alone."
Perform the visions: restore a Whitman presence in Our Mother,
who is willing to give holidays their due, and then
to eat alone, to sit and swing her leg, uncovered leg;
old women with bare legs.

Mothers, not face lifts.
Mothers, not liposuction,

poems that are the bodies of our bodies, are worships
that America gets hungry for. Gets starved. O, Walt,
your singing. Take us in your throat.

5. *Perform the Visions*

(This on Dia de los Muertos) —"O the beautiful rain!"
Her gray hair, curled. Her pink print dress—the many,
many tiny flowers on that dress. Pink sweater but
no umbrella. Could be my own Nebraska grandma here
on Finley north of Franklin Avenue where I'm out walking
early in our rainy season. Her hands spread out in praise.

My street's called Mariposa, butterfly,
the angel of the psyche. Place I live and
love a husband who's a poet, who's an actor
in the dreams we call The Movies.

Virginal Midwest: Me, depressed and angry teenage girl
in calf-length skirts. In garter belts. In pincurls and
in menstrual blood. Seventy-five cents an hour,
my first job's pay. I sold blouses, hosiery, sweaters,
plastic earrings shaped into the 50s rigorous belief
in femininity—daisies and their stems, straight up the ear on
many little wires, prolific cuteness. But I knew

how my mother died in pain, cancer which the 50s couldn't
cure. Ah, those cashmere sweaters that I sold (and wanted) woven
from the hair of special goats—years later

I would dream a goat who was The Mother of Us All—
the Goddess not as metaphor, but as animal—

Behind each shop girl purchase stood a flower or animal,
a meaning; stood the Indians' emphasis on sacrifice.
My mother, sacrificed—and so is everyone
who's standing in the rain, her pink dress getting soaked,
who praises, anyway.

No more the possibility to grow up to be Lakota Chief,
and yet I did attack the single-minded fate
the 50s had arranged for me:
I wouldn't study shorthand. Never
chose a pattern for my married silverware.

Americans can persevere. A shapeless girl can have
a future where she'll live in full view of the Griffith Park
Observatory where the heavens are decoded, where
everything celestial gets its due. The fated planets who
eventually sent her into poems have brought her to a house
with husband, cats and food—good, black beans are cooking at
this very moment. Our neighbors cook, as well, rich salty meat,
an oniony tomato broth. Armenian. Across the street,

a Filipino boy who brought us our lost cat.
Peruvians are in the corner house, people who enjoyed
my husband's son when he was growing up, had a son just
Dylan's age, provided snacks and videos. The daughter
now has multiple sclerosis; as her mother says, "God's will."

Dia de los Muertos—not my language, but my city's
language, anyway, so mine. My city's sugar skeletons to eat.
Day of the Dead, the dead who dance around, get close
to us, want altars made exactly for their preferences:
their photographs; the marigolds as orange as suns;
a hundred, flaming candles; tall can of beer for Uncle Somebody;
a box of chocolates that the kid who died too young would like.
Sweet death. I read my list of ghosts out loud each year
and burn my single candle, light the rose-smell incense.
Get weepy-eyed. It does us good to honor tears;
America forgets—ignores—its tears so easily. Think

about our murders. Cancers of our softest organs.
An epidemic, AIDS, that halts our thousand
thousand friends. O, Jim. O, Lee. O, John.
The ghost-scroll lengthens. We'll be there,
too, as soon as possible. Bad seafood, or pollution,
or lungs smoked black by cigarettes. The heart, the
precious brain, the colon. We're paying for our murders.

Perform the visions:

This poem's goal—to be the buffalo,
which is to be communal. And a history.
And a looking forward, the way my recent dreams
suggest both death and also something jumping
out of death to sprout: Listener, what
would you sacrifice to rescue honesty?

What word is my white face?

ARRIVAL

1. *Los Angeles, 1960 and Onward*

Swollen moisture, that Midwestern heat,
an enervation, killing
riskiness; my tiny college islanded from big Detroit.
My mother: dead. My father married to another woman,
just like the fairy tales. The crumbs,
and anger over bathing suits, new curtains for my bedroom.
Elvis Presley singing in that closed-door room. Why
shut the door? Because I'm young and this is Michigan;
nothing waits but drowning in the suffocated green, vast trees,
deciduous, their seasons: turns to years-long winters, frozen
body in too many clothes, another way to drown. How to go,

get out,

away, like Kerouac: I don't even think
that I can't do it, only wish for how, just how, in
whose cramped sports car from the little college town (at least
away from family here) to fast Detroit, me lying in the not-
backseat, against the window, folded into any space
that takes me fast, away.

America, your romance: We can escape.

The person I admire is Marla,
college roommate, hair an auburn beam
against the winter. Wears black tights, a long
loose shirt. She has ambitions for the theater,
has the nerve to be important to herself.
Her bright hair melts the cold.

I'm not her vivid shine. But she encourages
whatever leaps across the stage in me, and so

Detroit, her home, is practice. She leaves our school,
gets into acting—"Peer Gynt" every weekend. I pull
lacquered chopsticks through my tucked-up hair, wear black,
and go to watch her every chance I get.

I like a folk singer named Tommy. His hangout is The Cup of
Socrates, a coffee house. I like the coffee house—where I can
listen, smoke, and sip espresso even though it's bitter in my
naive mouth. I like the city's bite; I like its stores. Marla
makes me buy a small, wood Chinese god of happiness—more money
than I'd spend, plus shoes, plus skirts

much shorter than my pleated college plaids.
American: To change the length, the look,
the whole idea. Marla's been to California. She won't go back,
although she says she will, to theater and David, older man
she loves who sends her roses from his San Diego sculptor's
studio on New Year's Eve. It's me,

ungifted, undramatic, who will take the country's edge as mine.

Los Angeles, Los Angeles:
cactus, succulents and wild tobacco. Jimson weed.
Newly arrived, I learn these plants that promise
danger, or know how to hold their nourishment
a good, long time. I am a virgin, loving uncompanioned walks.
Summer, to be twenty-two years old; there's nothing better

than the dry, unbruising air, inhaling night and cool and jasmine,
thinking how to say a couple things in Spanish. I came
by miracle. I came the minute, just a month ago, I finished
college. I came by car, by singing all the way the folk songs
Tommy sang. I never miss him. How does the naive self
know what to get away from, never mourn? Thank God, it did,

it does—

I'm here: My rented house is just a room and then
another room and then a bathroom in a city built on air,
Los Angeles—the angels as its temperament. Completely
unfamiliar, just like heaven, what's above us and beyond
but not a fantasy because the strangest stuff is real—
is Esther Williams in a coffee house called Positano's

way above the coastline off of P.C.H., up a narrow stretch
of road, a winding climb to music, where she sits,
tall clarity, Fernando Lamas at her side. He laughs.
Los Angeles, incomprehensible, and yet I know it in a breath:
Its immorality is this: Everything stands visible. Such

jam-thick salad dressings, different colors:
they're chartreuse; or ivory-white with blue cheese thickly
mixed around. Within a year, I'll like the taste of scotch.
But in July and August, 1960, I can only love big salads and
folk guitars at Positano's up that coast—oh, endless
coast—the coffee house where people play my kind of music.

No, not mine. I haven't earned one note of it:
scratchy moon, bad love, goodbye forever, scented jealousies.
(All that will come.) I have long hair, and guilelessness,
and I get in and out of cars at scenic points along the coast,
allowing two or three new friends to tell me what a sandpiper
is called, and ordinary gulls, and when the grunion run.
It's swish, fresh swish of waves, the lyrics
I can listen to, can memorize.

Some nights, somebody will drive us to the hills above
the Sunset Strip, through streets that crowd themselves up
to the highest spot and when there isn't room to turn
another time without a plunge, here come the vibrant, sparkled,
fablioso city lights below, spread into patterns
infinite, inhuman, wonderful:
the brazen, holy, hedonistic
city thoroughly embedded in itself.
Simple electricity enhanced by zillions.

This is where I've come.
The marveled lights, an ocean of their own,
give me fast ideas about mortality:
live and live and hurry up. Divinity will come and go,
can easily go dark, the switch flipped off. And yet recurs.

The immigrant amazement:
pride in upheaval, re-moving
ourselves from the place we
were born to be born in the place
where the salads are gospel. Signaling
more California, the fields and the groves—
Midwestern wheat traded for oranges,
for artichokes stuffed with those mushrooms which grow
right near Oxnard: mystery thrives in earth's shadow,
dense mushrooms, dream-swollen, near mountains.
In ten years, I'll walk into mountains like everyone else who
seeks spiritual ending for grief.

But now, it's the great Whitman meal.
Garlic by truckloads. More lettuce
than you've ever seen. I have to have all the ingredients
angels can mix in my brain.

1960: America decides it will be gracious Kennedys.
I look like Anglo passiveness, but I'm about to buy
a lot of purple clothes. I learn to call more plants
by name: bougainvillea, shrimp plant, donkey tail.
I have a job. I take the bus. And I don't need
another thing except these names,
vocabulary conjuring the mystic city, constantly in bloom.

How can this be a home? Because I'm not the one who
looks like me. My inheritance of snow has made its opposite,
the girl whose element is heat. How easily
I turn my back on winter, my palest self.
(America's large health depends on revolution.)

Inevitable, though,
the fall, in such a fabled city.
Through lightest light, too light
to hold me now, I drown again.

My ignorant virginity assumes
my eyes can see, even when I'm so far under water.
This city's element is strangers, and I am one myself, and
then I marry one, and blindness is the story,
all the way around.

I would have gone on,
thrilling myself, the virgin, unshattered. *But he wants me*

to love him. His cold fragility, his narrow face,
Greek wars, advanced degrees, and literally
eyes that could go blind in not too many years.
He wants me to look at those eyes, *say*
that I love him. The virgin's foolishness includes
the ocean's generosity, boundless tears of pity. But
pity isn't heat. Pity hates its victim. How can I,
though, be hateful when *he loves me?* He's going blind.
He's working on his coldness, sees a therapist.
He's bird-thin, decent, doesn't lie about himself.
I cannot pull myself out of the blur, the water,
marriage to false sight.

I give up Positano's, my belief that music
has its pulse in me. The Michigan I left
has never left. Coldness is an education there;
everyone must suffer. To please oneself is decorative
selfishness, immodest, sinful as the blackest lingerie.
Music is a life of driving where you want to go, instead
of living out the rules. The Puritan in me chills even
bougainvillea, even my enthusiastic start on adulthood. The fall,

the plunge directly from The Garden

(lush Los Angeles) into scratched-out moon
unvirgined not as much by sex
as by unlove, the greatest sinful ignorance.
It isn't purity that's good—purity defiles
the living mess we need to thrive, the open
window, brash emotion following its voice, its own,
until immodesty is gorgeous, is the blatant
bird of paradise, official city flower, orange and
purple crested fantasy but actual, prolific, and long-
lasting. Longer than this marriage could survive.
Two summers without breath and then
confession and then guilt. I'd thought I'd known
Los Angeles, its visibility:
Sparkled, holy, marveled lights.
The other L.A., though, is not forgiveness but the way
Los Angeles refines its strangers
in raw desert air, scrapes meat right off the bone.
I'm smaller, less efficient, more
familiar with the odor of decay.

2. *Where Is Some Music?*

From marriage into Eastside hills—my Echo Park—
and on one hill, the house, its windows:

West—a bamboo field with city lights beyond.
South—tall weeds, the downtown buildings in the distance.
Another side—a Russian church I look at while I eat.

Poinsettias grow their long-tongued, floating leaves
outside the door. And there's Elysian Park, half a block
above my hill; I take a book, take sun, take walking by myself
through yellow weeds. L.A. as yellow—productive
as an egg, a chance, Charles Olson's poem that finds
itself not as plan but as discovery. Each line
grows fonder of the next as it progresses down the page.

Paper made from aster leaves. And marigolds when autumn
comes: *el dia* of the dead. The everlasting marigold
down the stairway to the soul, right up the slope to parks
named after heaven. Elysian. I pay my rent with cash.
I clean the little rooms on Saturdays,
and finally

I'm invited to go out for music on a Sunday,
piano at The Music Center. I think I'm making history,
gathering myself as someone, but we cannot own
a history in America; the angels flap it all away.
On Sunday, I am introduced to my next self—to be
a friend of John and Gary's, the ones who have the tickets;
to be a woman closer to the arts, closer to the 60s,
meaning Vietnam, and protest marches, and the cliched cop—
that flower in his hand, stuck there by hippies chanting,
"We are one, all one..." John, architect, an Aries always
twenty steps ahead of me, asks who's my favorite poet as
we dash into the concert. I say Wallace Stevens, haven't
said that name out loud since Michigan. Suddenly—the way
applause comes up to praise the music—I love these

two gay men, these gurus in the revolution called
our merging hearts. As Ginsberg wrote, "Soul identical
each to each..." about Jack Kerouac, and here I am again
in music as a worthy thing to live for, confessing that
I do love poets and pianos and some scotch at intermission.

1965: I meet George Prado, second husband, all because
of Marla and her now-husband in Poitiers, France,
the army base where George plays in the U.S. army band,
and Jim works on the army newspaper. When George leaves there,
Marla says to look me up. He's coming to L.A. from his home
town of San Antonio, driving the old Chevrolet he's named
The Rocket, going to make his mark here as musician.

Marla.
Marla, even in post-army life with two small kids,

is never far from my own map. And now she draws a crossroad
on my solitary page, Chicano man who moves into my Echo Park,
my house, with two large, upright basses and one box of clothes.

George drives a European/Texas road to get to me; soon,
we'll drive with John and Gary
up and back and up and back to San Francisco for the marches
there for peace, against the war in Vietnam. 1966 and 7 and 8:
When I look back along the street at rows of marchers,
we are thousands. And I'm "the soul identical," the fervent
cause, the truth, at least
for this quick clock, the 60s.

George plays me Miles Davis records, plays John Coltrane;
we are never unaccompanied. His bass can play us into clubs,
to friendships with musicians—somebody in L.A. he knew in
France; somebody he met right now; somebody early out of jail
who's vegetarian, can hardly talk, plays drums. Nolan Index
plays piano. Rondelone plays reeds. Zoe's boyfriend Ron plays
sax. Mike Hurwitz plays the trumpet, gives us our dog Wigs who
once lived in Las Vegas with Mike's musician brother and a lot

of fancy poodles. Gregarious America, all this music—melody,
improvisation, words like "chops" and "changes." Words like
"my old lady," "babe," and "groovy." I can listen to his army
stories. I can listen to his boyhood as an Eagle Scout and how
he grew peyote in his yard. His father phones long distance,
calls me pretty Spanish names. I shed my socks. We cook
menudo, enchiladas. I don't think to ask a single question. I
just listen, then applaud.

We have the dog; George brings home cats. I wake up,
a new one in the bed whose name is Wayne. Wayne Shorter.
Always, a surprise, a happy gift; a way to make a hang-out
on the roof, to tell our friends and have a party. We rent
a cheap, upright piano. I play Bach and Bartok, exercises,
and Bill Evans' "Waltz for Debby." I'll start to write in

two more years. He'll start to see another woman. George
backs off from nothing. Fabulous Los Angeles has everything
a guy could want, a young and talented and funny guy. A guy from
someplace else, like me, who wants as much as I do to not
stay the same, not to be where I was from to start with.
Not to be whoever I turned out to be. To be

instead
improvisation.

Soul identical? Soul wildly sharpened, cut away from hills,
from anything Elysian.

3. *The Solo*

George leaves as suddenly as he appeared,
as if he only came to make it certain that
I'd be alone again. I spend two years of weekends,
summers, in the mountains:

Sierras, Rockies, Tetons, mountains where another self
is barely seen inside the rock, the self
who doesn't even know what holds her to this life
except the trail she puts her feet on. This isn't
younger drowning, isn't wet. It's work. It hurts,
but I can't cry; I don't want ocean.

Solid trail, then ground beneath my back in sleep:
Gradually, my bones gain weight. Finally, a mirror
shows muscle in my neck. I recognize a privacy
that listens to itself without a melody. I am those
porcupines who come to hop around my midnight
campfire—gnomes who chew up salty meat-bits
dropped from cooking. I am released

from weddings, high school teaching, people
coming to our house and coming to our house.
The 60s,
hashish smoke,
lift into air, curl
and disappear.

No history ever vanished quite like this,
dropped so suddenly its paisley skirts,
its headbands and its love beads,
all that patchouli incense called right back to heaven.

We are not One. The cop forgets the pretty hippie chick who
thrust the daisy in his hand. The Haight is hard core drugs,
is murder. Nobody says
he's going to learn to play the sitar anymore.

John and Gary split apart. Gary, who will be my lifelong friend,
keeps moving from apartment to apartment. Invites me to have
breakfast, dinner, anywhere he is. We celebrate our birthdays,
holidays, but I'm not gay; I can't follow him in that direction.
I stand aside, excluded by the facts.

And Marla, never far away, *is* far away in Indiana
with her husband and her children. Then, he takes off
for Florida, doesn't get in touch for years. She moves to
Cincinnati, finds another husband, rarely phones me.
When she does, she's always drunk; it's three A.M.,
her time to tell me we're best friends, but I'm just sleepy,
angry, want her to

hang up.

Each revolutionary, naked, starting over.
The war in Vietnam ends badly, but it ends.
Lorraine, my downstairs, former-hippie neighbor,
decides to have a baby; make a living from good food:

sells vegetarian tamales cooked right in her kitchen,
then expands. She rents more space and hires some help.
We all become another age, the choices more American
than ever—family, business—

I learn I really can climb mountains;
I really can take care of language on a page.

I find a small, upstairs apartment: When I type,
I face a flat, white wall. I face the page, my thoughts,
and getting thought to word through body. "Each Stem
Its Own Fruit," I call one piece I write. I'll have
six years of this excruciating luxury: the self-
containment of a plant who grows another self.

Los Angeles—I got here.

We can become
the strangest, most acute and crucial versions of ourselves.
The air in 1960—dry, unbruising—turned out to be
the unrelenting winds that swallow little girls. Why
did I stay? The jasmine's fragrant spell; my citrus-bitten
sense of taste: loving what both soothes and stings,
the everything which shifts
as crazily as earthquakes, mudslides, brushfires, and those

heatwaves throbbing on into October: there is no possibility
of leaving because there's always more to eat and to be eaten by.
You Santa Anas and you Arctic winds—I've been your meal.
I'l be here till I die, till L.A.'s angels close my eyes, then
wrench and shape my breath into these same winds that
roil, offend, release, inspire. Look

straight ahead at Griffith Observatory on that hill.
Everywhere, a hill from which to see the "brazen,
holy, hedonistic city thoroughly embedded in itself."
Look. Look at the planets far above the telescope:

There's Mercury, wild god of chance and change,
the god with wings right on his feet. I've been
his jokes; I've been his testament. I was a girl, and now,

mid-1970s, I'm another someone I have never seen before.
She's stopped applauding. She lets a friend take photographs
of her: her shortest curly hair; a wine glass raised; a gypsy
smile. Nothing but her own ripe mouth will tell her what to do.

AMERICAN LOVE

1.

We are real.
"Love is form." (Charles Olson)

February 12th, 1996:
My husband smoothes my shoulders
as I sit over news—
Lincoln's birthday; his
hat is on display and thousands stand
in line for hours to see it. Smith-
sonian exhibit hits L.A., brings
Abe Lincoln's stovepipe hat, the one he wore the night he died.
We Angelenos stare at that historic night, now
visible at our Convention Center. My husband
rubs my shoulders, leaves his touch even when he goes
away, sits, now, in bed, reading news himself,
calls out, "I feel drawn to you!" a joke,
line from the daily horoscope. He makes predictions
true by giving voice to them. ("Taurus: Someone says
today, 'I feel drawn to you,'") We are our voices—

and our shoulders, and history which
still has substance in a hat.

American epiphany: Make real. Manifest your thought.
Two days more and we'll have valentines,
every lover's offering a *thing*—a card; a heart-
shaped box of treats; those roses upped in price especially
for this day of love. Profit, that's American. We make
and spend good money to buy the visible, the proof.

2.

Valentine's Day arrives:

Street vendors two blocks up the street—
a woman and a man—set out their white,
stuffed animals, as tall as I am, with red
ribbons tied in bows around their necks.
The woman hurries. It's already 9:00 A.M.
Cars are going by too fast. Please stop; please
buy your valentine a huge, white bear. Love's proof.

3.

My husband and I celebrate with
sandwiches, the crusts cut off. (Refreshing
cucumbers, dill and cream cheese on the bread.)
Our view, expansive February, Southern California
garden—lawn Matisse's green.
Naked goddess out there with her cupid, stone redeemed.

Private mansion into public beauty.
Altruistic? Or
just wanting to show off.
American success must have The Visible.
Love collects.
Love eats

the pretty food and then another platter
rushes from the kitchen: fresh pineapple and
cantaloupe and honeydew. We eat again. And then

We cannot do without our later afternoon
in bed, the sex we've always given each to each—
my body keeps its flesh alive for you,

and yours for mine; the room has light enough
to see that we are
yes
ourselves.

The body—

4.

never tired of itself.

And now days past that afternoon
a window finds him walking toward our house;
such pleasure in the hat he likes, a summer Panama
but worn in winter. The stride. Key in the lock,

unlocking.

America, a never-ending search for home,

for form.
Hat shaped to match
a head. The body, restless,
walks along the sun, a brilliant
morning after rain. Start out.
Move toward and toward. Then turn,
come back. Love demands return:

Marriage—

The tongue which circles genitalia's roundnesses:
Creation does perpetuate its forms,
in love with how it's made—
planets who live out their prescient orbits.

We make our poems and our house with distance
and return. I buy oranges now because it's winter,
their best season, and I suck the juice
while Harry reads to me how Corso would burst in
on Olson's class, demanding to be kissed.

Be home.
We breathe our country's breath, molecular,
historical, and inexhaustible.

5.

Thursday, talking about death, but later
I have coffee and some cream of carrot soup.
A coffee house—I see the table in the corner
by the window holds two lovers—man and woman—
Angelenos, tall, "attractive," as we say, and
kissing (just a little) after food and tea. Iced
tea, as if the chilly, gruesome day has not affected them.
There isn't any death when you are tangled in his arms.

No shame. Their longer kissing, kissing.
The handsome colors that they wear, the two of them:
earth-browns and mossy grays. Her long, red smile;
his blondish, urgent hair. Love is justice for the endless
sorrow under every life. Oh,

I try hard to read good Robert Duncan's poems (also love)
but keep on looking over at the corner.
The kiss,
the shameless L.A. afternoon,
with no one disapproving in this city where we all
are, all have gasped at being miles and miles
away from where we started and it's getting dark.

Our Andrea: her body falters, dies. She isn't old.
"To leave," she says, not ready to say, "die,"
and yet the body, finally, decides,
not our objections to its choices. I want
her as she was those thirty years ago when we
attached ourselves to friendship. This cafe's name:

"Revival." Can that be true?
The couple over there, this moment brewed
from their own bodies, irresistible.
The wind-pulled sunlight comes indoors where air
has shape, presents me with two of the most blatant feelings
I have ever felt:
Each second brings loss closer—Andrea—
and every shift of tongue between those two is ecstasy.

Two weeks later, same cafe, this time
a different soup and lousy service,
but the corner booth continues to amaze:
An eighteen-year-old girl, an elfkin, waits
alone. Her profile as she watches out the window
shows itself as dance—ballet—a discipline she echoes
in those tall and limber legs she folds into herself
and that loose sweater, white, its neckline casual,
designed to be put on right after long rehearsal.

This youngest woman at the window thinks she
invents the gift of isolation; she's not used to it.
She is waiting for a boyfriend. My newest book,
compassionate advice (Tibetan) about dying.
I am waiting for enlightenment, the slab of stucco
I can see across the street becoming message, beauty,
meaning. My heart, American, believes in healing.

Today, there's only this young woman who's alone
and has a body just like everybody else.
I take to her sweet throat, its purity of bone,

the sweater gently, barely touching flesh.
Such tenderness should not be introduced to failure now.
Hurray. Here comes the guy—black leather jacket, serious.
Our city and our world insists on sex,
also on stretching our whole bodies
into dances we were never meant to do.
Standing on one's toes. Grand leaps.

6.

L.A. Times, March 18th, 1996,
two days before the vernal equinox:

There is no love.

Two kids have thrown themselves
into the ocean off the coast of Palos Verdes.
A boy and girl decide that SOMETHING
feels too terrible to be endured.
White kids, and privileged; her dad says
"She loved life and lived it to its fullest."
Really?

mid-air/ their jump/ breath's end/ their minds
now crushed on rock/ are nothing further that can grow/

those children take away the pulse-risk, wild-hearted
possibility/ they take away the country, our whole country.

7.

Teenagers kill themselves enough for suicide
to be the second leading cause of death
in adolescents. Teenagers hurt themselves
with piercings in their ears, their
noses, tongues and genitals;
with piercings in their nipples and
their eyebrows. The shapes art conjures every generation:

Charles Olson's city, Gloucester, Massachusetts,
gave him ocean, ships and people, solid forms. America
is where we are and what we see. We struggle to see
anything, given as we are to action, doing, traveling,
working; to mistrusting thought and insight.
And what our children see appears as holes
in their own bodies, and in the "body politic."

Pierced criticism aimed at us—the kid who shoves
his car into my lane, ahead of me, leans out his window,
shows me in his laughing mouth the tongue with four big metal
rings stuck through it. He's had his victory for today,
to get ahead of me, old lady in a Geo Prizm driving west
on Third Street. Is that enough? America, is that
enough for us to offer him as true rebellion?

8.

Love's forms,
the body,
and our treatment
of our own, (of yours,
America). The trees grow sun
outside my window now; it's early

afternoon, a Friday. I've been reading
recipes. My mother studied nourishment in 1945
when men came home from World War II,
and women were encouraged to be homemakers again.

Love's gratitude,
the body, how my mother fed us
every night at 6:00—a sacred trust,
that meatloaf and green beans; her spongecake
or canned peaches for dessert. Midwest's abundance.

Fresh housedress
just before my dad came home.
A dress she'd sewn herself.
Smart red lipstick: She always was a city girl who'd
studied some ballet before she was a wife
and mother. Taught me how to do the Charleston on an
afternoon a lot like this one—nothing much to do,
too early yet to think about our supper—it's spring,
and she remembers how to get the knees exactly right
and shows me, laughs. The serious routine of cleaning,
cooking, sewing interrupted by a dance in which
you hold your knees together in a funny way.

Love's dreamy passing-on of hopes. I took ballet
myself a few years later, even though I had no talent.
Anything is possible when we're well-fed. Nebraska taught me
love as form: each recipe love's coming-into-being,
transforming of ingredients from raw uselessness to
what is on the plate, what's eaten, carried in the body
as its fuel, its reason to keep dancing while the sun
fills up the tree these fifty-some years later.

America: your multiplicity,
and yet we each
inherit this—a single body
urgent in its destination.

9.

Embodiment.
The breathing
in of self.
America's democracy
embodied in each citizen.
Of course there's love. Or?

Four years before the year 2000.
Am I decent witness to millennium?
I just hear mostly how the builders of our L.A. subway
cheat—inferior materials causing tunnels to collapse.

I love my city and my country, map of my own personal
obsessions. Do I love enough, forgive the waste,
the lies? Graffiti's desperate signature: I paint
across it time and time again; step across

the woman
opening post office doors for every customer;
she wants money, manipulates us with her gesture,
desperate kindness. Give her a buck for her trouble—
she's homeless; she needs our help.
I don't like her. I don't want to help.

To love the weakest image in the neighborhood:
Does that make subways safe for all of us?

The FBI has caught the Unibomber,
or at least we think so—will that make
the P. O. woman happy? Is she safer now?

How are we safe, our bodies and our sanities?

We are the city's/ nation's tunnels, labyrinths,
streets that will collapse or else be strengthened.
We're never free from where we live.

A flyer at the Onyx coffee house announces,
"Killer Cosmic Riots in Outer Space," some kind of
dance or party, something I don't understand.
Young woman sipping cafe latte says,

"Again? Didn't
they just do that one? I went to the 70s one
but only about three people came in costume."
Disappointment. Nothing new today. The same old
cosmic riots. She does assert her right to jaded
fingernails, vampiric purply-red. She does assume
variety is democratic, that repetition of the same
pat entertainments can be as bad as changeless, rigid Biblical
interpretations, or too many carbon-copy autocrats in Congress.

No love: Some tunnelers complain. Safety rules aren't
being followed. Nobody wears protective gear; carbon
monoxide fills a tunnel at double legal limits.
The foreman says he only wants to get this project done.

Does that hard-hatted, crusty foreman love enough?

Do I? No soul is saved unless we all are saved,
then saved again. I do not have to like the P. O. woman,
but I have to give her credit for her citizen's equality.
To not get meaner—that's the task. To find democracy
embedded in the merest act of sanity. On Wednesday,
now May 8th, two men say, "God bless you." One, begging,
weaves his way through cars just off the Fairfax exit
of the freeway. I do give him a buck; he's old and limps.
I think he even calls me "ma'am."
The other one is in the Xerox place. Black, middle-aged,
and portly, with a line of chatter I find irritating.
But, my copies done, I wish him a good day, and he, then,
says, "God bless you."

I'll believe that we're embodied in our words, that we believe

in language, which is breath, and which assures us we're
alive, American, and suffering, in need of anybody's
blessing. Embodied. Olson:

"one loves only form,
and the form only comes
into existence when
the thing is born . . .

born of yourself . . ."

America: Each mouth be born.

—*for Harry E. Northup*

AMERICAN FOOD
(LOS ANGELES, CA, 1996-97)

Santa Monica Farmers Market, Wednesday, October 23, 1996

The ocean a block away, ancestor who shaped us
as we are, we eaters shoving toward the carrots,
green beans, broccoli piled high along the aisles—
the body's concentration on itself,

here are our gods: goats whose milk (thick pungent mood,
like prayer) produced this cheese; the avocados
(true America, given meaning as both "testicle"
and "alligator");

pumpkins—flagrant, heavy callings-out to worship
in this season when thin spirits dress as us, when death
appears and cries for sweets. We know the dead are hungry.

I'm reaching for red peppers, hearts.
I need their love and what they can be filled with:

rice
and goat cheese
onion and tomatoes
pine nuts.

At home: Marriage includes food forever food
day after day. If we are empty stomachs, we are also
alchemists: Raw peppers take the magic well, *prima
materia* into dinner that we bow to.

I brought home
eggplant, too. And cantaloupe. And three huge cups
I'll give as Christmas gifts (the largest size, necessary
for enough strong coffee, soup, herb tea, spring berries,
custard, or a bunch of fragrant, just-picked sweet peas).

Vampire in Vons Supermarket, Sunday, October 27th

Santa Ana winds: warm and violent wishes we've forgotten but to-
day they give us headaches do their witchery inside our dreams of
burning hills but no that's real—along the coast the thousand thou-
sand acres set on fire by wind or arson-craziness. We all imagine set-
ting something valuable aflame to just get rid of righteousness. Dry
crackled leaves for hands, and teeth want flesh—our kindnesses our
generous vocabularies drop away let's burn let's make the wind pay
off.

He's wearing a long coat too woolen for the temperature. He's in the
aisle of reds: tomatoes diced or whole or spiced or crushed—his
basket's red; he's got tomato sauce six cans then seven then a dozen
cans of sauce as fast as he can go he's throwing all these cans of sauce
into the basket. I understand obsession and I watch him, drawn to
those who can't resist whatever their temptation is—he sees me watch-
ing him he says sardonically sarcastically (a handsome war torn face)
"excuse me please excuse me just excuse me." I think he'll drink

all this tomato sauce a substitute for blood the way an alcoholic in
recovery gulps a virgin mary and regrets he can't get drunk. He can't
smash up his car. He can't burn down the houses of his enemies.

Hallowe'en: East Hollywood

107 homemade oatmeal/chocolate chip cookies.
3 large bags of "Fun Size" Snickers bars.

Eat for the dead:

my mother and my father whose good food
remains my standard of appreciation;
ancestors and uncles and the aunts and one child-cousin gone;
three friends who died of AIDS; Liz Brown, so long ago,
that tumor in her brain; and just this year
I've added four more souls: Bob Flanagan, a poet

I'd known for over twenty years;
Andrea's mother, Euna; our neighbor Helen,
right across the street, who moved into
her California bungalow in 1938; and then the woman

killed by the police this summer here
on Mariposa Avenue when they shot her trying to escape,
trying to drive their own cop car away, run over
one of them. Young woman shouting, then just dead.
Shouting she was not a hooker. Not a prostitute.

Eat anything that's sweet. Eat night.
Eat tragedy. Eat up any promises
to lose ten pounds, to cut out fats and sugar.
Eat to feed the hollow pumpkins, hollow platitudes.
We die. We're ghosts. We need our nourishment.

Mary's Food, End of October

Beef on the bone or chicken legs long-cooked with onions, broth, a lot
of salt, plenty of food for her and her husband and their two children
and whoever comes by to say hello, and plenty for us which we tell
her we don't need and doesn't she want to keep it for herself but she
brings it anyway in large plastic containers. We try to reciprocate but
we never make up for the food she brings. We aren't even

Armenian; she and her family and other families on the block hang
out together, speak Armenian, buy from the Armenian vegetable truck
that comes along every morning, and from the bread guy who comes,
too, every day, shouting in Armenian that he's here. We aren't in-
vited to parties or to morning gossip or to anything Armenian and yet
she gives us her food. Once when I told her not to, that it was really
too much for the two of us, Harry and me, to eat, she said in her
enormous, throaty voice, "I do it because I love you!" Why would she
say such a thing?

Who does she imagine we are that we're so lovable? We yearn for peace and quiet while she and our other Armenian neighbors make all kinds of noise, play their Middle-Easterny-minor-key-romantic music at top volume, yell at their kids, let their kids yell and bounce their balls against the side of our house so we hear the repetitive, torturous thump thump thump until we're forced to go out and tell them to stop. Why, with so much going on that's more interesting than we must seem, does she love us and feed us? Does she believe we're deprived, can't see the beauty in communal living, loud and energetic conversation, letting your children know you adore them because you're constantly instructing them, paying attention to them, saving them by screaming at them? Does she notice that we don't eat big hunks of meat on bones, don't weigh as much as she does, are frail and weak and puny, wanting solitude when actually it's human heat will save our pale-ish Anglo Saxon souls? Oh, Mary, please forgive us our

ungratefulness, our picky nibbling, the skimming off the fat before we eat.

The Possums

come at night,
eat food we set out
for Jan's cats.

Making Pesto, November 14th

Summer months brought theft,
spilled death right here at home,
but now: the garlic and the pine nuts
and the parmesan, combining olive oil into the
basil—greenest rescue in my garden—
to do a meal with fingers, spoons,
a laughing jag, old joke my husband says
right out of sleep this morning.

These leaves:
inherited appreciation of themselves. Each seed,
investiture. We do go on in spite of crime.
The pots of basil live where they can see it all,
and yet they don't forget what they were meant to be:
real nourishment, the way I see my wedding
ring—it's continually gold. The plants begin
to fade in autumn, but I'll have seed to use again
next spring. Why do I say these things
so often to myself? Why is hope this possible in me?

I am American by birth which gives me rights:
to live in this enormous city with its urban sins
and yet to cook with what my own breed has inherited:
Be educated and be brave. Try any recipe which stands
its ground. That freezes well. This pesto does.

Free Turkey—Ralphs Supermarket, November 16th

Is this American, or what?
Spend a hundred bucks on groceries, get
a turkey free. It's perfect. It's the deal
we've all been waiting for—a free symbolic bird
to brighten up Thanksgiving. You can't go wrong.
And so I go to Ralphs and buy a lot of food
the way I always do, except I never get this kind of present.

I'm excited: Even though we won't be cooking
on Thanksgiving, I can put the turkey in the freezer,
save it for a day we're really hungry. Not only
do I get the turkey, but I get to keep it for awhile,
savor my terrific shopping acumen, Ralphs' generosity,
American promotion, loyalty to Mother Country and her
holidays. Twelve pounds of meat and bone: my just reward.

Cooking Ralphs Free Turkey, December 11th

Lunch with someone loved.
Coffee: real espresso—
she and I are L. A. kids; we like it
tough and foreign in a cup that stains.
She's very ill; she's doing everything she can, is
taking charge. But I have dreamed

my plants are stolen, cat's found dead,
old car and driver's license gone, people
in my life for years just turn away.

Last night's new storm won't let us get home easily.
These flooded streets. The sky

a blot, with nothing I can quite
call "day" involved. I give my friend a book;
she gives us—Harry and me—a finely painted box,
its ocean life, its artichokes another dream:
She'd live next door so I can take her some
of anything I'm cooking, every dinnertime.

When I get home, I put the turkey in the oven,
a plump, young hen—bird sacrifice, that
gruesome truth about the lives we take to stay
alive. Our own: let go, the wisdom says. Give up
control. I've heard it, haven't you? A million times—

sacrifice what's precious. My generation, now,
is winter. Year's end will strip off every feather,
leave me just the way it wants me—
a woman who's unarmed. The one who drinks
that stain the coffee leaves behind.

The Possums

eat every bite;
shove the cat's bowls
all the way to the street.

Three Lunches Right in a Row: December 18th, 19th and 20th

In such a suffering world.
How does it happen, joy?

Tomorrow, winter solstice.
Bold promise, and

it's true—new sun, glossy, makes the wooden table
pretty here at Mamma Mia, where I can have
my favorite sandwich, vegetarian.
They don't put in the usual red
cabbage chunk but do include some carrot rounds,
sliced mushrooms. Yesterday,

I ate Say Cheese's tuna melt,
so rich with tuna salad and hot cheese
that I could hardly lift it with my hands.
And Wednesday I was at Revival, spooning

their resilient onion soup
into my mouth. How easily

I chew.
How wonderfully
my teeth and tongue and throat
cooperate. (The miracle of swallowing.)

Oh, sunlight, you do polish up the wood;
you press into the whole wheat bread
and so I eat the light itself.

My task for my old age is this—

take a table by the window. Ask for extra napkins.

The Possums

slurp up all the water, too.

Christmas Day—Geoffrey's Restaurant, Malibu

Perfect:
blue
ocean its Mediterranean best.
A woman eats
by herself, facing perfection. Her simple
black pants suit's set off by her red velvet shoes.
She starts reading a book I remember: *The Autobiography of a
Yogi.*
She sits straight in her chair and eats slowly—
beef Wellington done in a puffy, baked crust.
This bite, then

pause, then
the next one while reading a spiritual book and wearing
red shoes with embroidery across the smooth toes, making
a Christmas her own. Later, dessert is an airy souffle
with one berry on top. She savors this, too, in small spoonfuls.
It takes time
to taste that it's lemon; it's tart and
it's sweet. Christmas: Spirit born into flesh.
Our bright, guiding stars are our stomachs.

Early January Winds, 1997

I lift out handfuls of dry stuff that's flown from the Italian cypress
tree into the pots of herbs in front of the house. I throw away the
debris, then sprinkle in black, grainy fertilizer, poke it into the soil of
every pot: sorrel, sage, oregano, rosemary, arugula, Italian parsley,
ornamental chilis. The mint looks as if it's dying, leaves sparse along
the skinny branches, but in spring, it will perk up. The summer basil's
gone—I pull out a few bitter remnants. The roots are loose, easy to
dislodge. Life's willingness: Be lived, be used.

Sage in the meatloaf.
Parsley on the steamed potatoes.

Elaine has come to visit, my friend for thirty-seven years, biologist.
After dinner, she tells us, "Possums have done really well adjusting to
urban environments because—well—because they'll basically eat
anything."

Harry wants to know exactly where the winds begin.
But, he says,
it's not precisely facts he's after. I understand.
The accuracy we treasure lives in reality but has to
get its nourishment from insight. Is the possums,

and is also mystery: Where do they come from and where
do they go when they're not around? What do we feed when
we feed them? Our snuffling, short-sighted souls,
nocturnal and ancient? Adaptable. Hardy—

the herbal self, embedded in its seasons. The friend who
visits twice or so a year with information, sure affection,
and dried beans with spices packed by homeless women
to make money. Put the beans and spice into a pot of water,
cook, and we'll have soup. Add whatever we can grow;
whatever we are thinking about getting a new start.

I don't make new year's resolutions.
This year, I didn't even pray about protecting us,
our home, our animals. Some language has been lost to me,
the way Ma Nature can take over, shut me up while she plans
rain more rain more rain. The wind has changed to water.
That must mean we're getting clean enough to wait, be lived,
be used, assume the new year wants us.

—for Elaine Brooks

Jello Instant Butterscotch Pudding, February 3rd

Creamy
as those years right after World War II,
how proud we were, our victory, our modern
progress: white bread I was sent to buy. The loaf,
squeezed in its waxed paper, gave off
a sweetish, yeasty smell. My farm aunt baked her bread
but my mother—city woman—thought store-bought bread
had class, was up-to-date. The war was over. We had plenty
of canned soup, and jello, and the latest innovation:

oleo margarine. We kneaded a white lump of it, then
squished and added in a yellow pellet for the butter color.
There was nothing but the future,
nothing but improvements—cake mixes, homogenized milk,
electric mixers, home freezers bigger than refrigerators.

And here is still a modern miracle: Toss the pudding powder,
white, into two cups of cold, cold milk and stir.
Suddenly, it's vivid orange. It's thick. It's luscious,
poured into these little dishes, eaten
as we settle on the bed; we're watching movies on TV. The wonders

of the 1940s,
the oath I took to be a technicolor miracle myself—
Betty Grable's life, the much-loved movie star, seemed
something any girl could have.

Then,
though, it was 1952: My father

moved us north. 1954: My mother died.
I got used to dieting, to no dessert.
I wasn't overeating for myself, but for the times
I spent in kitchens with my mother and my aunt,
women who had shaped my body and my knowledge
that to feed your loved ones was your most

important job.
The pudding: Harry wanted it.
We both came from the heartland to L.A., city that gives
all us immigrants a chance to be invented, glamorous as fate
allows, our mouths alive, each spoonful new. Nothing
into milk, then stir. You watch yourself, an innocent,
change texture, shift and shift again—now, into
thickened work you've done. That old, absurdly
hopeful promise to myself as Betty Grable was sheer fantasy,
but this—oh, this is present years in which I always
eat dessert. The sugar in my life helps

take the edge off missing, still, my mother and
Nebraska, of knowing how the future broke itself.
America today: Margarine is just as bad for you as butter.
The noise increases in our neighborhood. So much graffiti
asks to be erased. The chained-up dogs: I'm wide awake at 4 A.M.
to hear them keeping watch. Pudding won't take away the barking,
but its smooth creaminess reminds me I've seen ragged times,
and worse, and so has Harry. So has everyone I know.
We're eating, still. And we can say it's good
when it is really good. I even buy some more.

Mary's Food Again, and Her Daughters, End of March

She never gives up. This week it's special because her husband's home.
Often, he isn't We haven't figured out where he goes, sometimes for
months, except we do know he went back to Armenia a couple of
years ago when his mother died there. And the other day, while I was
out in front sweeping the sidewalk, one of their two little girls said,
"My daddy went to New York and took food." Are there Armenians
in New York who yearn for Mary's soups? Who insist that her hus-
band carry them personally all the way from L.A.? But he's home
now, and this week's big, hot bowl delivered to our door by Mary is
filled with tomato-y, spicy broth; shredded cabbage cooked to ulti-
mate tenderness; a single chunk of meat; onion; green pepper. "It's
her best," I tell Harry.

The little girls are four and seven years old. They like to hang around
while I sweep outside or tend the garden. They usually catch me on
Sunday mornings while they wait for a van from their Armenian
church to pick them up for Sunday school. Spring's here, has been for
three days. This Sunday, I'm doing my annual rock ritual, picking
out all the decorative stones—black, brown, blue—I've scattered along
the periphery of the garden between the cactus and succulents.
They've gotten embedded in the soil, are really dirty, hardly show.

I dig the rocks out, put them in a bowl, bring them in the house to wash them off, then scatter them again. It takes some time, and they don't even look great, the way I wish everything in the garden would and never does, but they're O.K. It's too early to plant seeds. I've been cleaning up this week, even got rid of the ugly rabbit's foot fern that's been an eyesore for years. The girls are out ahead of me today. They wave and say, "Hi," when they see me, excited that I'm here, even though they see me every day of their lives. The seven-year-old talks non-stop: "I'm going to the dentist in North Hollywood. He gives you candy, but only if you're a kid. People at church will get up on the stage and sing. I wrote a letter to Santa. We're coloring eggs today." Then, she sings a chorus of "Joshua Fit the Battle of Jericho," which her sister joins, although the little one speaks hardly any English yet. I sing, too. The girls are amazed that I know the song; like all children, they believe they've discovered everything in the world by themselves. Then they sing,

"Jesus is king of the jungle/ Jesus is king of the sea/ Jesus is king of the universe/ Jesus is king of me." I ask about Armenian Easter, wondering if it might be on a different day from our American one, the way their Christmas is. I don't get any information about the date, but the older girl tells me, "You can celebrate Armenian Easter, too!" I'm impressed. Not only can I have my Easter, but hers.

This morning, the littlest girl sticks close to me, tries to help pick up the rocks but mostly just giggles. The older one stands aside, not wanting to get dirt on her shoes, and fills me in on what she thinks I need to know. I can't always keep track of her fast-moving monologue, but I do hear her say somebody came to visit and tried to pick a flower—one of my now-gone yellow tulips, I imagine—and she told him not to, that "the plant manager" would get mad.

"Plant manager"? She's made up a title for me. The word "manage" is related to "mano," a word for "hand." I'm out here, putting my hands into things, managing the tiny bit of space I can make useful with plants and care, and two children think I'm hot stuff, worth talking to, singing with. Finally, as their van's arriving, the older one asks, "Do you want me to bring you something green about Jesus? It smells nice." I say, "Sure," not understanding, then getting it. It's Palm Sunday. At church, she'll get a branch of palm to bring home. She knows I'll go for anything green. When it gets warm enough to plant seeds, I'll put in herbs, and plenty of extra basil, which I use a lot. Mary likes to cook with it, too.

Easter

A dream I've just had: Tulip bulbs
are actually asparagus tips. We eat
this beauty, all of it.

Now, Mary's youngest daughter joins me
while I plant French tarragon—twigs,
bare sticks, dull brown, on top of skinny roots.
Will these mute nothings really grow
into an herb to flavor summer's fish?

The child watches carefully the tucking into dirt
of every little root. She stands as close as she can get,
and when the roots are finally covered up with soil,
sings out: "Alleluia!" So, the season wishes us new breath,
new earth. "Alleluia": praise from Latin, Greek and Hebrew;
from Susie, straight to Easter's tender ear.

ESPERANZA:
POEMS FOR ORPHEUS
(1998)

RILKE AS DOOR

his chest thrilled, stretched against
god's breath.   poetry

needs excess: Orpheus finds a man,
a woman, fully opened in the spiral
cypress tree, by wood as flesh

by paper where the tongue licks
nothing
into Word and no thought can stop
the pulled and pulling roots from

shattershatter:

the wrench of salt, and yet from grief
the music: Orpheus
kept singing when his body disappeared—
like all the ones whose stories we forget
to tell, he comes as great, incessant breakage.

WHAT IS EXACTLY GOING THROUGH

tree-hooves, the possibility,
and falling green, as in uprooting:

something changes everything.
Orpheus made the trees get up
and dance.   I do remember stumbling
right behind the god, his music climbing:
here are the earthworms, then the wheat,
and then the balconies.   and next a woman's
hair as cliffs.   who does make everything

transform itself?   dust.   be careful of your nakedness.

THE TALL, UPHEAVING ONE

the cypress that I pray to:
it can fly. nothing is a single
species. we're made of bark, then
avalanche. Orpheus can make us anything,

can make us god's own door. cypress
or oak or black: to be accepted there,
across the boundary, as when I leave the house
this morning, walking—nothing painful
in my legs. I tell misunderstanding,
"this is our last year together," then,
I see, just up the street, that planets
are our bodies; their mouths slam through
my wrists. I was a child who practiced
jumping from the top of anything right
into the air. music was a swirl of vines
and leaves that left my throat.

I'm calling. and I'm waiting.
and I'm called to.

this black, the pure unknown which finds its way
exactly like the song you can't get rid of,
the one I start with now and won't give up.
the god, obsessed with worship that is memorized,
abiding, until the prayer itself moves inside
out, converts these worlds of sliding rock to fragrance.

I'm calling and I'm calling and I'm called.

FLOWERAGE

our pulse is flower-pulse, death-pulse.
we are so many everywhere at once.

an out-pouring: two eclipses in three
weeks or less. nature slams us thick
with jobs. I shove my hands into the pulp.
potential suffocation. or renewal. who
can know, when everything becomes Druidic
trees the demons have to answer to? what is

this year for us? what does it mean
to follow: to waste my time, fall into these
reveries that do nobody any good, except they
do—the demons find their chairs and listen,
just like any servant. my job arranges
little bits of shattered stuff into the dug-up earth.
will I get lost again? I am already. the thousand
broken seeds. to be them.

THE OLDEST HABITS

the one who has the strongest
noise to make. in this wet
year, my thoughts can be arranged
more easily than ever. Orpheus,
you're welcome here, on any path
you choose to take. it's not so much
that I need knowledge. I need the presence
of that bird, the strange one in the tree
this afternoon, a voice like pounding,
then a chuckle. then, more hammered song.

nothing is forbidden. you leave us
everything we do with mouths. that bird
is in the cypress tree for moral purposes.
you have enlivened
that whole beak to teach us
to believe in prophecy. you make us
spirit-smoke, and yet red sunlight, too,
fostering this paper. there is a difference

between me and wings, but you don't know it.
you come in, no matter if it's flesh or
trance. you break our sleep. the god
inside the mind, wishing. the curtain,
now, decides to be a man, hands on his hips.

COMEDY, AND THE TOMATO BEING EATEN

the feminine explosion—the cosmetic
gist, these summer clothes a white
that's absence, never solid foot
on solid curb.   the thing to learn
from Orpheus is prophecy: be

right here in your signature; be
there, where orphans call across
the graves and know the future
like a schedule of baseball games.
they will be played.   we all
are

lost, alive, the audience, the
dead, the brandished fork
above the warm, red flesh.

THE CHORUS

"oh, sure, the hummingbirds
are always here," she says.
I imitate a woodpecker, a bird
she saw up north. she's heading
that direction now, for good.
forever: is there such a time?
the cup my grandma never knew she
gave me, and out of that, my hair cut
much too short, to let my mind
sail through. it's right
to think the present day is
absolutely harmless, filled
with several incarnations of
ourselves. this Orpheus as
summer, what we think the birds
can tell us, what we understand.
even why I'll never come into
this yard again. why, now, it
turns invisible: the friend who
leaves us and the inside of my
painful neck. when she is gone,
completely gone, I'll be her
dream: she moves one single thing
among a hundred single things,
and that makes every sea align itself,
become the home's new shelf. and so
the scarf flows loosely, and so there's
reassurance that we live beyond one wing.

—For Terry Preston

VAN GOGH RECOVERS

in France?
the French that makes itself from
fields of lavender, the town where
nobody remembers violence done
to self, to self, to self.   the god

is not obsessed.   what
takes its turn now that it's free
to think about its opposite?   above the ocean,

someone's having a bad day, rejected by
religion, stepping out of that into
the sun I found another time when I was sick
at heart, at breath—and sun becomes
the noon that leads us to the sirens
and the Orphic poet.   this stone
they're made of is so old it's flesh,
her fingers curving at her chin.
the other's fingers agile, gesturing
toward wings.   his mouth a little
open, ready to imagine how we all began.

obsession's opposite is art.
intense composure, like the rose.
the private tunes of light inside
the inside of our wrists.

extend this Southern California day,
a France, and let the god be not
exactly Christian, not exactly not:
Orpheus believes that joining with a god
can save us trouble, and that's true,
if we just take it easy, don't insist on
glowing in the dark.   narcissism thrives,
but has that rose to be humiliated by.

don't lift that knife. don't laugh.
but slowly turn your head and watch
the way the swirling, dizzied mutilations
calm themselves, transmuted from our sickness
to another species. I give myself to herbs,
admiring what can grow from dirt,
and as I walk along the garden,
row to row and bloom to bloom,
I want my lunch. I want to be
just human. also more. someone
who will hear creation but has not created
anything. the viewer. and the one
who touches stone as skin, as thrill.
the health of kneeling and then getting up again.

WHY I WRITE

the dog whose teeth
catch dinner, and
it's raw, the blood
just starting to give off
its nourishment.   I write

about my mother dying:
I write that now and ever.
other faces smash against
the high, lost wall, but
turn around and love the sun
as much.   I never turn.
it's all those motorcycles
parked across the street.
not smiling, and with women,

with our mothers who would leave
the house as quickly as they died,
would be with gods who picked them
out of crowds to drive into the air.

to lose their daughters in the trees.

I'll never get her back.   Orpheus
gives meaning to the horror, gives meat.
the hell-dog has a multitude of heads,
and so do I.   keeps breaking its own skulls.

lament.   that protein.

MY MOTHER ENTERS THE UNDERWORLD

she tells it:

in death, no fear of death.
no substance, but the clean,
sure fact: the dog is now
behind us. we've come through
teeth, his gate. and here we
are, with royalty. we know that
Hades is invisible, but here
in his own home, his face shows
eyes that move—black liquid
more than mineral. his mouth
is not a law; I'm given sand
on which to rest and dream,
the element that shifts,
that roams. we are not fettered
in direction. rumors that his wife
would hate us, new arrivals,
prove untrue. she washes off
our cuts, the teeth marks, with
fresh water from a stream that
flows beside her throne. I was
a woman who could understand a
daughter. she seems to notice this.
and if we have no bodies, she still
believes we do, queen who travels
to the upperworld, herself, in spring.
she takes a little time to dry my hands
inside her hands, is less than solemn.
"make your own thoughts here," she says,
and not as if we have to keep this secret,
as I did when I lived, when thoughts were
wars. I don't regret a thing. my daughter
needs to find her single moon. the privilege
of the dead: the cruelty of distance.

AT THE SAME TIME

it is someone who runs,
not in panic but only because that's the way
these things move.   not deliberately hiding,
but nothing like color or bone.   and yet
not so indifferent to us.   I could feel that
this one intended I see it as much as I could,
which was one startled breath yet no question
about it.   not the god but from that part of life,
where inside is lightning, not blood.

later, I dreamed that I'd have to be fair to myself
as a woman and also to laws, and to others who
trust me.   or don't.   it was decided that I would
take part in a ritual justice, combining
my face and the face of a tree.   whenever

my chest gets so tight I can't think, then
I pray to the god, to this kind of poem
which reduces my personal names to the pulp
that we write on.   I have seen the whole
world that runs next to our ears.   it looks
back, as if it would stop if it could, but
its music compels it to be where it is.
it isn't a shadow.   it isn't a ghost.

SURROUNDED

who was sitting in the van beside
the curb, watching to be sure I
didn't steal the yellow rose?

three essays made of art, extolling
splash, obsession and the power of smell
to thrust us back and back.   once,
I stole in anger.   later, what
I didn't have meant "wait," the truce.
you, god, our Orpheus, tell us that
the peace from which we make your poems
rises from our lack of hands.   the rose
is light I can't take home.   it will not
mend the table or the window.   what
completes us is the everything we never
took.   we never stole.   is there.

"DO NOT TOUCH THIS TREE. THE MANAGER DOES NOT WANT YOU TO TRIM IT."

I set my neck against the bark, the rain-grown
smell of cypress.   the good hill's language

pushes farther up, then up again.   a stranger's
face: he lets me see how much his own doubt
means to him.   which makes it confidence.
and here's the city's glamour; here's the city's
merciful compassion.   I can talk out loud to
hair, to skull, to god.   the shapes

today make curves against themselves, excited
bouncings-off.   I lap the water and I climb.
I'm your tame animal—you, the god within
the prism—we can't be anything until we tell
you what the world forgets, until you sing it
back at us and then we sing it even weirder.
"weird," it's true, means, "fate"—

and "strangle."   one poet gave his tongue.
another one will be here soon, be born from
cock and cunt, that health.   thinking isn't
how the truth imagines union—that is known
by bringing this tall hill to meet the lilac
bushes I was told won't grow here.
my nose against their fists.

A MAN KNEELS IN THE GRASS

if he prays, it's for peace,
for his dog, large and white,
the convert to faith.

the thoughts of a man who is
bowing his head to the earth,
who listens to music so deep
in the ground that even the dog

understands.   a language of trouble,
made seed.   a language of conflict, made milk.

SOMEONE HAS DIED AGAIN

Orpheus has turned and sent
his wife back to the other world.
it is the place where we can't speak.

but she can.   when a death's
this close, we hear her fragile
note, an instrument without an

instrument: her welcome.   and
instructions—how to be the air.
how to greet your family, all
as clear as that which lives
without the breath, nothing in the way.
can you believe in anything
that simple?   that uninjured?

THE CASSATT STRING QUARTET

we heard the last note as we left.
it's almost winter, and we feel
as married as we ever will. "I'm
holding you as close as I can hold you."
the music is four women who've become
a season all their own—no one can
interrupt or throw them off. long
practice and its obvious results:
see the way her knees come open
to receive the cello. the way
the other's head leans to the violin,
her love. each one initiated to devote
herself to measure after measure after
measure. years and then more years, and
here we are together, hurrying away into
another world, our own, the night time drive
across the city—no one will ever know we
talked about the seafood we would like to eat—
into an understanding that we really have become
enough, can do enough, are not inadequate.
our car slides through the map, and when we
get there, I will have the pasta, which
"we make ourselves," the waitress whispers,
while some poetry goes on, an old friend's
lines, good luck and bad, no reassurances,
but after all this time, who cares? we won't
give back precision—how to make a mess squeeze
out its sense, its knowledge of the northern cities.
goodbye, goodbye. and then we're not attached
to night, and then it's one month down the line:
it's Christmas with those asked-for books.
completion. music. wonderment. I hear

the women play again inside the ear I call
keen memory.   young women with so much to do.
like us, such fever, and such satisfaction.

—*for Harry E. Northup*

ORPHEUS AT CHRISTMAS

these ornaments are gold, are pears
with faces. a shine. a boldness:
sand blown into glass and painted
with the sun. or butter. and a rose.
this is the body crossed with clouds.
with trances. but it's right here.

it has to be a god.
"real" equals another country
brought to our very laps. can it sing?

can the dead god's head keep telling us
ourselves? gold pears: I'm following
that trail of mouths. the eyes we think
are not alive: they have to be—Orpheus

gave every rock a throat. gave
Persephone, queen of trouble,
queen of pain, into her own great beauty,
where she lies with Hades, where they
make the soul. where Jesus wakes
to animals; where animals become
the god and talk all night. telling us

our bodies mixed with flutes, the bird-
bone instruments those centuries and
centuries of mouths have touched. think.
think about the voices hanging on the trees
this time of year. the trees we bring
into our houses, the trees that Orpheus
inspired to dance. the feet we send
across the continents in sleep, in prophecy.
we are these golden flakes.
we are the language sewn into the fruit.

IS ALWAYS PHYSICAL

sandalwood's the odor of the day,
the most familiar incense, what I read
as how I am the same exotic and yet
earth-bound heat I've always been;
quick hope and longer burning, the way
the things I see stay with me, some
forever: buffalo, those icons. not
the clever artists but the shaggy
animals who might redeem, if we are
ready to be awed by blood we eat.
the taking-in divinity—as crude as
fire, repulsive and then purified.
eyes closed to carve the temple
decorations, which are women, who
are dancers as they ride across
our shoulders. we are nothing more
than weight, sustaining god's idea
that we can speak—and those long robes
of skin, hand-painted, used in ceremonies,
give power by lightning and by absolute
belief. we pray to bare our throats.
to lift them up. to offer them.

Justin

ESPERANZA

I remember the night when
we pulled at our roots.
when we drank all the water
then sang. we were beautiful
trees; we were roads to the
next simple town. they had
waited for us, both the people
and stars. we were made into
hymns. nobody wrote them, but
no one forgot. and then
we weren't trees anymore;
we were families of sparks.

you will be next.
you will be you, and then not.

WHERE HAVE I BEEN?
(1998)

WHERE HAVE I BEEN?

For Toke and Barbara, who pose the question: "Where have you been with your writing in the past twenty years? (1978-1998)

1.

In the garden in front of my house in the middle of Los Angeles, with its big pots of herbs, vegetables, and, this summer, a moonflower that never stops putting out white, trumpet-shaped blooms. Twenty years ago, I'd just moved to this place on Mariposa Avenue in East Hollywood, knew nothing about maintaining a garden. I still don't know enough, but I have paid attention to the garden because the way it is shows me the way I am: in the casual arrangement of pots, the eclectic collection of plants, I see the kind of person who resists thought-out planning, willful organization, detailed outlines. This is the kind of writer I am, too.

The moonflower seeds were given to me by Diane Wakoski, a poet-friend. Diane, when she sent the seeds, wrote that people had trouble getting them to sprout. I checked the *Sunset Western Garden Book* to find out about moonflowers: the seeds are hard-shelled. They need to be soaked for a couple of days before they're planted. I did that.

So, I can be careful, at least try to nurture my life with a little information and insight. Yet my garden failures are countless. I don't know what to do when bugs eat more than their share and I can't force myself to get rid of them, or when I can't stop myself from watering too much, drowning plants at their roots. The fact that I do learn, that I have a great hunger for learning, is countered by my refusals—not deliberate—to become learned. I do things with one eye open, one eye closed.

What we make, any of us, reveals who we are: the conflicts being worked on through us; the strengths at our command. Here in the worst of a miserably hot August, in a summer that's been disheartening all the way around, I went out to the garden early this morning and cleaned up. Pulled out the crop of no more than a dozen baby carrots—the whole of the reward I got for planting those seeds in the spring and watching over them for months. I lifted impossibly tangled tomato vines, reattached them to their stakes, cut off dead leaves and branches. Got rid of the bolting tatsoi, which had been delicious for salads in its youth but had gotten bitter fast in the heat. Snipped off a dead moonflower bloom, noticed five or six more buds on the plant. Thought the oregano, rosemary, basil looked okay as they were. I swept up, carried the debris back to the dumpster behind the apartments.

Now the garden looks more like me coming to the end of a bad time instead of the bad time itself. I haven't gotten rid of my own personality, but I've made peace. Now, I can write. There's a cleaner, less cluttered person available for the page.

2.

"Pilgrim in this foreign land, on foot," is the last line of one of the poems in the Barnsdall Park series I've been working on since January. It's a lonely line, but I take comfort in it. It says the pilgrim in me, the seeker of the holy, feels herself in a strange country away from love and family, with her only true resource: herself, her own feet. This is everything writing is about for me.

A few nights ago, I dreamed of being in Barnsdall Park—the familiar, single hill that rises above Hollywood Boulevard and Vermont Avenue. As I dreamed, I was taking in the green trees, the Los Angeles Municipal Art Gallery, Frank Lloyd Wright's Hollyhock House, when a woman I know joined me whose relationship to the unconscious, the archetypal, is exceptional. She showed me what *she* was seeing. Through her eyes, I discerned another world existing simultaneously with the outer, physical world of the park: Medieval knights in armor and their horses moved among the trees, their silvery colors a contrast to the leafy greens.

The Medieval world, alive, inhabits my park. A larger psyche than my personal one has allowed me a glimpse of the Middle Ages, when pilgrims were everywhere, traveling from various points in Europe to Palestine and other far away places, sustained by their own faith in the holy. Knights, yes, on crusades, and others who were nobles; but, too, servants might be sent in place of wealthy employers who didn't want to make the arduous trip themselves. People of lesser station joined in— devout or simply adventurous.

Travel has no appeal for me, except within my own foreign self. Twenty years ago, I'd just turned forty, the time in life when you need more and more of what you are. If you don't know yourself, you'd better set out on the search. I was already seeking a self through writing. Psychologically, I was in pursuit of healing for old wounds. The knight's wounds? I'd been battling the world for a long time before my fortieth birthday; yes, blood had been shed. By the time I was thirty-three years old, I'd had two disastrous marriages. I'd plunged into teaching English in a public high school, a job which, after seven years, exhausted my physical and emotional limits. A different vocation had become necessary. I was able to write.

I could watch the miles pass on the pages I filled. Those written pages became the vast amount of territory I'd covered, surely as much as one actual pilgrim's journey from Caumont to Toulouse, then across the Pyrenees (which were heavy with snow), on to the shrine at Montserrat, then to Barcelona. Onward, sailing, to Majorca, and from there to Sardinia, Sicily, Crete and Rhodes. Finally, Jaffa. To Ramla, then Lydda (the spot most sacred to St. George). In Jerusalem at last, he took communion at the Church of the Holy Sepulchre and had the great privilege of being allowed to spend four nights in that holiest of churches. This pilgrim was even knighted there. Also on his route: Bethlehem, Capharnum, Jericho— and a swim in the River Jordan. (Pretty much the route of Nompar de Caumont, a pious nobleman, in 1419.)

Many years of poems, novels, essays—my public writing—count for a lot of my pilgrimage, but the journals I've kept between 1972 and the present are witness to the raw materials of the public work, and to much that will never be seen in the wider world. Behind my desk, made years ago from an old door set on a couple of cabinets, is a double, often triple, stack of journals, tied together according to year. I do intend to re-read the early ones soon, take in the strange sights again, find out what I make of them this time around, having had more experience of both pirates and generous sultans in the meantime. I know there have been despair and futility in my journey. There has been awe, as well, in the discovery of my own alien soul. But did I ever really get to the Holy Land?

3.

And why go alone? Why have I been so much the orphan, the exile? (One of the meanings of "pilgrim" is "an exile.") Why has this standpoint sustained me, leading me creatively to move into the unknown? Why has this unknown been fruitful rather than destructive, when it—the foreign land—could as easily have been unwelcoming, even deadly?

I was born an only child to older parents who loved me, allowed me the run of our Lincoln, Nebraska house, yard and neighborhood where I spent my early years imagining who I might be—the princess? Or the gypsy dancer—even then, I loved flamenco music, full of sex and passion, death and pain, not that I could claim much direct experience in those adult intensities.

When my mother died of cancer, I was sixteen. We'd moved to Michigan. My father, grief-stricken, re-married within a year. My step-mother lived on the planet earth. I breathed the air of another star, found in books; in movies; in music; in deep, unsatisfied longing. The first recording I ever bought for myself was Carlos Montoya playing flamenco guitar. I'd lie down on the living room floor after school, when my father and step-mother were still at work, put my head as close as I could to the portable record player my father had given me for my birthday the spring before my mother died and listen, and grieve, and listen.

Technically, I was an orphan; the loss of one parent qualified me. Alchemically, "the orphan" is one of numerous Medieval metaphors for the raw material of The Great Work: the beginning of the process of transforming one's base self into if not gold, at least a worthy human being. When I came to Los Angeles alone in 1960, I had a college education. I was free to find a job, rent a place to live, be acted on by whatever came my way. I knew nothing, even with my Phi Beta Kappa key. I stayed in this vast city in spite of the emotional mess I blindly dove into, in spite of the constant errors of judgment and wrong-headed choices I couldn't stop making. Or, rather than "in spite of," perhaps "because of." Girl, dear girl: what a fool I was. Yet I was determined to live by only my own experience, since others, loved ones, could simply die or abandon me, anyway.

I admit it's this insistence on self-reliance which has kept me ignorant. I will never be the expert gardener who has studied with the best horticultural teachers or followed the important rules. I always stay closer to failure than to mastery. Gardener, never perfect in my relationship to nature, I'm still grateful to have the faith to plant anything, believing my solitary effort will find an answer in nature's light, air, water, spirit. One lesson I've learned from my failures in every aspect of life: If I seek sincerely to do the work that's offered me, I am companioned by a Presence which nourishes. Those we cherish do die or disappear, yet we're still accompanied, aren't we, mysteriously? I'm not made perfect by this Presence. But it wants me to take meaning from all that occurs. Success has its charms, but what won't flourish instructs me more profoundly. More than beauty or goodness? We need joy, too, and pride in our accomplishments. But I know what teaches me the most: struggle, and gratitude.

4.

Yesterday, an editor phoned and asked to publish, in an anthology he's preparing, a piece of writing I did twenty-two years ago, "Staring at the American Buffalo." I agreed, even though I wanted to refuse. The buffalo piece shows me at a time when I believed a single image or idea could sustain a hundred takes on it—a thousand—my writing swirled with multiple kaleidoscopic meanings for any helpless object or person or animal caught in its path. The buffalo writing, although it didn't teach me another completely different approach, did force me to an attitude perhaps akin to the buffalo's own large, solid, mean-eyed stare. I had pages and pages to work with, each one rich with overly enthusiastic imagery. One afternoon, immersed in the proliferation of so much bursting language, I realized I was showing off. I wanted to prove I had an imagination. My childhood gypsy, the wild singer and dancer, the vitally emotional self, had faded in my late teens, in college, and then totally vanished when I was fighting through my first tough years in Los Angeles. The swirling imagery in my writing was supposed to establish me as a woman of heightened insight and energy, one who was entering the writing world late—in my thirties—and needed to make up for lost time, lost hope. I had big hopes now; I'd found the art that would sustain me for the rest of my life. I needed to assure myself I could pull language out of myself endlessly: the magician's scarves flowing from a sleeve, one after another after another.

The buffalo, animal totem of my Nebraska birthplace, deserved better. Instead of loading the writing with my need to be seen, why not step back and work for the power inherent in the buffalo itself? Why not edit the piece to reveal my subject rather than to hide my insecurities? I cut the piece ruthlessly, getting down to a truer shape. Now, when I re-read what I did then, I still find the urge to use three images when one would suffice, but generally the work has a decent honesty.

"prayer to the buffalo:

keep me chewing so that nothing gets lost by swallowing too fast keep me alone but close to the herd"

I was still the orphan, but I wasn't ignoring the power of learning from other writers, the ones I was meeting in those days, and the writers before me, too, the dead ones, the ancestors. (The buffalo herds moving in their long pilgrimage across the Plains.) I'd heard plenty about directness and simplicity in writing. It would be a lesson I'd continue to practice—sometimes successfully; sometimes not.

5.

Alchemically, the stages of The Great Work are Calcinatio, which burns; Solutio, which dissolves; Coagulatio, which concretizes; Sublimatio, which volatilizes; Mortificatio, which empties and kills; Separatio, which separates; and Coniunctio, which unites. Willingness to accept these difficult metaphors as living experiences can open a seeker to conflicts which then can be worked on creatively. Alchemy's lore is rich in drawings, poetical writings, mysterious recipes designed to appeal to the imagination. My own metaphor, the orphan, finds comfort not only in individual struggle but in belonging to such a creative tradition. One reward for being faithful to creative work as inner alchemical process has been the dream of seeing those Medieval knights and horses alive in my neighborhood park. I watched, in terms of the unconscious, through the eyes of the larger psyche: historical perspective, universally shared "story." I'm not—we aren't—alone, no matter how marginal we feel. We belong in history, our own and the world's.

Compared to the buffalo writing and many other pieces I've written, my most recent poetry, the Barnsdall Park series, has a directness I do take note of. I can't call the writing simple—my fertile mind still likes to put together more than one straightforward image or idea—but I see that I'm able now, as I age, to speak what I feel. The poems darken with a close, much-loved friend's death from cancer. In the buffalo piece, I wrote about another friend's cancer, taking the buffalo as an image of survival. I believed, as a younger woman, I could will survival, cure, health. I know now that I can't will much of anything. I couldn't save my mother; nothing I've done since her death has saved anybody else.

"the pungent eucalyptus smell—an herbal stringency—

which hits my nose as I pick up my notebook and my glasses,
ready to stop staring into God's blank cruelty. The odor
comes as medicine. I have my senses for right now,
my body for a little future, anyway. Am I thankful?
I have never answered that. Pilgrim,
in this foreign land, on foot."

These are the final lines from "Blue T-Shirts Saying 'Pilgrim' on the Front," one of the Barnsdall Park poems that talks about Andrea's death, about everybody's mortality. The question "Am I thankful?" holds a tone of voice I couldn't have written in twenty years ago. It's a voice that admits its puzzlement, not able anymore to hide itself in endless richness of imagery.

So, gratitude for the pilgrimage to this much honesty. And on, now, to the task of my present life, which is the discovery of a wider perspective, one that includes death not as horror but as an integral part of nature's structure. "Am I thankful? I have never answered that," deserves an answer in the affirmative, if I can manage it. My gratitude for my journey is definite; my gratitude for the suffering life inevitably offers is questionable. I'm curious to see what gets written next, because it will show me how I'm doing with this important concern of aging. Writing will show me, as always, my failures, and my still-strong hunger to learn.

6.

Will I ever get to the Holy Land?

I've been copying this question onto the various pages of this essay for days now. As I move it from one section to another, I wonder if I want to answer it, or if it can be answered. The first response which came to me is that it doesn't really matter—the alchemy of learning to write and to live, interconnected for me, is everything. My second thought says there's no absolute union with The Divine, anyway, on this earthly plane. We're human. The struggle toward union may fill our lives with value and meaning. But heaven on earth—not for this originally Midwestern, Protestant kid. It would be prideful to believe I could achieve the saintly faith necessary to meet The Divine in its own home, its Holy Land.

My third idea, though, is that I'm there. I've been in the Holy Land, even as I've searched for it. Writing inspires the numinous. By working creatively for many years, I've always been with what is holy, as a writer and as a pilgrim.

And the mysterious Presence, the companion on the trip? The accompanying Other who isn't exactly a teacher and isn't exactly Divinity and isn't exactly a comforter and isn't exactly great wisdom? But, too, is all this, invisible yet nearby, from time to time giving the right cue for planting Diane's moonflower seeds or re-seeing the buffalo writing. The orphan's mother—for I do sense this Presence as feminine—won't save me from my own stumbling but does answer my yearning to know the meaning of my sufferings and pleasures; then, by extension, to gain an understanding of a greater-than-individual meaning. I'm ashamed to not make my garden more wonderful because that means I can't make my relationship to all nature better than it is. This extends to the relationship we have as contemporary people to nature. We destroy, too often, what grows in our forests or swims in our oceans. Environmental horrors are familiar. I can't separate myself from them because I see right in front of my house my inability to respect nature. I'm not chopping down ancient trees or polluting waters, but I'm not aware enough or educated enough to get the best balance in my little piece of earth, either.

Nor can I get the best balance in my writing. I keep trying to improve. Still, I don't become vastly better at what I do or who I am. Early experiences formed me for my whole life: orphanhood and the orphan's need to be self-reliant, so that I don't learn from others as fully as I might. I'm also at the mercy of what is genetic, embedded in my particular share of intelligence, talent, stamina and perception. Another fact is that it's simply too late for me, at sixty years of age, to re-do what I've done. The work is the work; it's not over yet, but it's got more past to it than future. That past is within me. I can't deny or rectify it. I can only attempt to understand it, which is the whole point of asking, "Where have you been with your writing for the past twenty years?"

In the past twenty years what can I say really has opened profoundly in me? "Compassion" comes as a response not exactly my own. I don't consider myself a compassionate person. I consider myself self-absorbed. I'm not a woman who sacrifices her needs for the needs of others. The sensitivities necessary for making any kind of art require a relationship with a lot of pretty odd vulnerabilities. Art is no longer the province of one blessed (or cursed) person who's called "the artist" and does it for everybody in the tribe. In our time, many individuals are called on to serve the creative psyche. To serve, each writer/artist has to face the unknown, the foreign land, the vastly irrational yet brilliant unconscious. If the creative powers welcome you, you can become, eventually, compassionate. You've traveled the rocky terrain on your own—and with your companion travelers. The Holy Land is the piece of imaginative earth and sky we share with those who love the art we love, who practice it like prayer.

7.

It's October now. I've been out in the garden this morning, watering and tidying up. The glorious nasturtium that's given me months of orange blooms is fighting tiny, slimy black bugs under its leaves. Eventually, they can kill the plant. Every time I think to do it, I go out with the Safer's Insecticidal Soap and spray the leaves. I don't think to spray often enough, though. The bugs have won most of the battle, although a few hopeful, new leaves are sprouting. I've cut off the dead, dry-brown mess hanging helplessly over the side of the planter. I sprayed. I guess you could say I did my best, but I didn't. My neighborhood nursery would tell me what the bugs are—they've infested my nasturtiums for years—and give me the exactly right antidote to use. Why haven't I taken this simple step, gotten advice? Why do I stubbornly go on and on, thinking I know how to grow nasturtiums?

So, I'm stuck with myself, how I do what I do. But, in spite of the nasturtiums, I admit to pride this morning in the gathering of pots and planters. The summer basil—huge, green stalks in various spots, even planted in pots with other things because I bought way too many seedlings back in April—is ready to harvest then turn into pesto to freeze. Sage, rosemary, lavender, oregano, mint, sorrel thrive. When the moonflower stopped blooming, I cut back the overgrown branches, gave it a new, larger pot. A tomato plant had run its course; I got rid of it a couple of weeks ago. The large container it inhabited can be planted with cool-weather lettuce. In Southern California, autumn is a fine time for gardens, many say the best. My other tomato plant insists on putting out little yellow blossoms, so I can't uproot it. Chances are that chillier weather will do it in, but why not wait and see? The one I just dug out had lasted two fertile years.

On an afternoon a season or so ago when I was poking around the garden, a woman visiting the neighbors in the apartment behind ours walked past me, smiling, said with a heavy, Armenian accent, "You... flowers... love." There weren't any flowers then; she said the only word she knew for plants. But her remark meant a lot to me. The Armenians here in East Hollywood are prolific gardeners, excellent judges of "flowers." Because she was impressed and saw love in what I do helps me believe that not only am I reflected in my failures but also in my triumphs: to tend a garden which often does flourish; to get words on the page in satisfying—no, thrilling—order; to read books with a maturity of insight I couldn't have imagined twenty years ago; to teach in my own way, work with writers who trust my ability to move them in their particular creative directions; to be married to my husband Harry, deeply loved, a poet himself, who has been loyal to both my difficulties and my strengths for, yes, twenty-one years.

So, finally, I fully accept my relationship with my work and my loved ones: my lengthy creative life has brought me release from orphanhood. I may not be able to slough off old habits—stubborn self-reliance, mistrust in the general solidity of life—yet my years-long pilgrimage has convinced me that I am held to the pilgrim's road not only by my own two feet but by the grace which sustains faith, which gathers failures into ritual: poem, fiction, journal and other writing forms I've explored. Both failures and revelations become, at last, my own warm breath, expanding then dissolving then expanding again. They fill me the way any healthy breathing does: generously, continuously.

The 2000s

BARNSDALL PARK
(1998-2000)

(In Memory of Andrea Dyer)

Part One

CHAMBER MUSIC TWENTY YEARS AGO

We like consistency, the house
the way it was the day before,
Frank Lloyd Wright, historical, his hollyhocks
in formal stone along the walls; the stone
pressed nobly into stems which hold their flowers.

To stay among what stays.   But then
to not.   This happy park and yet
its olive trees are sick with smog.   Sick old self
who feels cool stone against her back, who sees
the artful hollyhocks against the wall;
she calms herself because there's nothing else to do.
Kids, now, shouting to the squirrels and Mom.
Sun on red sweater.   Then the sweater's gone.

Why so much pain in disappearance?
Why *bas relief* when really
truths are made from everything we've lost?
Fissure, memorized.
The loved ones: How they stood and breathed and walked away.

MOUNTAINS IN THE BACKGROUND

No one in the park.
Frail olive trees, their branches
gathered, thin, as if it's really winter,
which it never is in Southern California,
not biting winters I survived in grief,
my mother's death. The chill today, though.
But olives only grow in better climates,
and I have reasons to not fall into the blind,
blank warp my adolescence gave me. Ah,
a car pulls in and stops—

A couple. She's in the driver's seat;
he leans and kisses her. Why did any of us
come to California? Heat. The lying down
right now against the seats in that blue car.

Soon, I'll dream *my vampires*
say goodbye. I understand the female one
because she knows she suffers, knows just
what she is. Our monsters grieve, like us.
If there's no death today, if there is only park,
hope, going home to my fine husband, there's still
the warmth sucked out of me, and how I never

walk downstairs in front of my own mental aberrations,
no matter what they are. They lose control and push.
I come to trees to have a little peace, to watch
the olives hold themselves, even if they're thin.
I remember why I'm here at all. To be inspired. To think
of spring two years beyond myself when I will fully
understand we can be permanently changed. Cured?
At least, white sun above the peaks.

I'M NOT THERE

The rain, you know—it would only be
wet grass, just staring at the park through my car
windows. The house a testament to Frank Lloyd Wright's design:
Mayan temple, grand stone hollyhocks. But disrepair.
Oh, God, this unreliability of stone, and yet
I tell myself this is my world; it's real—not everything
will have to die. Dear Andrea,

I can't stop finding tears, although it's been eight months
since you did die, like everything, my friend of more than
thirty years, your body ruined by cancer. The last gift
was a black and silver pin you gave to me at Christmas.
Black: the new, hurt soul. And silver: women's moon,
the metal that has got to be kept up, a friendship,
polished every time it's worn.

Evening: The patio outside my living room has shifted
from green fern to silhouette of plastic-covered chairs.
The rain is gone, but more will be predicted for the weekend.
I want the park. I want the hill that lifts
above the city—L. A. view, the European look of houses
scattered on more hills right under Griffith Park,

the lessened raw collision of myself with Andrea's
enormous absence. And yet I've dreamed of her:
I understand that death is not a judgement, or regret,
or floating miserably in air. It's—who can know?
Those hollyhocks stand true against their weakened stone.
I can have faith in flowers rendered by an artist's hand
to represent the coming warmer seasons. But. Still.
I can't deny it's getting ever-darker out there on the patio.
She's nothing

but a box of ashes
covered up with dirt. She's nothing like a flower at all.

THE ENTRANCE FOR THE TOUR

Up close, the lamp post is the hollyhock,
original design by Wright.   I take a photograph—
this lamp post getting browner in the rain.
I keep the detail,

all we have of any weather.   The other side of Barnsdall
as I drive around: a spot where Andrea and other "dear ones"
(Gary calls us) came to celebrate my birthday with a picnic.
Years ago.   That detail, too.   Around,

around the park's one hill, cold rain a formula for grief.
Andrea: She liked to be here, take the painting classes,
loved to look at things—to look and then record them
with her brush.   My camera: a wish to keep exactly what
is in this little frame, to know it's there.   But where's

dead Andrea?   You, Nature, tell me now.   I stand here
at the lamp post in the rain.   Mother of our earth and art
and their destruction, present yourself and let me understand
why photographs, so intricate, precise, stay flat, no breath,

no friend.

Gary shares this death.   And Fred, and Harry, Ardath, Peter,
and Virginia.   When our whole generation slips aside,
who'll hang her painting of the yellow roses graceful in their
blue-green vase?   Or, who will be the one to throw away
the photos from the birthday picnic, not recognizing any

face or name?   The facts become just like the rain:
fallen, soaked into the ground, gone down and down until
there's nothing in our sight but air where sweet minutia
might have been.   Can I remember any of her clothes?   Only

the dress, cotton, pastel plaid, she wore as ghost when she
came home for my one dream in which we talked.   We sat all

evening but of course I don't know what we said. It's gone.
She's gone. The rain is not a blessing and the camera doesn't
help a thing. And yet I will look at the photograph, the lamp
post, browned, historical, and feel my pleasure in the human act
of taking time to look, to notice what is standing by itself.
To not say "futile" underneath my breath.

BLUE T-SHIRTS SAYING "PILGRIM" ON THE FRONT

Downs Syndrome kids, round-faced, stumbling together,
running on a flight of stairs. ("Eddie! Eddie! Eddie!
Hey! Hey! Hey!") The sun picks out each fat geranium
along the gallery's wall—all shining here for those
who cannot even know they have a destination—even Eddie,
center of attention. These pilgrims flow in snakey
inabilities, eventually complete their circle of the park,
gather for instructions, happily believe the teachers
who are telling them it's time to go. Go where?

Four quick days until my dead friend's birthday.
I want the afternoons we had in 1965 when "pilgrim" meant
we'd trek across the rough-earth stretch between her house
and mine, a field belonging to another park, grandly named
"Elysian." How serious we were, in weeds grown to our ankles.
Our dialogues about This Life included evenings at our
neighbor Ann's, the Ann who once was married to a matador,
his body muscled, gifted, praised

until the bull that killed him came along.

Andrea and I across the field: We called each other by our
living names as sun jumped on our arms; we called the way
they shout again, again, for Eddie, leaping Eddie, happy Eddie,
mortal Eddie. These gestures nonchalantly made by Chance:
the shapes we're born to and the illnesses we nurture
in ourselves. Make a civilized, warm-hearted bowing down,
I guess, although blind luck is shit. And yet I recognize

the pungent eucalyptus smell—an herbal stringency—
which hits my nose as I pick up my notebook and my glasses,
ready to stop staring into God's blank cruelty. The odor

comes as medicine.   I have my senses for right now,
my body for a little future, anyway.   Am I thankful?
I have never answered that.   Pilgrim,
in this foreign land, on foot.

IS THIS A SONG?

The day, bi-lingual, pleasant to ourselves.
The woman on the bench, whose name, I hear,
is Jane, gets up to greet her friends.

Well-brushed, sniffy dogs run by.
The doggies' mistress speaks in Spanish;
then, a crow-voice answers her. Good manners.

I guess it's all okay right now, religiously okay.
Jane's friends are here on time to tour the house.
The bougainvillea so cerise, magenta, bursts in front of
yellow that's chartreuse, which swings into a lot of bushy,
leafy branches, colors brash enough to hurt my eyes.
To make me happy, too.   It's not so bad today,

the sadness I can always give my breath to.
It's spring; old vibrant goddesses, their realm the fields,
return from death in highest spirits even with their knowledge
of the coming seasons when they have no power to rule.
Oh, let them have this much at least:
Both doggies let me pet their heads.
Even as a stranger to their language, I reach out.

OUR LUNA

Purple moon, painted in the left hand corner. Later,

outside the gallery, jacaranda blossoms, gods so lavender
I want to stare until they blind me. Forever, then,
inside my eyes pure rapture filling up the sky.

I turn instead to watch kids over there on rollerblades—
a girl, a boy enjoying this June 4th, right after my friend
Celia's father died. She's home, another city, crying.

A dad, or this nice breeze, or where the skating girl is now
that I can't see her—she speeds away before I've written
just one page. The fine Latina painter paints, she says,
her miseries then hangs them, sets them in their frames.
Her purple moon is lifted to its place

as if we can. Do that.

We're doomed.
And yet we do have time

to learn what color means.
To do things well, invent a month called June, for Junius,
a Roman clan, a family like the ones we have ourselves,
remembered as I take another look at gorgeous jacarandas.
I yearn to climb the sky; I can't.
I hate not understanding what's beyond our flesh
or what it means to finally join the moon. I pray to

blindness as it opens different eyes on different trees,
a wilder zodiac which aims the lunar fire to show us
how our orbits run—cruel, specific, beautiful.
Our Luna. Always where we need to see her,
attached to myth that guides us up and up.
I'm not the guardian of Mystery, only

a practitioner of staring, thinking what is sent to me to think.
"Circle" is the word that comes;

perhaps it is the end which has beginning in its mouth.
When I arrive here, at this word, we've gotten to
another August heading on into September:

The jacaranda trees are not in bloom. Celia's back
in California now and has been for awhile, not relieved
of sadness but with friends, at least, who've all had
fathers, too. We're made of time. Moon's roundness
when she's full, but yet she starves on other nights.
We're lovely. Then completely emptied, far away.

Do we need, when we become the substance of the moon,

to even be remembered, painted, held as human selves?
Is what's beyond our flesh that gravity-less dust
Our Luna offers as our transportation, no matter where
she's going? I realize
we're going with her, finally:
blind, reflected light.

(with thanks to the paintings of Patssi Valdez)

Part Two

HALLOWE'EN

So, it's true: things change.
The little girls sing "wanna, wanna,"
kick their legs and jump. They jump
too close to me. One smiles, or sort of does.
I'm sitting on this bench for my own purposes,
trying to ignore her yellow T-shirt, bright
red pants. I look away,

and then I can't.
Wild sun today. It enters hard concrete—
the bench, and buildings there beyond the park—
makes the hard stuff almost beautiful. These kids
are Andrea, my friend who died, her childhood back again,
past grief. I wanna wanna wanna
smile the way she smiles at me—the girl who prances,
shows off how much she loves her ankles; long, smooth feet.

On Hallowe'en, the souls arrive.
Andrea comes in children's voices, sounds like herself
again. Arranges all those rows of eager chairs
across the grass for people
who will come to listen to

more music later.

FAIRIES

(The original meaning of "fairy" is "one of the Fates.")

The place with roses.
The cottage with quaint English stuff.

It was my birthday, some year gone.
Hot scones, and little sandwiches. Clotted cream, of course.

Afterward, we noticed Pasadena houses echoed
England in their pruned but wildish gardens,
gardens welcoming to elves and sprites. (Shaded, moss-green
thicket near the low-branched oak.) Andrea, you never fit
into the plain world's alphabet. You wanted spells,
believed that we can take the consequences of enchantments.
Now, you release

the quick spice rushing through my kitchen;
your ghost stirs up the scented air. Again, I'm drinking
from that British cup—fine Earl Grey tea with sugar.
We didn't know, but finally

you'd suffer with a hard, cassette-thing strapped around
yourself to drip big chemicals into your body, ones
you thought would save your life. Who wants

this life?
It's torture. Death must be the widest grandeur,
birthday, leap into all Nature's bloom. There's nothing
here to miss. The sandwich really in my hands is simple
lunch, not grand, high tea. Andrea, dead friend,
I'm glad you're close, but my advice is this:
breathe as the dead do breathe. Breathe wings.

HOW WE FILL OUR LUNGS

Twice today, some roses.
Not the park but I am thinking

just what "park" involves:
I see a woman, fat, in a pink
T-shirt who holds roses which she's
just been given. Roses from a garden.

"There's God," I think.

And when I go into the pricey florist's,
the man I haven't seen before says,
"Happy New Year," smiles as if it maybe

will be new.
Roses come in lavender, along with
white and pink and yellow in a bucket and
because they've been around awhile they're
cheap. Here's God again—roses made affordable.
I take a dozen home. Their lessened freshness
gives them perfume, subtlety of age which senses
winter now but not forever. Turn aside.
The minute you turn back, there isn't doubt but
violent color and the way they crowd the vase.

ON CHRISTMAS EVE,
YOUR BODY ALL REBORN

A few days after new year's I'm inside
the house that Frank Lloyd Wright designed.
One ceiling—lovingly restored—shines copper,
gold and green. My dream, dear Andrea, was this:

I find you naked in your bedroom: round belly, curving
thighs, richer in flesh than when you were alive before.
You've gained the weight of women who will never die again.
I bring you a Christmas gift which you don't need;
your cancer's gone.

So, as I tour these outer rooms, I understand the park exists
to prove existence does hold on. Abandoned, left to ruin,
then rescued by the faithful. I buy gold bookmarks
made to be the hollyhock design the house is named for:
abstracted, graceful, bold. I want to take home beauty,
which is how the living fill themselves. Andrea,
you'd come here to the park to paint, but now,
season of miracles, you are the truest art yourself.

I look again into the brilliant ceiling,
some kind of heaven; then, I leave. Outside
here's sky, sheer endlessness. You'll never be
forgotten, Andrea. Death's made you sun. You walk in me.

"UH, UH, UH, OO, OO, OO"

The mentally disabled kids today but different ones
than I have seen before. They whoop.

Then people walking, man and woman, moving swiftly,
dressed in fresh, blue clothes.

The children hunch, inspect their sandwiches.
They rock—their bodies tidal, forced to crash against
the shore then slide away again. The man and woman
head for art, their privilege of symbol, abstract thought.

One keeper puts a hand that holds a sandwich toward a mouth.
"Will you stop screaming?"

The walkers leave their art; they come my way.
I see they take the time to read brochures.
The children hoot. This is their language,
an attempt to join us. Crows
start their own noise in the sky.

"Easy, easy, easy," a kinder adult says.

I don't feel hungry for big bites of what I've had before.
I slam along the coastal self a lot like those who have
no minds. The walkers wait to tour the house.
Architecture has its lovely walls

to keep the necessary boundary between *in* and
outside where the screams come from. Let's move on

to crows, who fly above us, watching without judgment
what we do or do not eat. I lift one of my veiny hands
to signal God or Goddess, Crow; I'm waving to whoever

guards the sacred roominess between art's genius
and hunched madness, moves in us as balance, a dream
that's finally understood. Look over there—

another woman slips into a coat the color of the noontime light.
Exactly everything we need, yet nothing much. Equality of light.

ART INSTALLATION

Clay which once was earth is music now.

Outside, the wall is swept with light;
many palm trees' shadows make themselves
much different palms. They sway, shift into angels
patterned through a crowded sky. Yes, we can discern
one hundred twenty thousand hairs on everybody's head.

Young man right over there performs his exercises—
sort of Tai Chi, sort of push your shoulders to
the tree as hard as you can push, turn angels into
muscle you can use. The weight, the faith we need
to be art and miracle and nothing but ourselves.

(With thanks to Mineko Grimmer's Vessels.*)*

Part Three

PLAIN PAPER

Just to stare.
At? This hour, half erased,

and did
the stain I left at home to soak come out?

I look at bottle brush then squirrel then jacaranda.
"Hi," I say. "Hi, squirrel." It dashes toward a ripened smell.
The radio today says women still aren't seen, need fleshier
assertions. All I've ever done, though—get visible,
be present on the fabric.
This summer,

the hours are less themselves. The jacaranda tree is less
in bloom because our spring was cold. Still, lavender.
Enough to notice. Staring is the poetry of age.
The newest birds

talk constantly: here in the park as crows,
and when I'm home as mocking birds and blue jays,
mourning doves. I wake up at 5 A. M. to hear their news.
Not what I'll do today or did when I was young,
but bird-events, that urgency. Time, commodity we always
think we need more of, finally removes us from the whole
idea of "hour," of self. I think

this is relief. Memory rubbed back
to paradise, to unflawed water.

THIS SEMI-ARID, WING-DRENCHED CITY

I guess it's thirst, cactus who insists on shape,
can even bloom. And standing on the park's far side I see,
I'm sure, as far as Santa Monica, white statue of the saint
before the ocean starts. Here's everything I've learned:
Swallow constantly,

take it in by gulps. Think of Christ, His fish and bread—
why not thousands fed from nada, zilch, impossibility?

Jan, my neighbor, died a month ago. I think about her
sitting in her car some evenings after work until
her breath came back and she could walk up to her door.
The faith to sit
and wait to
live a little longer.
This climate takes our tough ones in its stingy heart,
gives them that croaky laughter Jan was really good at.
I can't get grief to hurt me;
she's still my neighbor Jan, her ashes in the ocean but
her real self on the stairway, step by labored step.

Everybody's stubborn, mythic trials. This week, a woman
I have liked has given up. A saint could help. Monica's not
listed in my books, but she's right there, right at the end
of Wilshire Boulevard, waiting for the ones whose tears flow
freely, who get so tired of holding on. The ocean says,
"surrender"; the desert says,
"survive."

Strawberry Hedgehog Cactus, Saguaro, Miller's Pincushion, Barrel,
Buckhorn, Devils Fingers, Rainbow, Prickly Pear.

Dry, hurt throats. I understand Jan's friend sneaking into
her apartment—5:00 A. M.— to carry out her microwave.

It's not perfection which makes character.
It's letting Nature take Her course: Jan died. Her buddy
has to eat. We have to think of Christ who feeds the least
deserving of us all. That's why I'm here:

for contradictions. And for miracles, those Biblical
amusements with our puny faith. The way the cactus grows.

Los Angeles, you show me everything exists at once
and multiplies. Good fortune in your fractured, milky wings.

A WOODEN PLATFORM WHERE
A DANCER MIGHT PERFORM

Young squirrel straight up the tree. The morning cop's
a woman with blond hair. Now, squirrel has got
a squirrel friend. They squeal and chase and chase.

I like my work: to see what's here; to see
what isn't. I was a child who longed for Hallowe'en
when souls, our truest metaphors, come right
to doorways, porches, fields. But now I know
Soul's boldness always stands beside us—searching,
breathing—if it doesn't accidentally kill us
with its force. The park allows me its good will;

the souls do listen,
welcome human voices who will try to hum in tune.
May old wounds feel that woman's bright blond hair
slide quickly on their faces; take pleasure in the
little animals inside their feet. Oh, faithful magic.
Everything unseen appearing on that empty stage.

A LOT OF CAMERAS IN THE PARK
THIS AFTERNOON

The woman with the handsome shirt—
she disappears. Her friend stays visible
next to a man who's taking photos of the house
designed by Frank Lloyd Wright. But wait.
Here comes my woman. No, she's hidden by a tree.
Palms and melon-colored sunsets fill the shirt; I do catch that.

It's August now, when everybody travels. Who do we think
we're meant to be, away from home? The shirted woman turns
the corner, comes this way, is her

but is an adolescent boy. The friend's his mother. His father
takes the pictures and they all have British accents.
How skillfully
we cross each other in imagination, gender, country, time—

how wavy palm trees on the shirt suggest this California,
or could be
Haiti, Cuba—maybe Costa Rican birds. Everything around me
slips into its feathered dress, lifts afternoon's long squawk
across the boundaries, adorned with our new thousand years.
Think

of how your family name will be pronounced when toucans
learn real English. What will choruses of small black
olives falling from the nearby trees compose when
they have been genetically combined with larks? I am

a teenage boy who lives in London, visits Southern California
in an August when he's ready to become a woman,
shoulder blades receptive to high flight. Look up.
Fly into the lens. There. Your photograph reveals your northern,
island ancestors—and yet the tropics pulse along your back.
The park

itself is scheduled for renovation:
My old familiar entrance changed.
New pine and olive trees. New irrigation. Seismic repairs,
as if such things protect us from the shifting earth within
ourselves. Turning the camera to my own broad face,

I see no one. No one I recognize.
This is not an afternoon like other days,
the ones I finish knowing how I'll start again tomorrow.
This afternoon is breath exchanging breath with languages
nobody speaks—not yet, at least. I'm being readied
for translation, my own long, autumn travel. Some place
unrecognizable, the words I need will come to me, Tiresian:
words that have both beards and breasts. Can understand
completion—a whole, changed world made from

a shirt's repeated sunsets, palm trees which are feathers,
which are messengers who lift us far above our own pale
outlines in the fading air.

SOLACE

Barnsdall Park
In Memory Of Theodore Barnsdall
1859-1917
"Our Fathers Mined For The Gold Of This Country
We Should Mine For Its Beauty."

Aline Barnsdall

Pink bushes with small bees.
A child croons nonsense, tiny adorations.
Old pools beneath the plaque have gotten filled
with rain, debris. I sit here on the edge
copying the message. Aline envisioned art,
this hill, utopian. I still believe her,
even with the stagnant water: water's reflection
shimmers up the wall—hazy, mesmerizing.
The ugly pools create the beautiful. The toddler
scoops up dirt enthusiastically, has his own ideas
of what's art. He moves the world. No,

just the opposite. The world

moves bees and kids; and difficult Aline
was disappointed, left her hill unfinished.
Right now, though, her father's image does stand out
among the old wall's cracks—his moustache and
his formal jowls. Her dedication firm as ever,
read or not. I want Aline to know

this place she couldn't live in still holds gold
embedded in the dirt the child digs out. He thinks
the earth is worth his effort. He may find
Gorgeous Nothing, but remembers it as treasure when
he's fifty-eight years old, the age her father died.

It's not what we accomplish, Good Aline, that matters.
It's our ruins. They turn to someone else's happiness.
I sit to think on gold, which, when I get home,
I write as godl. God. And L.

L for what? For lineage. Loss. Pink bushes
tended to by bees. Who carry pinkness everywhere.
Buzzing, getting fat.

JACARANDA BLOSSOMS
ALL OVER THE GRASS

"Oh, park. Oh, park. Oh, park."
I'm breathing hard as I climb up the hill.
Spring Taurus turns to Gemini—
the destined, sudden zodiac removes
our bodies to thin air. Every tree now, only breeze.

Today, and I can't stop her,
she's leaving me again, Andrea,
my friend who's dead. It's going to be

a summer full of weddings; cousins; brewing sharp,
black tea that's called "Awake." I'm learning
to rejoin the other ones I love. My husband.
And the mother cat who can't resist herself,
arrives with kittens. Andrea is way beyond us animals;

she knows the place the trees have gone.
She doesn't care about romantic gifts I send the bride,
about the birthday when I make that tea.

Farewell, Another World. This is the season
when the sky-lit twins take over, bringing
reconciliation—and ambivalence.
Oh, park. I hate this arm of mine:

it waves goodbye
without my ever thinking I have lifted it.

LOVE: POEMS FOR HARRY
(2001)

(FOR HARRY E. NORTHUP)

HARRY, TODAY YOU'RE GONE
FROM 9:30 A. M. UNTIL 10:15 P. M.

I'm busy on Tuesdays with teaching; how can I say I'm lonely?
But after lunch I stand at the sink, washing the glass my
soy milk was in, and feel you behind me, as you so often
really are, in this small kitchen. Sharon, this morning,

told me about her son and his girlfriend wearing each other's
bedroom slippers. "They're just starting out," she said.
That painful, hopeful look on her face—we can't know
the future, although we know we've had most of our own.
When you and I were just starting out,

all I could do was to write our first mornings together,
how we kept eating papaya and mango. I called you my Puritan
Outlaw, which you were, which you still are. We'd slept on the
floor—why?— of your West Hollywood apartment the morning I
woke up, rolled toward you, said into your still-sleepy ear,
"Stay alive." Late summer sun warmed the hardwood floor.
Now, this afternoon, standing at the sink,

I think about Sharon, the look on her face when she spoke
of her son, the knowledge we have as we age: Things can go
wrong. You and I have fought since 1977 abut everything we
want to change in each other, have never changed, don't expect
to change at this point, but can't help getting mad about,
anyway. As I wash my glass and feel your spirit-self behind me
even as your physical one is taking your friend Paul to the
doctor out in Venice, my body empties. I miss you.
How can I miss you? You'll be home tonight.

But I miss you as if you were never coming back. I miss you
as if we'd never met and I realize as an old woman that I lost
the greatest love of my life by not meeting the man who would
capture my solitary self, get her to pay attention to baseball,

the Dodgers, the beautiful unfolding of a game in which there are
rules but no predictable outcome. A baseball game takes as long
as it takes. You and I have taken, so far, nearly twenty-four
years. The first years, we talked about driving up and up the
coast to escape our routine; these days we talk about dinner—
cherishing the routine—and about your own son, recently

married, with his own unknown future. So long ago, waking up
on your sun-splashed floor, Dylan was eight years old. He's my
son, too, now, the only one I've had, the only one I need.
At his wedding, I looked at you in your tuxedo, his best man,
thinking, as I do all the time, how handsome you are.
Your handsome spirit moves around behind me in our kitchen
today while you're gone, and I can't stop missing you.
When you do get home after the workshop I teach that's over at
10:00 P. M., you've seen yet another movie version of "Hamlet,"
which you didn't particularly like. I know

how you feel. "Hamlet" is a good story but sometimes people
try to force it to go one way or another. Usually,
they shorten the original. But it takes its own time, that story,
like a good baseball game, or long-lasting love. Harry,

our future is ourselves, right now. What lasts, lasts.
Let's have some more.

HARRY, YOU OPEN THE CUPBOARD
DOOR AND I BANG MY HEAD

I'm tired. I'm chilly. I just want a cup of coffee.
You want coffee, too. While I'm trying to make my own coffee,
you're trying to get sugar for your coffee out of the cupboard.
Ouch, ouch, ouch. The cupboard door is wood, and it's wide;

I don't expect it to be open. So I hurt my ear
and the side of my head when I collide with it,
not looking, which I blame you for, but I don't
say anything except ouch, ouch. I go into the study,

sit in my rocking chair, start to cry because I'm tired,
because you crowded into the kitchen. You come into the study
where I sit holding my ear, which still hurts. "I'm sorry,
I'm sorry," you say, "I should have warned you.
I should have told you the cupboard was open."
I want to get self-righteously mad, even though
it wasn't really your fault; it was mine for not
seeing the door was open. I want to make a fuss

because I'm tired, because things hurt so often,
which isn't your fault but the fault of life,
plain old life, which I bang into all the time:

I fear the worst, like the possibility, a month ago,
that you had an "unidentified mass" in your stomach.
When your doctor ordered a CT scan, what could we think,
except cancer? A deadly, alien, awful something-or-other.
It turned out to be nothing, blessedly

nothing. But it could have been, might have been,
possibly and potentially was...

Harry, we're in our sixties. We're healthy.
We're lucky. My ear stops hurting. It's Sunday,
with two major football games for you to watch
on TV. I have puttery things to do around the house.
Everything is fine. On the wall behind my desk
here in the study,

I've taped a photograph of four Guatemalan women
in brightly patterned skirts and blouses. Three
balance big rocks on their heads as they walk
along the street. How do they do this?
Wear such beautiful colors and carry such large burdens?
I remind myself that banging my head on an open kitchen
cupboard door is nothing. What matters, Harry, is this:

You didn't mean to hurt me, and I kept my mouth
shut. Not getting angry is a spiritual task I practice—

when I can. This morning, I managed it, carried the weight,
held onto blame. It's nothing to be especially
proud of, but I am, a little. We have peace now,
which Sundays should remind us to work at,
us Christians. Let the cupboard door be a prayer,
then, for what we've got: pain which turns out
to be nothing, blessedly nothing, but peace.

HARRY, IT'S RAINING

Your knees against mine as we sleep. 5 A. M.—
ah, there's time, still, to stay here in bed.

When I do get up,

I sit at my desk in my pajamas with two candles lit
and Tibetan peace incense burning. My prayer lifts
with the lively twists of smoke:

May the day pass smoothly so we can get to evening
when we plan to eat out, then see a movie, then come home
and go to sleep again. What an ordinary prayer, I hope
not an insult to the Tibetan Buddhists who made the incense,

who built a floor-to-ceiling mandala for Universal Peace, all
by hand, infusing it with everything they, enlightened monks,
understand about peace for the entire world. But isn't
creating peace

in one's own life a step toward the whole? Aren't our knees,
gently touching, a mandala forming peaceful symmetry?
Maybe tonight we're doing our best for peace when we eat
at Zumaya's, then settle in to watch an Italian movie about
the Mafia. Kurt Vonnegut once wrote that if there are angels,
he wants them organized along the lines of the Mafia. I agree.
Tightly-knit bands of angels could surely do more good than
flittery, independent-contractor angels. As the incense
smoke curls, I believe in angels; in Buddhism's intricate cosmos;

in Catholic saints; in our own plain, Protestant carpenter-
Christ. He said "Love." That's it. That's my prayer,
breathed into the sweet-smelling incense. Love. Peace.
Nothing new, but so what? The day opens itself as I pray for

our knees, my darling, which touch each other with the
delicacy of folded angel wings. We are saving the world
with our knees. Knees for peace.

LACMA: "MADE IN CALIFORNIA"

One hundred years of California history
at the Los Angeles County Museum of Art,
which you and I both want to see, but I
end up going alone because you've been
so busy this week. The first weekend

we ever spent together, we saw a Richard
Diebenkorn show here at LACMA. His "Ocean Park"
paintings pulled us into one another;
you stood behind me, pressed to my back,
arms around my waist. Neither of us
could move without the other.

Art: the collaboration between God and body.
Love: the same thing.

These many years, we've taken in the stunning California
light that Diebenkorn could paint, enthralling us,
a couple of Nebraska kids who found their way to art.
Sometimes, we drive around our city saying thanks—

because you came to be an actor and accomplished that;
because we found ourselves in poetry—
and then each other. California, now,
is made of us: Los Angeles, the ocean coastline,
mountains, desert, all this light. No weather can erase us.

Before I leave for home, I find the gift shop with its
posters, postcards, books that would remind me of this afternoon,
but I don't see a thing I want. Or anything I want to bring
to you, except the knowledge that we haven't wasted
what we found the day we saw those Diebenkorns and
knew we didn't want to move a step without each other.

Art: Cohesive vision. Love: The same.

APRIL

carey

You're making your famous cheeseburgers tonight.
You went to Farmers Market and bought the exactly-right
amount of special ground beef you always get,
and, soon, we'll eat. Whoever's at Burger King
three blocks away would rush to our house if they
understood that food's not just any brown stuff on a bun.
It's driving to the Market; attention paid to weight,
freshness, taste. When your son was young,
you made his salads with such care:

lettuce in a roomy bowl. Cucumbers, tomato.
Inevitably, blue cheese dressing, the only kind
he liked. When you fixed peanut butter with Ritz crackers,
every cracker had its own spot on a plate delivered
as your boy watched afternoon TV, waited for the dinner
you would cook. We never
ate bad pizza from a cardboard box. In time,

your son himself and I made pizza. He patted out the dough;
I made the sauce. As I remember this, I get weepy.
Come on—I'm thinking about cheeseburgers and pizza.

to the reader

No, I'm thinking about my mother. Her April birthday.
Your mother, too. I know you miss her. I hear you now,
out in the kitchen, the hamburger in your hands.
Slap, slap—meat between your palms, becoming patties.
You can't find the garlic powder, a ritual ingredient,
but then you do. In our small kitchen, The Mothers
send their spirit-hands to move our own.
What I can do

in memory of everything is eat,
nourish our past with this new April's food—
your perfect cheeseburgers, served with freshly-picked asparagus.

"Shall I feed the cats?" you ask me, when you've
finished up the patties. Of course I answer, "Yes."
Harry, you feed us all. We're hungry, and we're yours.

THE "SOUL TRAIN" LINE

A favorite dancer wears her tightest tight black leather pants
with long black fringe around the waist which flips and twists
ecstatically every time she shakes her butt. And she does shake
it—

while in the men's row, guys do somersaults.

You say the "Soul Train" line's the best five minutes on T. V.
"Call me when it's time!" I shout to you.
"Pretty soon—two minutes for commercials!" you call back.
Butt fringe, somersaults: the styles and moves don't vary much,
and yet we don't get tired of watching them. The commercial
right before the line is always what it is, backed by
Don Cornelius' voice. His sultry bass makes me believe
McDonald's even might have soul. Later, in the afternoon,

you and I make love, although I'm wearing nothing
more exotic than an old plaid flannel shirt. We're so familiar
with each other that it has to be arousing. I watch your face;
nobody sees it in the act of love but me. Nobody else,
these thousand, thousand times. The more we move together,
the more I want to move with you. You say, finally,

how happy our life makes you feel. I'm glad.
I'm totally exhausted with the elegiac side of things.
I want soul wherever soul appears—in butt fringe,
strapless sparkly tops. And in the guys' wild acrobatics,
even when they can't quite get their legs to follow
their imaginations. What could be more soulful than

a Saturday at home, doing what we always do?
I know that when it's time, you'll call to me.
And there will be Cornelius' honey-darkwine voice
announcing, as he's done since God was born,
"The Souuuuuuul Traaaaaaain Line."

IT MUST BE AUGUST—WE'RE
AT A DODGER GAME

We're with my cousins, and with John and Jill.
Friday night, forty-one thousand fans to watch the Dodgers
beat the Mets. Sheffield's having a good season;
we are, too. Nachos and homeruns. I don't like summer
much, but I like this. Favorite cousins visiting
from out of town; friends we never get to see enough of.
We'll convert John yet, we tell him. He's a Boston man,
can't give up his Redsox. There's hope, we think:
the view at Dodger Stadium impresses him. The Dodgers
give it everything they've got. We come to games
to cheer our hometown team, but mostly just to sit together,
you and I,

looking out at timelessness. Beyond the wins and losses,
I see a sweet eternity: green, grassy diamond, always ready,
always waiting for another then another then another game.

Next time we're here, we'll celebrate your birthday.
All you've asked for is a Dodger game and Greenblatt's cheesecake.
During the late innings, I'll go into the gift shop
to buy Dodger Dollars, put them in a card for you at Christmas.
I do this every year. It gives us a head start on top-deck
tickets. This is where we always sit, relishing the vantage
point, better than expensive seats. Baseball:

Nothing in our sinful world makes this much sense.
I wouldn't say it's our religion, and it isn't,
but I'd say the game extends our souls, those subtle
yearnings toward a larger good. After the ninth inning
on your birthday, there will be fireworks—fountains and
mandalas and great floral bursts. They make us gasp.
How rare it is to gasp, to be completely taken in by
beauty, by its quick profusion. Of course, that fades.
We're never innocent enough to think it won't.

So what? Satisfaction doesn't have to be perfection.
Sitting here with you is plenty, knowing that the nachos
matter—salt and crunch and cheese. The cousins. John
and Jill. Yes, everybody else—tonight is blessed:
no guy bigger than an SUV in front of us;
no kid wearing a blue foam rubber hand, its "We're
Number One" finger right in our faces. No bunch
of business people from some office, here to socialize,
not watch the game. We're definitely watching, eating,

laughing. This is summer. You were once a baseball
player, played up to the semi-pros. Here's to boys
who want to play as well as they can play. To skill,
to pure devotion to the game. Here's to Karros, to
Lo Duca, to Shawn Green. Harry, here's to you.

HARRY, I'M THINKING AGAIN

about that morning when I leaned to you and whispered,
"Stay alive." Clear August sun fed the room.

These present August days, I'm reading my old journals,
gathering, then letting go. Great moments, though,
refuse to be released. New morning, early love,
isn't memory but spine, holding me in place.
Light came with us everywhere. You and I
have gotten through a lot of days
that weren't our best, but ones that were—

your Havenhurst apartment, and later, coffee,
as your little boy was waking up—

those days have made me—restless, bullish—
into a patient woman. I'm always sure

the brightness will return. I'm saying,
"Stay alive," this minute, and I mean it
just the way I meant it years ago. The light hums
through the window, knowing all it's known about
our history since it found us then. And when I spoke,
then you spoke, too:

"I love California," meaning how you loved
the possibilities this place carries at the edge
of everything: You and I were possible together.
You and I and your young son were possible.
California loved us, too.

Your shoulder brushes mine again as we begin to move
to make the coffee that first August. Time isn't time:
it is the ever-open window; light-quickened bones
which strengthen worlds. And when we are no longer bodies
we'll be the light itself, glad to vivify the best we waken:
lovers, rising to the possible. So may it always be.

SEPTEMBER 22, 2001

As fall comes—4 P. M. in California—you and I
are walking fast down Wilshire Boulevard, leaving
what we couldn't bear to watch: a movie full of fiery
airplane crashes, World War II heroics. Up on the screen,

a long-gone war, alive again. Out here on the street,
a new, hard tragedy for us, our country. Driving home,
cars zip past with flags attached. New patriotic
unity, honoring the people caught in terrorist attacks.
Some in the hijacked planes called home to say, "I love you,"
before their loved ones, watching morning television, saw
those planes collide with awful fact, explode and burn.

Autumn brings Persephone's return to Hades,
King of Souls, deep in the old Greek underworld.

Harry, tonight we'll say, "I love you," as we fall asleep.
We always do. In case. In case of what? In case of heart attack
or stroke, fire, or random murder. In case

Persephone needs company
as she descends to meet her husband for another season,
our flimsy bodies given without warning to the darker gods.

Can there be another autumn myth this year?
A harvest myth, offering
great cornucopias of apples, pears, along with
pumpkins carved to glowing faces? Children dressed
as ghosts, just kidding, aren't real ghosts at all.

No. Not even multitudes of flags can cancel what
the season holds: sun, now, much too quickly going down
as we get home. More TV news. More families pasting
photos of their missing ones on New York walls.
Will hundreds upon hundreds suddenly emerge, alive,
from tons of wreckage? No. This year, faith will not

turn ash to living breath. We are each other, Harry,
and we are the dead. Just as

Persephone begins her necessary journey—so will we all.
We are going farther downward than we had ever asked to go.

POEMS
(2002-2003)

THE PRIVILEGE OF THE ORDINARY

Twice this week, comments about the air:
"It's good here." Up in the hills, Griffith Observatory
watches over us. We're lucky for the coolness now,
before an unrelenting summer hits the city.

Alertness to our air has come from women,
old women who know language is the power to say
what's good, what isn't. I've had a dream: creation's
essence is a rich gold paste of seeds and honey,
all that's made within our fertile hives. For once,
no ambiguity about the meaning. I can hold the dream

as part of this sad spring which now is freshening
to "good." Walking, twice, outside our house with women
I adore, who tell me that what comes into our lungs brings
health. We stand, inhale the planetary view, and also sense

the rain tomorrow, unexpected, out of season, the blur
which presses boundaries through themselves. One says
she'll just tell death everything about herself.

The other says, "I like the wine we're drinking."

NATURE

has lifted the veins in my hand:
an old woman's love travels fast in the summer—
heat raises flowers on the branches.

Nobody knows what a solstice will bring,
but it moves all we own. Gives it to sun;
gives it to age—veins carry

fragrance, attracting the bees who
won't sting what adores their wild
buzz of prayer, their bodies surrendered
to service. Theirs is the victory:
pollen reborn as honey,

as gold which still holds its flower,
its source, on the tongue. In the blood.

PERSEPHONE RETURNS
TO THE UNDERWORLD

Wine over stone. I'm welcomed.
The young ones dance in their abstracted way—
dead too soon but, always, Soul moves itself, and
I exchange clear beauty for Hades' cool embrace.
Wine, pears, cheeses deep with age. We pray,
we eat, we listen to the music taken from
a single string. Forever, the same note.
I miss

the doting, fleshy mother-arms of Demeter.
Her wheat-hot fields. And laughter.
My husband's kisses never hurt me but are
simply Soul, which takes no side, is never
partner to fierce love, to all the wild
exchange of human feasts. Mother, hear me—

Pull this cave a little closer to you now.
Bring me to some clarifying window where
the worlds can see each other, can accept
unbargained truce. That, at least. Help the youthful
ones, so sorry to be here, to understand that even
in their slowest dance is pulse,

is promise. Seasons drop; they lift. We're ghost,
we're shadow; but we rise. And carry upward
what we take from Hades: We are not only sex
and blood but swift, hard thought—the book,
the law, the fine black kernel at the center of the pear.

THIRTY-THREE YEARS AGO,

a vision of old men who stood in the garage.
Long gray coats I thought were European.
It rained outside. They gathered in a circle.
Five or six old men from somewhere else.

They were my mind, ordering itself after great loss:
the husband who just couldn't stand me anymore.
These old men

settled down in me that winter, waiting out the rain.
Not ghosts. Not ancestors. Simply what they were,
a patience I had no idea I had: They let me know
that I'd get old. The men, I guess,

had watched me stare into an insurmountable pyramid
of brown potatoes at the grocery store when I decided
I would die. Leave my shopping basket in the aisle,
go home and die. It was

their coats that saved me. Closely woven dark gray wool,
the kind of coat so finely made you never have to buy
another one. I could sew, myself. So, I did. I attended to

how patterns fit together. How seasons stitch themselves
through time. And here it is, another winter. I realize
that early love's abandonment gave me more than it could take:
rescue moves within us, isn't anybody else's choice. Is in
the pockets where the old men kept their hands to warm them.
Deep, deep in the inner, unseen lining which I never
might have touched if I had kept the young self who,
I thought, was all there was.

Now, I hope to stand in someone else's mind. Old woman,
warmly dressed old woman, a companion, helping
to wait out the storm, the pain.

EVERY TIME THE PHONE RINGS,
ELAINE HAS DIED

Mushroom stain underneath my fingernails—preparation
for tomorrow took all morning. When I call her,
we say less and less. It's down to
"Hi. I love you." She's too tired for more.
I'm completely out of language, anyway. Tomorrow:

Dia de Los Muertos. My altar holds bright marigolds and
winter wheat; a *calaveras* has a violin—whenever there's
a breeze, he plays. Such good things

in every hollow mushroom, ready to be baked. And now
a piece of light someone's been saving enters on
our old wood chest, the place I keep Dia de Los Muertos
tucked away, except November. The phone—

it rings just once, then nothing. It's the ghosts
to say they like the altar. Why do we want more,
always more, than we can have?

More years for our Elaine. More mushrooms to put in the
mushrooms. More than the light's little sliver on the chest.
But I admit it's light. "Never use 'dark' in a poem,
and never use 'light.'" I'll do what the skeleton does—

play when I'm shaken, say "mushrooms" and "dying" and
"light." Light which has now disappeared, leaving
without me, so I have to say, "dark." Which is how

things just are when a friend can't have more than
she's already had. The leaf-driven plant, though,
where the skeleton lives, has grown to be higher than others.
Well, anguish. Well, beauty. The stains rubbing into my skin.

—*for Elaine Brooks*

MUSHROOM RESEARCH

The clouds today:
so fat I could stare
at them forever. I mean
forever. Sky

as earth—and even farther
underneath—old underworld,
the musky stairway down, then
one quick breath and up again
to flight and air: imagination never
settles on a definition of itself.

A mushroom feeds
or paralyzes. You take
your chances every day.
The mind as heaven, then
that smell of fresh-turned dirt,
of graves. White lotus cloud.
Or, *A. virosa*: deadly joke.

MARIPOSA AVENUE

Our oldest cat:
he's breathing,
then breathing.

How is Creation as large and as small as
the gray and white cat we spent weeks, once,
trying to find? He snoozes, pushed to my thigh. There is—

all I can call It is Presence, creating the room
in this minute and then in the next. Transforming
atoms of breath into cat, into woman who asks:

What shall we do, God?

I wait. I wait a long time, thinking:
Here is our earth: Children who wind explosives
around their small waists—suicide, murder,
the worship of blood. The Blood God

is thirsty. And real. But so is the One
I call God, Who, if great mystery, is also great joy—
creating this miracle cat, and the way I can think,
and our neighborhood sun held in the curtains.

I am waiting. And asking:
What is the space, God, between You and us?
Today, I believe there's a moment like crossing the street,
crossing spilled blood toward the promise that You are
our witness, and care. You want to be with us in finding
the lost. You promise The Word. Oh, God,

what Word? What loud Word can we say that is You?

MEMENTO MORI

The old woman upstairs
has moved out. She'll never be back.
My garden is gone,

torn up by workmen. One of them
stole the stone rabbit Andrea gave me.
My friend, dead, now, six years. Our cat
pokes at me with his claws, kneading.
He wants some comfort. Dear cat,

this world shifts every second we breathe.

The old woman was married to Sarkis.
He planted the fig tree in back,
a tree I got bowlsful of fruit from each summer.
Sarkis is dead. His wife is too weak to live on her own.

How can I tell the new renters to pray
to the spirits of Sarkis and Mary, respect
what they've left in the air of the upstairs
apartment? 1254 ½ North Mariposa.

Sarkis appears as a white butterfly in the plants
I did rescue. When he comes, I say "hi," watch him
flutter and bow. When Andrea drifts through my dreams,
I talk to her, too. And I won't forget Mary's home-grown
Swiss chard. So, we all keep in touch.

Goodbye, fig tree. The workmen will pay for the theft
of your life, of my happy stone rabbit. The world
as it spins does remember. There's tragedy; then
there is justice. Dear cat, your claws give me pain
yet your purr is sheer love. Here's where we are—

in every address that we've had;
in mouthfuls of black-purple fruit;
between this single instant and stars.

LAPIS

I look to the patio doors. My ghost self is there—
my reflection. This Whateverlasts has begun her
long journey. I can still see her—she wears
the old shirt that I do—but she's moving, gradually,

farther and farther away,

though at the moment my hands and hers lift a glass
in a toast. When I meet her again, the wine will be gold,
much more gold than this cheap chardonnay I have poured
for myself. Losses are given as promises,

finally collected, embraced—the self who has troubled
the world with her flaws is also earned history:
the ancestors crowded behind my reflection. Remember?
They packed all their graves with shimmering beads, plates, and
harps; wedding rings, hammers, paintings of gods. Blue lotus
goblets just for that wine. The Whateverlasts

has created herself in the marvelous cells of my visible
body and in the bodies of millions who live in the delicate
air; in this odd, carnal evening which shifts past its flesh to
my rare understanding of everything, everyone. I look again
toward my ghost self, still in the patio doors.
She turns away as I sit:

her hair has grown white. She carries red roses,
cradles the blooms against her black dress as she
walks through the patio, then past the low, curving wall

then disappears. I am left here to wait—
left with belief that never escapes from our blood:
human insistence on scarabs placed over the heart, small
sacred barges, food for the journey to Somewhere. On red,
pulsing and fragrant, pressed against black.

ABOUT THE AUTHOR

HOLLY PRADO grew up in Nebraska and Michigan but has made her home in Los Angeles since 1960. *These Mirrors Prove It* is her eighth book.

Her poetry and prose have appeared in numerous publications for the past thirty years. For nine years, she reviewed both poetry and fiction for the Book Review of the Los Angeles Times. For three of those years, she wrote a column reviewing new books of poems.

Recent honors include First Prize in the 1999 Fin de Millennium L.A. Poetry Award, sponsored by the Los Angeles Poetry Festival and Poets Anonymous. Additionally, she was a winner in the "Sense of Site" project for 2002: poems by eight Los Angeles poets to be printed in an edition of 10,000 postcards and distributed throughout the city.

Her poetry is available on the solo CD "Word Rituals" (produced by Harvey R. Kubernik, released by New Alliance Records).

Presently, she teaches creative writing both privately and in the graduate writing program at U.S.C. She lives in East Hollywood with her actor-poet husband, Harry E. Northup. She and her husband are founding members of Cahuenga Press.

ALSO FROM CAHUENGA PRESS

Specific Mysteries, by Holly Prado (OP)
You and the Night and the Music, by James Cushing (OP)
Ordinary Snake Dance, by Phoebe MacAdams (no ISBN) $10.00
The Length of an Afternoon, by James Cushing
    (ISBN 0-9649240-6-4) $12.00
The Ragged Vertical, by Harry E. Northup
    (ISBN 0-9649240-0-5) $15.00
Sacrifice, by Cecilia Woloch
    (ISBN 0-9649240-4-8) $12.00
Esperanza: Poems for Orpheus, by Holly Prado
    (ISBN 0-9649240-5-6) $12.00
Homelands, by Jonathan Cott
    (ISBN 0-9649240-7-2) $12.00
Dreaming the Garden, by Anne Stanford
    (ISBN 0-9649240-8-0) $15.00
Reunions, by Harry E. Northup
    (ISBN 0-9649240-9-9) $15.00
Tsigan, by Cecilia Woloch
    (ISBN 0-9649240-7-2) $13.00
Livelihood, by Phoebe MacAdams
    (ISBN 0-9715519-1-X) $12.00

For each book ordered, add $5.50 tax/shipping/handling.

Cahuenga Press
1256 N. Mariposa Ave.
Los Angeles, CA 90029

Most titles also available from

Small Press Distribution
1341 Seventh Ave.
Berkeley, CA 94710